Sure Foundation

Sure Foundation

by

DONALD COGGAN

HODDER AND STOUGHTON

LONDON SYDNEY AUCKLAND TORONTO

British Library Cataloguing in Publication Data
Coggan, Donald
    Sure foundation.
    1. Coggan, Donald, *Archbishop of Canterbury*,
    1974–1980
    2. Canterbury, Eng. (*Diocese*)
    Title
    283'.092'4   BX1599.C567

    ISBN 0 340 26357 1

Christ is made the sure foundation,
Christ the head and corner-stone.

(7th- and 8th-century hymn,
tr. by John Mason Neale)

Other foundation can no man lay than that is laid,
which is Jesus Christ.

(1 Corinthians 3:11)

Dedicated to:

David A. C. Blunt
Michael W. Escritt
Douglas W. Cleverley Ford
Michael Kinchin Smith
John D. G. Kirkham
David S. Painter
James A. G. Scott
Colin C. Still
A. Michael A. Turnbull
Hugh Whitworth

in deep gratitude for their friendship and loyal help during the York and Canterbury years, 1961–80.

Preface

This book is a successor to *Convictions* (Hodder & Stoughton 1975), which was a collection of lectures, sermons and addresses given during the thirteen and a half years in which I was Archbishop of York and during my opening months as Archbishop of Canterbury.

In this book, as in that, it will be seen that I have not been over-careful to eliminate marks of the spoken word—some parts have been written up from notes. There are also very wide differences of style—from the almost monosyllabic simplicity of *Stars on Sunday* to the more sophisticated style of University lectures or Cathedral sermons. That, perhaps, is not altogether to be regretted, for it reflects the variety of work on which an Archbishop is engaged and the differences in audiences which he addresses.

I have sought to eliminate too many repetitions but a certain number still occur in cases where their omission might spoil the thrust of the passage concerned.

Sissinghurst, Kent   Donald Coggan

Contents

FOREWORD

The Archbishop at Work

AN ARCHBISHOP OF Canterbury, by the very nature of his office, touches life at many points. When I was Archbishop (1974–80) I noticed how deep was the interest, on the part of many people, in the nature of the work which that office entails. Perhaps it cannot be helped that to some the Archbishop seems a remote figure, generally seen on television or in the flesh at some great ceremonial occasion. Others see him at closer quarters when he celebrates the Eucharist or preaches in a parish church or institutes a new vicar to a benefice. But if such people were asked how the Archbishop spends his time and what are the activities which make most demands on his energies, they would be at a loss to answer.

I hope that this book, consisting as it does of lectures, sermons and addresses delivered in my years at Canterbury, may serve to cast some light on some of his activities. But they will be read with deeper understanding if I preface them here with a brief description of some of the areas of life he touches. I may describe them in terms of five circles.

The first circle is that of his *diocese*. This comprises three areas, Dover, Maidstone and Croydon, each with an area bishop and an archdeacon. The heaviest burden of the episcopal work falls necessarily on the shoulders of the area or suffragan bishops. Nevertheless, the Archbishop does what he can. In doing so, he finds that the pastoral care of a diocese, involving him regularly in such activities as the celebration of the Eucharist, the preaching of the word, the care of the clergy, the institution of vicars to new "cures", is a means of grace to himself. While he has such responsibilities, he cannot become just a managing director or an organisation man. He is a priest. He is *servus servorum Dei*. The diocese is the field in which, at the most intimate level, he can fulfil these functions. It may be that the area over which he has supervision is too extensive and should be reduced in view of other demands which are made on his time and energy. I believe this to be the case. But that his office should be shorn of episcopal oversight is a concept which I would not like to contemplate, even though there are instances of such a shearing within our Anglican Communion.

The second circle is that of the *Province*. The Archbishop of York has the care of the fourteen northern dioceses, the Archbishop of Canterbury (though his title is that of Primate of All England) is primarily concerned for the other twenty-nine. This large and densely populated area makes demands on him not only in the consecrating of diocesan and suffragan bishops for their sees, but also in visiting the dioceses on occasions when their bishops or others invite him.

The third circle is that of the *Anglican Communion*. The twenty-seven Provinces which contain the seventy million people who are Anglicans are independent of Canterbury and of one another, but nevertheless form a family whose allegiance to the "Mother Church" of Canterbury means much to all concerned. The unity of these Provinces is witnessed in and strengthened by the Lambeth Conferences which are held, roughly, every ten years and which, hitherto, have always met in England. The Archbishop of Canterbury is, by courtesy and by the circumstances of history, regarded as *primus inter pares* among the metropolitans of the Communion, but he has no authority to decree what should or should not be done in any part of the Communion. In recent years, Archbishops Geoffrey Fisher and Michael Ramsey and I have travelled extensively throughout the Communion and our visits have been warmly welcomed. There are those who feel that in the future an even larger part of the Archbishop's time should be devoted to such journeys and that his other duties should be adjusted to meet these demands. It is not too much to claim that these journeys can constitute a kind of "adhesive" influence in a far-flung and widely variegated Communion.

The fourth circle is that of the *world-wide Church*. Whether or no the Archbishop of Canterbury is at any particular time one of the Presidents of the World Council of Churches, he is deeply concerned with the great Christian world outside his own Communion. By visits, by conferences, by constant correspondence, he must be kept in touch with Rome, with Istanbul, with Geneva and, in England itself, with the Free Churches. He must play his part in the ecumenical scene.

The fifth circle is that of—the *world*! While on his shoulders there lies the burden of "the care of all the churches" and he is mindful of the fact that "Christ loved the Church and gave himself for it", he carries also the burden of a world much of which cares little for his Master; and he is mindful of the fact that "God so loved the *world* that he gave his only Son . . ." This being so, he must refuse ever to become a narrowly ecclesiastical person, wrapped in the cocoon of the institution. If he is threatened by this possibility, he must break out from it, maintaining contacts with the thinking that is going on, the thought-forms that are operating, the lives that are being lived in the wide world. His work in the House of Lords, his meetings with leaders of other nations, and his visits to factories, prisons, universities, schools, the Forces, and so on, together with constant interviews with people from all strata of society, keep him in touch with the complex web of a rapidly changing world. Thus, in his own person, he can do something to kill the image which all too many people have of God as a kind of super-ecclesiastic, only remotely interested in the everyday life of ordinary people.

It is within these five circles that the Archbishop of Canterbury seeks to fulfil his function. The very variety of his work means that the demands on him are heavy. He cannot begin to meet those demands without a team around him on whose members he can constantly call for wisdom and advice. During my time at Canterbury I was wonderfully helped in this way. The readiness with which experts in their own field were willing to put their expertise at the disposal of the Archbishop was a source of immense strength and enlightenment, saving him from taking false steps, and fructifying his mission.

It is my hope that the chapters of this book will enable readers to see how one (very unworthy) occupant of the ancient See of Canterbury addressed his task in days of great change and perplexity. Through these chapters he may be seen at work among the clergy, in the General Synod, at great national occasions, in ecumenical outreach, on radio and television, in and about his diocese.

I laid down the reins of office on Friday, 25 January, 1980. Thanks to the kindness of the Deans of Westminster and Canterbury I had been privileged to celebrate the Eucharist and to preach at farewell services in Westminster Abbey on January 17 and at Canterbury Cathedral on January 25 respectively. The addresses which I gave on those occasions are printed in this book (pp 19–25 and 31–34). But between those dates, on January 22, 23 and 24, I spoke briefly each morning on the BBC *Thought for the Day* programme. I called these talks "a retrospective thank-you to God"—first, for *ministry* (the infinite privilege of being called to minister in the Church, in my case as deacon, priest and bishop); secondly, for *friends* (I instanced, from a wonderfully wide circle, two women and two men who had inspired me); and thirdly, for *Christ* himself, who had brought meaning into my own life, giving inspiration to my thinking and strength for my action. These talks are printed on pp 26–30. No wonder that it was with a profound sense of thankfulness that I reviewed the forty-five years and more of my ministry.

No one—least of all the present writer—can look back over such years of ministry without seeing that some of the building which he has done has been shoddy workmanship, poor stuff to offer to the Lord who called him. As he does so, he can only use the Jesus prayer: "Lord Jesus Christ, Son of God, have mercy upon me, a sinner", and leave the work, such as it is, to the infinite pity of God. But at the same time he can utter a prayer of thankfulness for the foundation of all his work, which is Christ himself. Hence the title of this book—SURE FOUNDATION. I have put it in the singular, not only because the words recall the first line of the hymn

> Christ is made the sure foundation,
> Christ the head and cornerstone,

but also because they take us back to the Pauline affirmation: "Other foundation can no man lay than that is laid, which is

Jesus Christ" (1 Corinthians 3:11). In so far as a man keeps true to that, his work will stand. When he departs from that, his work has within it the seeds of decay.

A further word must be added. The strains entailed on the holder of the office of Archbishop of Canterbury are considerable and the demands unremitting. That needs no elaboration. Perhaps the title of this book may be seen as the writer's tribute to the unfailing grace of him who calls a man to ministry, and the cross on the cover (the Canterbury cross) may be a witness to the truth of St Paul's insight when he wrote: "God forbid that I should glory save in the cross of our Lord Jesus Christ" (Galatians 6:14).

I
FAREWELL TO
CANTERBURY

Westminster Abbey

IT WAS ON January 25 five years ago that a service was held in this Abbey to welcome the man who the previous day had been enthroned as Archbishop of Canterbury in his Cathedral. Now by the kindness of the Dean and Chapter we are met for a farewell Eucharist.

Many times during those five years I have had occasion to come to the Abbey, sometimes to preach, sometimes to share in a service of thanksgiving or of national importance. Always I have received courtesy and, more than that, a warmth of welcome which has moved me much. Though I have a close link with the church at the top of Ludgate Hill, a link which is *sui generis* in that it is the Cathedral of my ordination, my link with this Abbey Church is also close, going back at least to the days of Dean Alan Don, who used to ask me to preach here back in the forties. So I am thankful that my last big service in London should be here in the Abbey.

On the day of my enthronement, the Lesson which was read was taken from the sixth chapter of the Epistle to the Ephesians. Part of that Lesson shall constitute my text tonight: "Our fight is not against human foes, but against cosmic powers, against the authorities and potentates of this dark world, against the superhuman forces of evil in the heavens. Therefore, take up God's armour; then you will be able to stand your ground . . . Stand firm, I say."

The background against which the drama of these last five years has been played out has been a dark one. Internationally,

17 January, 1980.

the background of the last scene of my archbishopric is darker than that of any former scene. Only during the last few weeks we have watched the rape of Afghanistan, as twelve years ago we watched the rape of Czechoslovakia—watched, protesting but powerless to prevent it. The hordes of atheistic Communism have enlarged their territory while a shocked world has looked on.

Again, on the world stage, we have seen the increase of international violence taking the form of kidnapping and similar acts of brigandage. Even as I speak, some fifty unhappy men and women languish in Iran, and outraged America has so far been unable to devise means to secure their freedom.

When we look at the world of medicine, we can chalk up some considerable triumphs, in the easing of the human lot and in the prolongation of human life. But, from another point of view, it seems to be clear that, while some diseases are being obliterated, other forms of sickness, not least in the mental and nervous spheres, are taking on fresh virulence. Disease seems to be a hydra-headed monster.

In the countries of the West, where systems of social security are increasingly common and, thank God, inclusive in their care, the crime rate and the divorce rate nevertheless rise sharply, and a laxity of moral standards undermines the stability of the home and of society.

So one could go on, but I forbear. I mention these things only to illustrate the truth of what St Paul sensed in the first century and any open-eyed Christian can sense in the twentieth, namely the fact of cosmic powers, of superhuman forces of evil at work. We cannot and should not shut our eyes to this fact. The world is dark, the powers of evil potent.

"Watchman, what of the night?" What do the next two decades hold, ere a third millennium dawns? It would not be non-Christian, nor even sub-Christian, for a disciple of Jesus to answer: "Quite possibly darkness as black as today's or even blacker." For Jesus never promised, so far as the Gospel records show, a steady dispersal of the clouds until Utopia dawns. As he looked into the future, the colours of his forecasts were apocalyptically dark.

Is that all, then, that the Christian has to say? God forbid! Far from it. Whereas such a forecast would, if taken realistically, plunge the godless man into despair, it does no such thing for the Christian. *He* knows that, even if man, in his utter folly, should blow God's lovely world to pieces, God still reigns. There, in him, the immutable God of justice and love, is his hope and his confidence.

But the Christian is also aware that, while such a faith under-girds and supports him, it does not exonerate him one whit from engaging in the battle against darkness in the here and now. He is placed here for that very purpose, and provision is made for his battle needs—belt and coat of mail, shoes and shield, helmet and sword. Thus equipped, he can stand, he can pray, he can prevail. Indeed, in some strange and paradoxical way, he can rejoice in the midst of the battle, recognising, from abundant evidence, that it is so often from the heart of the battle, from the blackness of the darkness, that God brings victory and light. He knows that "when God intends to make something wonderful he begins with a difficulty. When he intends to make something *very* wonderful he begins with an impossibility!"

What, then, has this terrible realism of St Paul and his glorious God-centredness got to say to us in England at the beginning of this decade? I mention three things:

First, and above all, it says: *Put God first*. We preachers would not so often be grumbled at, nor would our hearers look at their watches so often, if we would preach about GOD! That is what our people want to hear and to be taught about. That is what *we* are here for. God in the majesty of his continuing creative activity; God in the glorious power of his redeeming mission; God in the lovely work of making men holy; God in his concern for society; God in his care for the individual. Put God first. Put him first in your synodical government; learn to trust a little less to parliamentary patterns and a great deal more to waiting on the revelation of his will; seek for a *consensus* without which there cannot truly be a *synod*. Put him first in the conduct of your business and of your family life. Put him first in the thought and conduct of your own day-to-day living. Put God first.

Secondly, get right into the fight. "Stand firm", says the Apostle in the text. *Wanted*—men and women in public life who realise that more than individual action is called for; that decisions have to be made in the corridors of power, and that those decisions can often be shaped by people who are prepared to take a stand for what they believe to be right. I think of the Houses of Parliament, the business corporations, the trades unions, the local councils—wanted *here* people who, at whatever cost, are prepared to give a lead against the cosmic powers of darkness.

Wanted, too, men and women who think on a global scale and are prepared, without a touch of paternalism but as servants of the Servant Christ, to put their resources into the alleviation of third world need—whether those resources be of personal service, or of money, or of willingness to let their young people go and carry the light.

Wanted, again, men and women who are prepared to think and work on ecumenical lines, glad to share with any who name the Name of Christ the vast task of evangelistic and social outreach. Faced with the forces of cosmic darkness, we need not, we must not, go to the fight weakened by division or rivalry.

Thirdly, use your armour. As well go into atomic warfare armed with bow and arrow as enter *this* warfare equipped with human armour. Nor is there need to do so. There is divine provision for superhuman conflict. Mark the pieces mentioned by St Paul—truth and integrity, the gospel of peace, and faith; salvation for helmet, and for sword the words that come from God. And, above all and through all, "pray on every occasion in the power of the Spirit . . . Keep watch and persevere, always interceding . . ."

Last Monday, *The Times* had a long obituary notice of Maurice Reckitt who has just died at the age of ninety-one. "His great cry", so the paper said, "was that the Church had three functions: to worship God, to bind up the wounds of the world, and to prophesy." I note the order in which this Christian sociologist, colleague of Demant and Eliot and Temple, put the Church's task—worship first, and then social action and prophecy. If in the eighties the Church of England could get this right—the primacy of worship and prayer—its contribution to the alleviation of world agony would be greater and the note of its prophecy surer. Pray God that will be so.

In this battle against superhuman forces, we follow in the steps of Christ himself—and we go in his power. We recall the words, and in doing so nerve ourselves for the battle, of an old warrior who fought hard for Christ in India:

> Captain belovèd, battle wounds were thine;
> Let me not wonder if some hurt be mine:
> Rather, O Lord, let this my wonder be
> That I may share a battle-wound with thee.

BBC Broadcasts

I

NEXT FRIDAY WILL be my last day as your Archbishop. So I'm particularly glad to have the opportunity of speaking to you today, tomorrow and on Thursday—and to do so in a rather personal way.

I look back over some forty-five years in the ministry of Christ's Church, more than half of that as a bishop. That's a tremendous privilege for any man. So you won't be surprised if, in these talks, I speak of certain things which make me a very thankful man today. You could call these talks, if you like, *a retrospective thank-you—in three parts*.

Naturally enough, then, my first "thank-you" to God is for the gift of ministry. I know so well what one of the New Testament writers meant when he wrote: "I thank . . . Christ Jesus our Lord . . . for appointing me to his service" (1 Timothy 1:12). You can't have a greater privilege than that.

I think back to a few years of work in the thirties in what was then a very tough London parish—when unemployment was widespread and there was no Welfare State as we now know it. I also spent nineteen years teaching theology in Canada and at home, preparing men for the ordained ministry of the Church. Then there was another nineteen years in Bradford and then York, as Bishop and Archbishop, and now over five years at Canterbury. How good God has been!

It has been so rich and varied, this ministry, here at home and in many different parts of the world. The supreme privilege of preaching in cathedrals and parish churches and in the open air,

"Thought for the day", 22, 23, 24 January, 1980.

seeking, with God's help, to lodge in men's hearts and minds some tiny bit of God's immense truth. The privilege of celebrating the Holy Communion in Canterbury Cathedral or in some little Kent church or by the bedside of a sick person. The privilege of visiting universities and schools, prisons and dockyards, regiments and ships, hospitals and mines, meeting people where they work, and laugh, and suffer. The privilege of administration—yes, "admin" is not a bad word; it simply means helping to keep the machine going with as few creaks as possible, and remembering that, behind every letter you receive (and I get a lot of them!) there's a human being who matters to God and who should therefore matter to me.

Happy the man who gets called to that sort of work! The number of men and women who are hearing and heeding the call of God to such work is increasing. We need them. God needs them—people who are prepared for hard training, hard work, no very great material rewards, but the deep, deep satisfaction of *ministry* in Christ's name, for his sake, to his people. To any such who may be listening this morning, I would say: "Be very careful not to miss God's call. Be ready. 'Lord, here am I; send me'—*that's* your prayer."

I've spoken particularly of the *ordained* ministry of the Church, because that has been my particular sphere of service, and still is, and will be till I die. The truth is, of course, that every Christian is engaged in ministry, for the word simply means *service*, the service of him who came not to be ministered unto but to minister. *That* ministry, in whatever sphere it is exercised, is a lovely thing when it is done in his name and through his power.

2

Yesterday I spoke about the privilege of *ministry*. Today I want to say "thank-you" to God for *friends*.

I'm thinking not so much of the friendship of parents, wife, sisters—these are the friendships which are basic, formative, more precious than life itself. One can never be thankful enough for them, and that needs saying though not elaborating. No; I'm thinking of friendships which haven't been as intimate as these nor, often, of such long standing.

There was that little woman in Islington more than forty years ago—she lived in a room whose chimney would smoke and nearly suffocate her, and her old age pension was ten shillings a week. Her sight was so bad that she might well collide with a lamp-post on the way to church, but never mind, she would battle on and there she would be, singing away like a lark with a sore throat, and gaining strength to live a life of exceptional grace. A good friend.

Then there was that woman in Bradford. She was the wife of a vicar. She was confined to bed—and had been for years. Consumed with self-pity, always grumbling? Not a bit of it. Her room was full of sunshine, the sunshine of her inner radiance; it was the power-house of the parish. One went to minister to her. One came away ministered to, enriched, humbled. A good friend.

Then there was William James. He lived in the Arctic. Not that he had any need to—he could have had a far more comfortable job in the more lush areas of a Canadian city. But he loved those Eskimos—loved them in the days when access to them was not by airliner but by boat and sledge and long, hard, bitter cold treks. He would come out, rarely, for furlough. But back he would go again and again—to love them, and serve them, for Christ's sake. Another good friend.

And there was Janani Luwum—big, black fellow-Christian, strong and gentle Archbishop. He was martyred a few years ago, because he stood up for Christ against Idi Amin in those terrible years in Uganda. He led his people, not only by what he said, but by what he was and what he did. He lived witnessing. He died witnessing. A good friend.

I've mentioned four friends. If I had time I could tell you of forty—four hundred! One of my biggest thank-you's to God must be for the friendship of people like these—members of Christ's Church who drew their strength and derived the sheer beauty of their characters from association with him and his people.

"I don't go to church—too many hypocrites there." So they say. I guess there *are* hypocrites there—who would deny it? But the Church is the factory where saints are being made, ordinary people like you and me, at different points on the assembly-line but moving on—by the grace of God. It's the Body of Christ, of

which we are limbs. It is his building, of which we are parts.
For all its faults, its pettiness, its sins, thank God for the
Church, the Body of Christ. Thank God for friends.

3

Tomorrow will be my last day as your Archbishop. On the last
two mornings I've been saying "thank-you" to God for the gift
of ministry, and for friends. Today I speak of Christ himself.

I'm in good company in saying this. St Paul, in one of his
letters, had a word for it. He wrote: "Thanks be to God for his
gift beyond words." He wasn't referring to money or books
or health, or even to his ministry or to his friends. All these
things were precious, and he was thankful for them. No; he was
referring to a Person, one no longer visible to the human eye,
but none the less real to him for that, the Person who had
revolutionised his own life, and through his ministry was re-
volutionising that of others. God's "gift beyond words" was
Jesus himself.

I've been trying to imagine what my own life would have
been without him—and I can't imagine it! From boyhood days
I've "heard him call, 'Come follow'". It was an inner conviction, deepening as the years have gone on, that life without him
is a poor thing; that self-aggrandisement is an empty bauble;
that he was – and is – the one through whom supremely God has
made himself known to men; and that in him, as in no other, in
his life and teaching and death and resurrection, life takes on
meaning; that by his Spirit in the Church, in word and in
sacrament, is strength and joy and peace.

This is not to say that, for the Christian, life is a bed of roses.
Far from it. Life's injustices and sufferings sometimes appear
worse to the conscience lit up with the light of Christ than to
others who care little for his teaching and are unconcerned
about his standards. The Christian disciple finds himself involved in the battle in some such way—though infinitely less
intensely—as did his Lord when he fought, and fought to the
death, against sin, and ignorance, and disease. That makes for
tough going! But—

> it is the way the Master went;
> should not the servant tread it still?

I don't want to sound "pious" about all this. On the contrary. I find myself, on looking back, infinitely in debt, a debt I can never repay. All too often, my service has been poor and my discipleship feeble. But all the time, under-girding, sustaining, upholding, has been "God's gift beyond words", Christ himself, the Word who discloses to us the mind and heart and will of the eternal God.

How do I say "thank-you" for a gift like that? Words fail. All too often the kind of life we live fails. Sometimes the poets get it better than we earth-bound mortals. Listen to F. W. H. Myers, in his poem *St Paul*:—

> Yea, thro' life, death, thro' sorrow and thro' sinning,
> He shall suffice me, for he hath sufficed;
> Christ is the end, for Christ was the beginning,
> Christ the beginning, for the end is Christ.

Better still, listen to St Paul himself: "I am persuaded, that neither death nor life, nor angels nor principalities nor powers, nor things present nor things to come, nor height nor depth, nor any other creature, shall be able to separate us from the love of God which is in Christ Jesus our Lord."

Canterbury Cathedral

Philippians 3:10
That I may know him, and the power of his resurrection, and the fellowship of his sufferings.

JANUARY 25 WILL always be for me a day of very special significance. It was on this day, twenty-four years ago, that I was consecrated a bishop in the Church of God. It was a bitterly cold day, but York Minster, snow-covered without, was full of light and joy, and of people, within.

It was the day on which, in 1975, after installation here on the 24th, a great service was held in Westminster Abbey to welcome and to commend to God the one who the previous month had been made Archbishop of Canterbury.

It is the day on which, by the kindness of the Dean and Chapter, I am allowed to say "good-bye", in the context of the Eucharist, to the diocese which I have loved and tried to serve, and which I shall always hold in deepest affection.

These events alone would make this day a particularly meaningful one for me. But there is a deeper reason for its special significance. It is, as every churchman knows, the day on which we celebrate the Conversion of St Paul. There is no other New Testament figure whose *conversion* is thus commemorated – St Paul stands alone in this regard.

For me, if I may be allowed to continue on a personal note, St Paul has, since my boyhood days, been a figure of towering stature and commanding mien. I say "commanding" because

25 January, 1980.

one cannot read his writings without seeing in one's mind's eye an imperious figure beckoning. Those writings of his are not to be read as it were at arm's length, with an air of detachment. If they are so read, they lose their main point—it is blunted, and they become part of the great literature of the Graeco-Roman world and nothing more. No: behind those writings is a man of massive mind, who dares to reach out into the infinite, to wrestle with the immensities of divine revelation, to speak of predestination, of sin and shame, of grace and redemption, of God's love and call, of a Holy Spirit's energies, and of a Church's birth, growth and mission.

Here is a man built on a big scale. He has all the marks of the human about him—now and again he brags; sometimes he loses his temper; sometimes he is obscure; often he shows how conditioned he is by the thought-forms and inhibitions of his day. Yes, he is human, all right. And then he takes wings and soars, and as we little people try to follow his flight we get dazzled because we find ourselves looking straight into the Sun.

The greatness of St Paul lies in this—that he compels us to face the things that really matter, in the here and now and in the long vistas of eternity. Let me illustrate.

If we ask him, for example: "Is it possible for a man, sinful as he is, to be right with God, holy and just as he is? Can we look into the face of God and laugh for joy?", he answers: "Now that we have been justified by faith, *we are at peace with God* through our Lord Jesus Christ. We have been allowed to enter the sphere of God's grace, where we now stand" (Romans 5:1–2). There is no doubt about the ground upon which the Apostle takes his stand—not the shifting sands of his own labours or merits, but the unshakeable rock of God's character and work. There he rests. There he abides.

Further, if we ask him: "Is it possible for a man to be holy?", there is no doubt about his answer. He roots it in the very purposes of God for humanity. "He ordained", so St Paul affirms, that we "should be shaped to the likeness of his Son" (Romans 8:29), that we should "share in the life of his Son" (1 Cor. 1:9). Nor is this some vague possibility for the hereafter. At work in the life of the Church and in the heart of the Christian is the power of the Holy Spirit, making the seemingly impossible a thing open to us all—holiness, likeness to Jesus.

We ask again: "Does belief really matter?" All St Paul's writings combine to assert that creed and conduct go together. The very shape of his letters—first doctrine and then ethics— points to the importance of basic belief, and that not merely in the sense of a series of propositions but of hard thinking worked out in daily commitment, prayer and worship. It is a strenuous and demanding recipe, but it is the only logical response to the God who has given us his all in Christ. This insistence on the relevance of a Christian's belief to his conduct is the final "no" to any suggestion that religion can be in one watertight com- partment and life in another; that a Christian should not "inter- fere" in the sphere where life's issues are worked out; that a man's faith does not affect his politics or his views on matters of sex, race, force, eugenics. To live as "children of the light" is to let that light shine in the very darkest and most problem-ridden corners of a very dark and perplexing world.

Or, once again, we ask him: "Isn't it possible for a man to be a good Christian but not to associate himself in any meaningful way with the life of the Church?" There can be no doubt about the Apostle's answer. The Church is the body of Christ of which he is the head. The Church is the building of which Christ is the foundation and Christians are constituent stones. Indeed, it may well be that St Paul's insistence on the centrality of baptism and Holy Communion, on participation in the life and witness of the Church, began when he, as a violent opponent of the Church, found himself persecuting *Christ*—"Saul, Saul, why are you persecuting *me*?" "Touch my disciples and you touch me—Head and body are one." Sinful and maddening as the Church may be at times, divided as it undoubtedly is, it is yet the Body of Christ, the Body through which, in infinite mercy, he wills to bestow his grace and do his regenerating work.

I speak of this man and of his message, in this my last sermon as your Archbishop, because I believe that our Church will only be great in fulfilling God's purpose for it and through it when it grasps anew and proclaims afresh what St Paul, its great Apostle, had nearest to his heart.

For here is a man *evangelical* in the true sense of that word— he has a message, *the* message of good news, centred in God's great acts in Christ, in his death and resurrection, a message which he must proclaim in life and if need be in death.

Here is a man *catholic* in his faith, for he has a gospel which he sees to be adequate for all the world, for all time, under all conditions; a message centred firmly in certain facts in recent history, made contemporary by the interpreter-Spirit, mediated by the word and sacraments, committed to and guarded by the Church as its most sacred treasure.

Here is a man *charismatic*, gloriously charismatic, in that he is open to receive and constantly to be renewed by the gifts of the Spirit—love, joy, peace, self-control.

Here in this man, small of stature, towering in faith, are the essentials of a message which never changes from age to age. May the Anglican Communion, and in particular the Church of England, ever be true to this gospel, faithful as I believe it to be to the teaching of Jesus himself. May the clergy, the Readers and the teachers of this Diocese expound it with clarity and joy. May the people of this land, this county, this city, heed it and live by it, for it is the way of health and wholeness and holiness.

Just before St Paul bade farewell to the leaders of the church at Ephesus, his friend "dear Doctor Luke" records that he said to them: "Keep watch over yourselves and over all the flock of which the Holy Spirit has given you charge, as shepherds of the Church of the Lord, which he has won for himself by his own blood." That is my farewell charge to the leaders of our diocese of Canterbury. And with what better words could I say farewell to you *all* than in his words to the Ephesians: "Now I commend you to God and to his gracious word, which has power to build you up and give you your heritage among all who are dedicated to him"?

II
SERMONS IN CANTERBURY CATHEDRAL

Rebuilding Walls

Nehemiah 2:17
*Come, let us rebuild the wall . . . and be rid of the
reproach.*

Ephesians 3:20
*He is able to do immeasurably more than all we can
ask or conceive, by the power which is at work
among us.*

A RUINED CITY is a terrible sight. Those of you
who served in Germany during the last war know what I am
talking about. We in England who were in London or Coventry
during the blitz have our memories. Those of us who have
visited parts of Ireland know all too well the sight of desolation
in cities ravaged by violence.

In the ancient world the picture of a ruined city was somewhat different, but it was equally pathetic. There were no
bombs or explosives, of course. But each city was surrounded
by a wall, and that was its main defence—the wall and its gates.
Once the wall was breached and the gates burnt, nothing could
stop the invader. The city was open to disaster.

This was the picture that met the eye of a man called
Nehemiah some centuries before Christ, when he returned
to the city he loved more than any other place on earth—
Jerusalem. A sorry sight it was—walls breached, gates burnt,
mounds of rubble wherever the eye looked. For three days
Easter Sunday, 18 April, 1976.

Nehemiah surveyed the scene. Then, taking a few men with him, he did a reconnaisance by night, riding on a donkey, unnoticed by any of the authorities. Then he said to the people: " 'You see our wretched plight. Jerusalem lies in ruins, its gates destroyed by fire. Come, let us rebuild the wall of Jerusalem and be rid of the reproach' . . . So they set about the work vigorously and to good purpose" (2:17–18).

There was opposition—what good work ever went ahead without it? There were sneers, and threats of attack. But Nehemiah and his band were ready. They divided the work into sections. Their tools were simple. The workers had three things—trowel, sword and prayer. A *trowel* to deal with the rubble. A *sword* to reply to attack. And *prayer* to invoke divine aid. They went at it, so the story goes, "from day-break until the stars came out".

Those tools are about all you need in any work of national re-construction—

> a *trowel*, which I take it indicates the will to work;
> a *sword*, which indicates the will to fight; and
> *prayer*, which draws upon the endless resources of God.

Last October the Archbishop of York and I issued what has come to be known as our Call to the Nation. We did so because we saw that the defences of the nation had been breached, the gates which should have kept out evil had been burnt, and our beloved England was full of rubble. The response was remarkable—and it still continues. A start at rebuilding has been made. Hundreds, probably thousands, of groups, all over the country are discussing the two questions we put to the nation: "What sort of society do we want? What kind of people are needed to create such a society?" This discussion must go on, and at greater depth. Plans are being made to see that in fact it does go on. Hard thinking provides the foundations for the rebuilding. But we must see to it that the response to the Call does not evaporate into a cloud of words. Trowel, sword and prayer are needed.

Trowel, by which I mean the will to work. I am not referring here to the need, on a national scale, to recover our pride in work well done, in turning out a first-class product and delivering it on time to the purchaser, though that, surely, is one of our greatest needs and without it there won't be economic recovery. No: I am referring specifically to work in clearing away the rubble of the spiritual breakdown and the moral decay of our nation and building again a society in which we can bring up our children without shame. It is no good saying "tut, tut" when we see things that are wrong, and asking why the Church doesn't do something about it! *You* are the Church, if you love and serve the Lord Christ. Nehemiah tackled his huge task by dividing it up into sections. Then as the sections did their local job, at last the whole city was re-built. That is the only way we shall ever do our reconstructive job in England—by doing it in our own locality and doing it together. I would say to Christians and men of good will in every area in Britain: "Define your local need. Muster your local resources. Use your trowels, and get to work. You will soon shift the rubble, and build something lovely out of the mess."

Sword. You are likely to meet opposition. Be ready for it. Indeed there are some things which call for a sword—dirt on the media and on the bookstalls, far too high an abortion rate, the cheapening of sex, a lack of reverence for life, unemployment of school-leavers, bad housing, lack of playing fields; you name it, for you know what is wrong in your own neighbourhood. Fighting is not pleasant work, but if the Church (that's you) is to do its work, it must be ready to smite, and smite again, when society tolerates things which the Christian knows that his Lord would loathe. Our weakness in the past has often derived from the fact that a vast number of people who know what is right tolerate what is wrong—*they will not fight*. "The silent majority" must become a vocal majority.

Prayer. Nehemiah's book is shot through with arrow-prayers. He kept in touch with Headquarters even as he worked. That was the secret of his final success, of the overthrow of the opposing forces, and of the rebuilding of his beloved city.

I speak to you on Easter Sunday morning. You may wonder why, on such a morning, I have spoken as I have, and have so far said nothing about the resurrection of Christ. I have done so because I have kept the best to the last. I should have no stomach for this fight for the rebuilding of our nation were it not for the fact that the Lord of the Church is the risen King of

Glory. "Do not be afraid," we heard him say in the second Lesson. "I am the first and the last, and I am the living one; for I was dead and now I am alive for evermore, and I hold the keys of death and death's domain."

This Call to the Nation is not a call to pull ourselves up by our bootstraps, nor a call to polish up our faded morals. The truth is that we have no power of ourselves to help ourselves. Our only hope is in Christ—incarnate, crucified, risen, all-powerful. "*He is able*", said our second text, "to do immeasurably more than all we can ask or conceive, by the power which is at work among us." This is the astonishing truth of Christianity— that the power of God which raised Jesus from the dead is precisely the power which is available to us who are sons of God by faith in Christ.

This is not a pious ending to an otherwise "practical" sermon. There will be no lasting renewal for our nation, no rebuilding of it, till those of us who are Christians wake up to the fact that in Christ is our only hope and that in him there are endless resources. Once linked to him, we use our trowel to clear up the rubble, we wield our sword to smite our foe, not in our puny strength, but with the resurrection power of the living Christ at work in us and among us.

No more dispirited Christians, then! No more jaded warriors! We need to hear again the word which came from God to Joshua who had been called to an immense task for which he felt singularly ill-equipped: "I will not fail you nor forsake you. Be strong and of good courage." We need to hear the word which Elisha spoke to his disciple when the opposing forces seemed so strong and all he could say was, "Oh master, which way are we to turn?" The reply came back: "Fear not: for they that be with us are more than they that be with them." We need to hear the word of Jesus to his friends: "Go forth . . . And be assured, I am with you always, to the end of time." "Strong in the strength which God supplies, through his eternal Son", we go with his name on our lips, his song in our hearts, his power in our arms. "Come, let us rebuild the wall."

> We rest on thee, our shield and our defender,
> We go not forth alone against the foe;
> Strong in thy strength, safe in thy keeping tender,
> We rest on thee and in thy name we go.

Babble and Blessing

I BRING YOU two stories this morning. Let me sketch them for you.

The first is a "once upon a time" story. In fact, in the New English Bible it begins that way. It comes from the book of Genesis and is told with a mixture of humour and seriousness—rather like a cartoon which, while it makes you smile, has behind it a point, barbed and meaningful. It is a story about Babel, which is the same as Babylon. Babylon stood for everything that is greedy, glamorous, gorgeous, shameless, utterly secular and godless. Well, here are the men of Babel, determined to make a great show of their materialism, their acquisitiveness, their shameless glory in their own works and achievements. "Come", they say, "let us build ourselves a city and a tower with its top in the heavens, and make a name for ourselves . . . !" God, so the story goes, got worried at this. Here was human pride and self-confidence at its worst. What would happen if it was allowed to go further? He must stop it. *How* should he do this? Hitherto they had had only one language. He would "confuse their speech" and give them in its place a *babble* of languages. They would understand one another no more. They would scatter all over the world. That would be the end of their overweening pride in human achievement and in the glamour of *things*.

That is the story. What are we to do with it? You can dismiss it as a bit of primitive folk-lore and leave it at that. You can take it as an elementary way of explaining the variety of languages

Whit Sunday, 6 June, 1976.

which do in fact make life difficult and communication well-nigh impossible. (Don't we who attend international conferences know it!) Or you can say—as I myself would—it is a cartoon story, written by a man with extraordinary insight into the nature of men and things; a story with a message of immense spiritual and practical significance. But more of that when we have looked at our second story.

Here is *no* cartoon. Here is a solid bit of history, though the events which it is seeking to record are so momentous that the telling of them makes almost impossible demands on human language, metaphor, description. Language groans under the burden, but the point comes through bright and clear.

We see a gathering of men and women. We know the names of some of them. They are all together in one place. They are waiting—silently, expectantly. Had not their Lord told them to do so? Had he not said that, when his bodily presence was withdrawn, he would not leave them orphans, he would come to them? But they must wait. Before long he would come. And come he did—not indeed in bodily form, for had he done that his coming would have been limited by conditions of time and space. No—he came invisibly, but infinitely powerfully.

Here it was that language was strained almost to breaking point! How can you put into words what you feel when you know somebody loves you? When you see a sunset? When you smell a flower? When you catch a vision? Any painter or poet or writer or musician knows what I am talking about. You must use metaphors. And so they did. They used two. It seemed like a rushing mighty *wind*—for wind breaks down things, wind sweeps away cobwebs, wind freshens a foetid atmosphere, wind is breath, is *life*. And *fire*—fire burns up dross, fire unites (as in soldering), fire warms the chill, fire glows.

So it was that day with the disciples of Jesus, when his Other Self, his Holy Spirit, came. The wind blew down the old barriers like a tornado, and they were one. It blew away their pride and complacency, in fact it burned it up. It freshened their thinking and enlivened their outlook. It blew down their pride and gave them a great and joyful surprise as they saw the loveliness of Jesus. And the fire warmed them, till they positively glowed not only with love for him but also for one another and for the world for which Christ had died.

Out they went—and preached. They had never been to theological college. They had never had a lesson in homiletics, in how to preach. But as they spoke—and spoke to a mixed multitude of people from a wide variety of nations—they found that somehow the curse of Babel, Babylon, confusion, had been overcome, and they were understood. Love had blown away, burnt up, the old and cursed divisions, and made them one!

Pentecost, in other words, is the reversal of Babel. Babel was about human power. Pentecost (Whitsun) is about God's power. Babel was the work of men. Pentecost, the coming of the Spirit, is the work of God. Babel was about confusion, confusion wrought by man's pride. Pentecost is about order, the order of God brought about by "the humility of the Lord our God descending to our pride", as St Augustine put it. Babel was about destruction, for man's trust in his own achievement always leads to that. Pentecost is about salvation, God creating harmony out of Babel, coming upon us in wind and fire, renewing and re-creating.

Here, then, are the two stories. We can see that the first is far more than a bit of primitive folk-lore. It holds within it some profound theological and religious insights which we ignore at our peril. We can see that the second is best understood as the reversal of the first—on the first Whit Sunday God stepped in in power to undo man's folly, to reverse his disaster, to rescue him from his pride. The first story is a cartoon of damnation; the second a story of redemption.

All very interesting—but what has it got to say to us in Britain today; to me in my journey towards eternity? It has much to say.

The message of Whitsun is the message of *power*. There are few things more powerful than wind and fire, as anyone will tell you who has experienced a tornado or seen a forest fire. And power is our greatest need in Britain today—power to rescue this nation from the curse of self-destruction, of self-centredness, of sin and folly; power to release individuals from bondage. The on-going response to the Archbishops' Call to the Nation shows that all over the country there are men and women open to the coming of the Holy Spirit, themselves centres of his power. There are multitudes more who, in their heart of hearts, long to be agents of his strength but so far have failed to yield their hearts to his allegiance. So we must press on, till men see that they "have no power of themselves to help themselves", that sin has undermined their moral fibre, and that their one hope lies in the Spirit of Jesus taking over, re-newing, vitalising.

vitalising.

This is what our second Lesson was all about. "If a man does not possess the Spirit of Christ", that is to say, if he is not open to his incoming and receptive at once to his demands and his power, "he is no Christian." It is when you are "moved", driven, activated, "by the Spirit of God that you are sons of God". Then you are able to utter the joyful cry which only sons of God can utter—you look up into the Face of God and cry "Abba! Dear Father." That relationship of glad sonship is the key to newness of life and power. New life comes even to our mortal bodies through the indwelling Spirit. We are, it is true, in for suffering now, for we share in the sufferings of Christ and the groanings of a created universe which is the victim of frustration. But we know that victory is ours even now, and splendour awaits us hereafter.

When the presence and power of the Holy Spirit become a living reality to the people of God, men and women will take knowledge of us that we have been with Jesus and will be attracted, not so much to us as to him, to find in their turn what it means to become sons of God and to live in the power of his Spirit.

Four Circles

St Luke 2:39, 40
They returned . . . to their own town of Nazareth.
The child grew big and strong and full of wisdom.

IF I COULD draw a graph of what I am going to say to you this morning, and show it to you from this pulpit, it would be a very simple one. It would consist of four concentric circles. If you wanted me to add a caption to the graph, it could be given in the words "The Family". That is what I want to speak about to you in this Cathedral and to any further afield whom my words may reach through radio or press.

The *first* and biggest circle is the circle of *the human race*—all mankind in its rich variety of colours and creeds, of wealth and poverty, of hope and despair. In this country we see a fair cross-section of the peoples who make up the population of our globe. If you go to the United States of America, you find a greater mixture still. I have no doubt that, as years go by and travel becomes even easier than it is now, this mixing up of peoples and races will increase. How are we to regard this? We can think of it as a menace, and view the man with a coloured face as a threat. If we do so, we shall sow the seeds of suspicion and hate. But we can think of it very differently. That man with a skin of a different colour from mine *could* be an enrichment to my life and to that of my neighbours, if I would not look on him as a potential foe but as a fellow-member with me of the human race, "created of one stock", as St Paul put it, "made", like us, *Christmas Day, 1976.*

"in the image of God" and equally dear to him. To look on these people as sources of enrichment is to lower the temperature of racial suspicion—and that is always worth doing.

On this Christmas morning our thoughts go out to members of our human race who will spend the day behind bars—not for any wrong that they have done to society but because they have fearlessly borne witness to the truth as they have seen it. I think not only of South Africa and of those arrested there over a long period, and even as recently as last month, but of those interned in Russia and other communist-dominated countries. Let us not forget them, and let us be relentless in the pressure we bring to bear for their release.

The *second* circle is that of *the British Commonwealth of Nations*. It is a big circle, representing the best part of a thousand million people. We shall, I hope, be particularly conscious of this circle in the coming year, when we celebrate the Silver Jubilee of the Accession of Her Majesty The Queen. Of that I hope to say more next year, especially in June when we shall, in a great service in St Paul's Cathedral, thank God for those years of splendid service (see pp 169–171), and when we shall meet in our parish churches to do the same with sincerity and joy. Those of us who live in Britain will look at our national life with loving and critical eyes. There is much for which to be thankful—our freedom to think and speak and write according to the dictates of our conscience; peace; comparative plenty; and so on. But there is much to make us anxious. Though I believe it to be true that, since the Archbishops issued their Call to the Nation some fourteen months ago, there has been a serious questioning which is wholly good, there is not yet that turning to God in penitence and faith which alone can lead to a healthy nation. "What sort of society do we want?" and "What sort of people do we need to be in order to achieve it?"—these were the two questions we posed—and they must lead on to other and even deeper questions. "What kind of society does *God* want? What kind of person does he want me to be if I am to take my part in creating such a society?" These are questions which matter supremely. What is my attitude to the God who created me, to the Christ who died for me, to the Holy Spirit who would make me holy too? Have I a living faith? If not, what am I doing to put myself in the way of finding such a faith?

These are the questions which increasing multitudes must ask if corporately we are to build the kind of nation that God wants and that we, at our best, also want.

The *third* circle is that of *the Christian Church*. It is a vast circle, composed of men and women scattered across the globe, declining in numbers in certain areas, increasing in others with enormous rapidity and vigour—men and women of every nation and tribe redeemed by the blood of Christ and owing their all to him. The media often seem to like to present this circle as one which is decreasing almost to the point of nothingness, impotent in a world of power structures which it cannot influence. I do not find this to be the case. As I travel in these islands and throughout the world, I find again and again glorious instances of men and women in the official ministry of the Church, and vast numbers of them in their lay activities, being in fact just what Jesus said they should be, namely, light and salt and yeast. That is to say, I find them penetrating the world's darkness, as *light*. I find them halting the world's rottenness, as *salt* stopped food going bad before the days of refrigerators—yes, and adding a spicy tang to man's existence. I find them acting as *yeast*—a ferment of opposition to evil and of encouragement to good. This is what I see, and I say, "Thank God for the Church and those who go to its make-up." I would add: If you are a critic of the Church, stop shouting on the side-lines and get into the scrum. There's any amount of work to be done for Christ. Let's be less shame-faced as Christians, and get on and do it.

My last and smallest circle is that of *the home*. Even as I utter that word, I think of those who today are homeless. A fortnight ago we sent off from the west door here a fine party, mostly of youngsters, walking to London in aid of just such people—*Crisis at Christmas* bears the homeless in mind. But I think also of one-parent families, where father *or* mother carries the burden that both should share. I think of families where tragedy has struck—the disabled, the unmarried mothers, the elderly women who have never married because they had elderly relatives to care for. We don't forget them at this Christmas season.

At the same time we think of the happy homes, where mother and father and children live together, and laugh together, and pray together, and plan together. These families are the very mainstay of our national life. May their number increase!

That ideal finds its inspiration in a home in a little village called Nazareth where the Child of Bethlehem grew big and strong and full of wisdom, where the Boy learned to pray at his mother's knee, learned what it meant to say "Our Father" and to nurture a passion to do his will at all costs, learned to apply the lessons of Scripture to the living of every day. There he learned to ask the questions: "What sort of society does God want?" and "What kind of person does he want me to be to take my part in creating such a society?" It was from that home that he went, in the power of the Spirit, to teach, to preach and to heal, and at the end to die and rise victorious.

To him and to the Father and the Holy Spirit be ascribed, this happy Christmas Day, our praise and everlasting thanks!

Service in the Setting of Eternity

St John 13:3–5
Jesus, knowing . . . that he came from God and went to God, rose from table, laid aside his garments, took a towel, girded himself, poured water into a basin, and began to wash his disciples' feet.

HOW STRANGE THAT your Archbishop, preaching on *Christmas* morning, should take a text which most of you will recognise as coming from a passage which introduces the *closing* scenes of the life of Jesus. Our Lord is about to enter on his passion and to die on the cross. But before doing so, he gathers his men around him for a final meal. He prefaces that with the foot-washing—he, their Master and Lord, does the work of the meanest slave and washes their feet.

That marvellous story might well occupy our attention this morning. But I shall by-pass it, in order to fasten your attention on the words which introduce it. "Jesus, knowing that he came from God and went to God, took a towel . . ." If you wanted a title for that, you could call it "Service in the setting of eternity".

There is a question which is troubling the minds of many thoughtful people these days. Put briefly and perhaps a bit crudely it runs like this: "Isn't it about time that the Church stopped talking so much about the third world and talked more about the next world?" Put a little more fully, those who pose the question—and they do right to pose it—feel that Church *Christmas Day, 1978.*

49

people have been dirtying their hands a bit too much in seeking to apply the Christian faith to everyday living and to the perennial problems which beset our tortured world, and have been giving too little attention to that other world with which, so they would say, Christianity is primarily concerned. Are they right or are they wrong? There is much to be said on both sides.

Let me briefly make their case for them.

Christianity is about eternity. If I believe, as I most surely do, that I am made in the image of God, destined to develop as one of his sons, made for communion with him not only in the here and now, but for ever, after this little life is through—if, I say, I believe this, then the dimension of eternity is of immense, of inexpressible, importance. Jesus, according to my text, believed that he "was going to God". When he looked at death, he did not use some vague phrase about passing away, but he thought in terms of *going to God*. If that is a fact, then being prepared to meet that God is about the most vital concern I can have. The Christian religion is about *that very thing*—how to enter into life by faith in Christ, how—in the words of today's Gospel—so to receive him that we become children of God. If a preacher fails to make that crystal clear, if he smudges the lines of the dimension of eternity, then he fails in the most sacred task committed to him. To a Christian, it is no morbid thing to be reminded on Christmas day that he is mortal and has to die. For if it is true that in the midst of life we are in death (and any newspaper will vouch for that), it is equally and gloriously true that, for the Christian, in the midst of death we are in life.

We have no business—those of us who seek to teach the Christian faith—to narrow the dimensions of our Gospel. We deal with the immensities of eternity.

But all great truths have their perils. This one certainly has. It is possible so to emphasise the importance of the life to which we go, the "other world" as some people like to call it, that we pay scant attention to *this* world—sometimes despising its joys and refusing to enter into them when God has given them to us freely to enjoy, and sometimes shutting our eyes to the horrors of life, the dirt, the deprivation, the disasters all around us. Jesus never did that. He knew he was going to God. On that, no doubt, he stayed himself as he faced the cruel cross. But that provided him with no escape whatever from the facts of life by which he was surrounded—that his disciples had dirty feet; that somebody had to wash them; that they were too proud to do it for one another so he would do it for them; that nearby was the traitor waiting to sell him for thirty pieces of silver; that round the corner was a howling mob, a cross, and a world needing redemption. For him, it was no either/or; no this world *or* the other world. For him it was both—*both* the world with the Father towards which he moved swiftly nearer, *and* the world of immediate need which clamoured for his intervention and his healing touch. We must go one step further. It was precisely *because* his vision of the other world was so clear, *because* the presence of the Father was so powerful to his consciousness, that he threw himself with such total abandonment into the griefs and sorrows of his fellow-men.

That is the message which I feel I must bring you this Christmas morning. No false antithesis between this world and that! No narrowing of the dimensions of the Gospel! No failure to look beyond this little life to the glory of the age to come! *And* no refusal to jump in, as the Lord Christ jumped in, to the realities of a world which needs the humility of a foot-washing and the redemption of a cross.

If Christmas has any message, it is the message of a Christ born in sordid circumstances, never afraid to dirty his hands as he grew to maturity and to be misunderstood for doing so, always willing to be available just where the point of need was greatest. He laid aside his majesty. "He took a towel, and girded himself."

That is the tension of the Christian faith, and therein is its glory. That is the tension of Christian living, and therein is its joy.

Happy Christmas to you all!

Newness of Life

EARLIER THIS MONTH, in this Cathedral, with the help of Canon Robinson, Dr Wicks and our wonderful choir, I recorded a half-hour service to go round the world twice over this Easter season. They say some sixty million people will hear it. I wondered whether I should preach to you this morning the sermon that I preached then. But it did not seem right. Sermons cannot be repeated just like that. What is God's word for one occasion may not be his word for another. And anyway, since we recorded that service, there has been a phrase which has kept repeating itself in my mind, and would not let me go. It kept, as it were, knocking at my door, and saying to me: "Try to preach about me on Easter morning in the Cathedral."

And so, by God's grace, I will. The phrase is *"Newness of life"*.

It is a good phrase to preach about in England on a late March morning. It has been a long winter—in some ways a hard one. Snow, and rain, and wind—and 'flu! But for some time now, there have been signs of newness of life. Earlier this week I watched an old lady burying her hand in a rather unpromising wayside hedge, and bringing out a little bunch of brave violets. Around us are crocuses, daffodils, fresh green grass where last month it was all dead and dirty. "Newness of life" everywhere! Life in place of death!

They took Jesus down from the cross. His body was limp and blood-stained. With tender care they wrapped it in strips of linen cloth according to Jewish burial customs. They laid it in a

Easter Sunday, 26 March, 1978.

new tomb, and rolled a stone over its mouth. Broken-hearted, they said: "That's that." There seemed to be an awful finality about death.

But there was no finality in this case. Don't ask me to explain the details. The Gospel records differ among themselves. Perhaps that is just as well—otherwise we might have suspected the writers of collusion in order to make us believe the tale they told. They say some very mysterious things about the nature of the body of Jesus which, they all aver, was raised by the power of God. But what they affirm with a total unanimity is this: that whereas there was death, real death with all its agony, now there was "newness of life". Death could not hold this Man. God ratified what he was and what he did by raising him from the dead. "If you want evidence," said St Paul, writing only a few years after the event, "ask the witnesses who saw the Risen Christ—most of them are still alive."

A few years after this crucifixion-resurrection event, somewhere not far from Rome, perhaps under cover of darkness (for Christianity was an illicit religion), a little group of men and women wended their way to a tributary of the Tiber. Stripping themselves of their working clothes, they went down into the water. It was like a burial—a burial to the old unregenerate life. Up they came—to be clothed with a pure white garment. "Abba! Father!" they cried out. They were in the Christian family. The old life was left behind for ever. Newness of life was theirs. They shared the life of the risen Christ—to the glory of God the Father and the blessing of the world.

This has gone on down the long centuries, from that day to this, all over the world. "Buried with Christ and raised with him too." For various reasons, the form of the baptism has not always been so dramatic or symbolic as that which I have just described and which St Paul refers to in his letter to the Romans. But "newness of life" in Christ—this is a reality which has been and is the birthright of every believer, you and me included.

There was released, that first Easter morning, a power which, so far from diminishing as the centuries pass, increases and spreads. It is fashionable to underestimate that power and to depict the Church, the Body of Christ where that power is uniquely at work, as effete and about to die. It is indeed true that, in places, the Church has the smell of death about it. But again and again, to those who have eyes to see, there are signs of newness of life and abundance of life.

I see this newness of life in so many people I meet—a Cicely Saunders giving her life to enable men and women to die with the dignity due to the children of God; a Trevor Huddleston going back to work in Africa at an age when most people would be thinking of putting their feet up in easy retirement; a young man, one-time art student, dedicating his skills to the furtherance of the Gospel by means of television and the arts; a young woman, trained as a nurse, turning her back on the comparative comfort of Western civilisation, to spend and be spent for the needs of a primitive race. I see these people with a purpose to their living, a drive to their work, a light in their eyes; and if you ask them the secret, there is no doubt about its source. They have found newness of life—in Christ, and want to spend it for him.

I look again—at the wider life of the Church. I see the Church in Uganda, undismayed by what it has suffered in recent years, inspired by the martyrdom of its Archbishop, experiencing in the midst of the fire the presence of One like unto the Son of God. At home, I see the growth of groups of Christians, of "fringers", of enquirers, meeting to study, to discuss, to pray, to find out whether Christ after all may not be the Way, the Truth, and the Life, and, if he is, how best to follow him.

I see an increasing number of men coming forward to offer themselves for the sacred ministry of the Church; and, unless I am greatly mistaken, I see already a determination, on the part of the members of the Church, to encourage them and to provide the wherewithal for their training and their maintenance.

I see, in many places, a new liveliness in public worship, a participation of the laity with the clergy in that worship as of right—for are they not all the people of God? I see a questioning, a readiness to experiment, a determination not to succumb to the standards of the world but to strike out into new paths—all very discomforting to those whose motto is "as it was in the beginning, is now, and ever shall be", but all very exciting to those who believe in newness of life in Christ.

I love to look at a newly-ploughed field. Great, heavy clods of earth, turned over by the plough, weighty with the soaking of the rain. But it will not be long before, with a daring and a vivacity which rebuke our faithlessness, tiny shoots of green break through the clods. A harvest is on the way! The powers of life are at work. Newness of life is a reality.

You, my brothers and sisters, if you are baptised into Christ and are at his disposal, are men and women of the resurrection, agents of his power, sources of his newness of life. Go back to your work and witness, this Easter morning, full of hope and joy, of peace and love, and let no one rob you of your heritage.

Homes

IT IS STRANGE, isn't it, how little we know about the home of Jesus. We know a certain amount about his Mother, her loving obedience to the supreme call that came to her, her thoughtful watch over the growth of her Son, and so on. Rather dimly in the background we discern the figure of Joseph; and there are references in the Gospels to a quite considerable family. We can be pretty sure that there was a firm discipline in the family—the Boy Jesus, when he went back to Nazareth after the expedition to Jerusalem, "continued to be under their authority", so St Luke tells us. There is no doubt that the family worshipped together regularly—Jesus as a young man "went to synagogue *as his custom was*", so St Luke again informs us. That meant a pretty firm grounding in the Scriptures—his own teachings show that he was extremely well versed in them.

Though we would *like* to know more, perhaps that is about all we *need* to know—loving discipline, corporate worship, basic Scripture knowledge of a practical kind.

I want to speak to you briefly this morning about *homes*, for Christmas above all other seasons is the festival of the home. Let me first of all wish you the happiest Christmas yet in your homes, and let me single out—I'm sure the grown-ups won't mind!—the children for a very special word of greeting this Christmas morning. I'll have a word more to say about our own homes in a minute, but first I want to mention two other kinds of home.

Christmas Day, 1979.

First—and this is rather an Irish way of expressing it—I would mention places where there are *no* homes, at least as you or I would understand that word. The sort of "home" I have in mind is the kind I've seen abroad—a few feet of space on the pavement, with a bit of tarpaulin or corrugated iron for shelter, and that's about all. My friend Archbishop Elinana Ngalamu of the Sudan was telling me the other day that in the south of his huge diocese they have got the best part of 150,000 refugees who fled into their country when Uganda was going through its hell. Think of finding—or making—homes for them! And there are the boat people, and the unspeakable conditions of Kampuchea! Don't forget the homeless this Christmas.

Secondly, there are the broken homes. How many there are! My heart goes out to the people in those homes—lonely persons trying to do double duty and to act as father and mother in one, in very difficult circumstances. Let's be sparing in our ostracism—that never helps much. Rather, let's see if we can do a bit to help in mending any broken home that we may know and, where the breakdown seems to be irreparable, lend a hand with the children ourselves and give a bit of strong and practical sympathy to the parents who are deprived of one another's help. And let's do a bit of pretty straight thinking as to *why* so many marriages break down, with dire consequences to the children. Don't our divorce laws need a good deal of tightening up? Are not many young people getting married far too young? Can we do something to arrest the spread of an attitude to marriage which at least seems to say: "Go through the ceremony in church or at the Registry office; it signifies little; you can contract out in a few months if it doesn't work out; little is lost . . ."? Can't we do something about that?

It will take hard thinking and serious action on the part of a great many of us if the present landslide is to be stopped. A country whose divorces have multiplied by four in the space of thirty years is a country in danger!

So I come back nearer to base. Since I became a bishop in 1956, I've gone round Yorkshire and this part of Kent and elsewhere confirming. On almost every occasion I have asked the parents and godparents of the young people I've confirmed to meet with me after the service. Quite often I have told them about our years in Yorkshire when we lived in a house a few miles from York where the garden abutted on to the river Ouse. On the other side of the river was a piece of open land across which the strong cold wind would blow with nothing to stop it. The garden, when we arrived there in 1961, was somewhat devoid of trees, and we planted a great many. We learned to be very careful how we did the planting. Not only did we see that the roots of the tree were carefully spread out in good soil and that that soil was firmly heeled in. But we also provided two firm stakes. To those stakes we tied the young tree—not too tightly, for it must have liberty of movement—but firmly; and we left those stakes there for quite a few years. Then came the time when the tree was so strong that the stakes could be removed and growth would go on as it should. As I told this simple parable, I could see by the faces of those who listened that little application was needed.

I hope to preach twice more from this pulpit before I retire. But I would like my last *Christmas* message to be a plea to parents to see to it that the homes in which their young people grow up are strong Christian homes. By that I mean homes where there is strong, positive and loving discipline—not a mass of petty rules, but a kind of simple structure which lets the children know where they are in moral matters and what is the meaning of the law of Christ. I mean homes where regular corporate worship can be taken for granted as the norm, father, mother and children going together Sunday by Sunday to the House of God. I mean homes where there is an open Bible and a place for family prayer; where Christ is loved and served in the gladness of Christian freedom. I mean, in short, homes something like the home at Nazareth where Jesus grew up and from which eventually he went out to minister to a needy world.

There, in homes like that, the young people will, in the words of St Paul, be "shaped to the likeness of God's Son"; and you can't want anything better for them than *that*!

Happy Christmas!

Happy Christian homes!

Happy New Year!

III
WHAT KIND OF SOCIETY?

What Kind of Society?

IN LITTLE MORE than two months' time, many of us will be assembling once again in this Cathedral in a service designed to celebrate the Silver Jubilee of the Accession of our beloved Queen. We shall thank God for these twenty-five years; and we shall do so with full hearts. The eyes of millions throughout the Commonwealth and far beyond will be on us that day.

It would not be out of place, therefore, for us who in our different spheres occupy places of responsibility in the city and nation to stop for a few minutes, in the quiet of this great church, and take a look at the nation of which we are a part.

Some eighteen months ago, the Archbishop of York and I issued what came to be known as our Call to the Nation. We asked two questions:—"What sort of society do we want?" and "What sort of people do we need to be in order to achieve it?" The questions were outwardly simple, but they proved, on consideration, to go pretty deep. The media were generous in the way that they responded to our initiative. A forum was provided for discussion. Groups sprang up all over the country to seek to find answers to the questions. Christians in places of responsibility have been activated to make their influence felt in the institutions they serve. It takes time for ideas to percolate society, but that a process of percolation has begun there can be no doubt. The Call of 1975 got something going. Up and down the country, in all walks of life, people began to be more

United Guilds Service, St Paul's Cathedral, 1 April, 1977.

articulate about the basic questions that influence the life of a
nation. And the process continues.

It matters to each one of us what sort of society we take a part
in creating. Do you want to bring up your children—or your
grandchildren—in a society where there are no guidelines to
health? Where they can rush, like the Gadarene swine, towards
the abyss and find nothing to stop them? Do you want the
nation to have laws to protect them physically and none to
guard them mentally, morally, spiritually? Do you want a
nation where sex is trivialised and life held cheap? Where
self-discipline is scarcely heard of, and "each for himself" is the
motto? To have such a society is the easiest thing in the world.
All we have to do is to keep silence when such issues are raised
in the circles where we move. Silence means consent, and
consent leads to disaster—personal and national. Our age, so I
heard last night, has been called by a young man of seventeen,
"the age of apathy".

But today, against the background of these eighteen months
of which I have spoken, I want to press our questions a little
deeper, and to ask: "What sort of society does *God* want?" and
"What sort of people does *God* want us to be?" For, after all,
the thing which, above all else, marks us humans off from other
animal members of creation is the fact that we are answerable,
able to respond, to the God who is our Creator, our Redeemer
and our Judge. That is *the* distinctive mark of our humanity—
answerability, responsibility.

If you say to me: "But the word *God* has no meaning, no
content, for me", I would remind you of the story of the man
who visited an art gallery full of priceless treasures painted by
the masters. Said he to the artist who accompanied him: "I
don't see anything in these pictures." The artist replied:
"Don't you wish you could?" And if you say to me: "I want to
see some content to that word *God*; I long to know what he is
like, if indeed he exists; I would even dare to line up my little
will with his if he would make that will known," I would reply:
"No such desire need go unanswered. For God *has* made himself known, *has* shown to man his likeness, *has* indicated his will
for nations and individuals. Listen to this word from St John's
Gospel: 'No one has ever seen God; but God's only Son, he who
is nearest to the Father's heart, he has made him known.'" God

is not a silent God. If we are deaf, we must not think that God is dumb. He has spoken, very clearly, very pointedly, in his Son, who is the Word made flesh, the mind and heart and will of God disclosed. If we are blind, we must not conclude that there has been no revelation on God's part. There has indeed. What we need to do is to put ourselves in the position of blind Bartimeus in the lesson to which we have just listened. Jesus said to him: "What do you want me to do for you?" "Master," the blind man answered, "I want my sight back." So deep was his desire, so great his longing for an end to his blindness, that he recovered his sight and followed Jesus on the road. It is, of course, all too often our unwillingness to follow Jesus on the road that leaves us with blinded eyes.

> 'Tis ye, 'tis your estrangèd faces,
> That miss the many-splendoured thing.

A week today and it will be Good Friday. A week on Sunday, and it will be Easter Day. *Good* Friday, did I say? *Good* Friday? Surely it was the worst Friday that ever happened, the Friday when men took the finest Man who had ever lived (to put it at its lowest) and strung him up on a cross and jeered at him till he died in untold agony. It only seems to make it worse when we realise that "Good" means, in fact, "God's"—it was *God's* Friday. Surely it was *man's* Friday—the day when man's beastliness outstripped itself and vented its awfulness on the Prince of peace and goodness. But wait a minute. Is there more to it than meets the eye? Indeed there is. It *was* God's Friday. For there on the cross, *God* was in Christ, reconciling to himself a world which had got itself all tangled up, which thought that power and money and possessions and position were the things that really mattered. There on the cross he humbled himself and hung naked and empty, the One who, as the Lesson put it, came not to be served but to serve and to give his life a ransom for many. Having loved his own, he loved them to the uttermost, even to death. And *that*, precisely *that*, has proved to be the most mighty power in human life and history that the world has known during the last two millennia.

Have we got a clue here to the kind of society God wants for us and for our children? And have we got a clue as to the sort of people God wants us to be? Yes—and far more than a clue. It is a key—the only key that fits our situation at all. For in the Christ of God's Friday, the Christ of Easter Day, the Christ crucified and risen, we see, as nowhere else, God's pattern for society and for us individuals who make up that society. His plan is that we should no longer be hard men, self-concerned, living on the surface of life, nor cluttered men, smothered in all the things we possess. *That* way, we become lonely, ill at ease, frightened that we shall lose what we have got, bored because we have everything we want. Life dedicated to being comfortable can be unutterably dreary. But life given, given to God who created and redeemed us, life given to God who is our Judge, life given in service to the needy for the sake of him who died for us all, *that* is the stuff of which the society is made which *God* wants.

You will have time, over the coming days of holiday, to give some thought to these things. What kind of nation does *God* want Britain to become during the Silver Jubilee year? What kind of person does he want you to be as you, through your own character, share in the making of this nation? Those are the questions which matter supremely.

A Christian in the Sudan was speaking recently of what our country had given to his. What did he mention? Commercial acumen, scientific knowledge, education, airways, fertilisers, power stations? He might well have listed these. But he did not. He said that we had given the Sudan a sense of nationhood, a spirit of self-discipline, and the Bible. Who is to say he was not right? Are not *these* the things which make a nation great—great in character, great in the contribution that the nation can in turn make to others? And are not these the things which the God of justice and of love revealed in Jesus Christ looks for, above all else, in us in Britain this Silver Jubilee year?

We look around at Britain.
We look up to Christ on his cross.

And at this holy season we turn our thoughts into a prayer—for the nation and for ourselves:—

Lo! the hosts of evil round us
Scorn thy Christ, assail his ways!
From the fears that long have bound us
Free our hearts to faith and praise;
Grant us wisdom, grant us courage,
For the living of these days.

Cure thy children's warring madness,
Bend our pride to thy control;
Shame our wanton, selfish gladness,
Rich in things and poor in soul;
Grant us wisdom, grant us courage,
Lest we miss thy kingdom's goal.

Responsibility

Psalm 8: 4
What is man, that thou art mindful of him?
and the son of man, that thou visitest him?

THE WORLD IN which the English-Speaking Union operates is a *shrunken* world—the discoveries of science have brought us to the point that we live in a global village. It is a *frightened* world—we are scared by the works of our own hands. It is a *divided* world—torn asunder by problems of colour, of inequality, of prejudice. And it is an *exciting* world— with all kinds of prospects and possibilities opening up for us and our children, if we have but the wisdom to exploit them rightly. How important it is that those tens of millions of us who share the English language and who acknowledge the ideals of our founder, Sir Evelyn Wrench, should hold together and seek to spread that international understanding for which the Union has stood for sixty years! This must be one of our clearest objectives in the coming decades.

The Commonwealth still holds, thank God. There are ties of loyalty to the Sovereign, ties of blood and of sacrifice which bind the members of the Commonwealth very closely together. Similarly, the ties of history and of close intercourse bind us in these islands with our brothers and sisters in the United States of America. For that too we can thank God. It is vital that nothing should loosen those links.

The English-Speaking Union, Service of Dedication and Thanksgiving, St Margaret's Westminster, 12 July, 1978.

But today other fields of co-operation open up before us, in a way which our founder and his friends could not envisage. We have entered Europe, and the Channel has almost ceased to matter. We hope and labour for closer European unity. Here at home, already ours is a multi-racial society. It is up to us to see that fact not as something to deplore or to moan about but as a challenge to our inventiveness and to our care for human beings, whatever the colour of their skins, whatever their religion, whatever their race. Co-operation must be strengthened at this point. To concentrate too exclusively on our unity of speech, on our "Englishness" or our "American-ness", *could* be to engage in a selfish operation and indeed a soul-destroying one.

All of which drives us back to a fundamental question—a question, I would suggest, compared with which there are few others of like importance. The question is an ancient one, and a perennial one. No one of us can afford to by-pass it. Three monosyllables pose it: *"What is man?"*, or—to put it more personally—*"What am I?"*.

Many answers have been given. One of the ancients, impressed (or perhaps I had better say *oppressed*) by the brevity of man's spell on earth, said: "He is a breath—a puff of wind." Just that—and he's gone! Another put it even less pleasingly: "He is like one of the beasts that perish." "What a piece of work is a man!" said Shakespeare. Well—yes. But it all depends on what sort of tone you say it in!

But there have been other answers. One dark night, some centuries before Christ, a man emerged from his tent in the Near East and looked up into the sky. He knew very little about the immensity of the universe as modern scientists have revealed it to us, but he knew enough to be impressed by the vastness of what he saw. As he looked up, he found himself engaging in a kind of conversation with God: "What is man, that thou art mindful of him? and the son of man, that thou visitest him?" What would you expect him to have answered? Presumably, he would answer as some of his fellow-nationals had done or were doing—"a breath; a beast". But no! This is what he said, speaking to his God: "Thou hast made him little lower than the angels, and hast crowned him with glory and honour. Thou hast put all things under his feet . . ."

This was a mighty insight—something of a revelation. Man as God's vice-gerent, put in trust by God with nature and its resources, answerable to the Creator for what he makes of nature, and of his relationship to others, to God and to himself. This is a great and powerful concept. According to this, man is not just a puff of wind, not just one part, even the highest part, of the animal creation, not just a mêlée of desires. He is a responsible being, that is to say, one who can make response to God, who is answerable to him. Here is his uniqueness. Here is his essential dignity. Here is the *humanum* which separates him off from the rest of the created order.

So far, so good. But this poses another question. What do we mean when we speak of "God" in this connection? We do not have to go very far in our search for an answer. Our Chairman, in reading that Lesson from the book of the prophet Isaiah, gave us a picture of the kind of God who awaits response from his creatures—a God of wisdom and power, of discernment and of justice. The second Lesson described that *love* of which God is the author, a love totally removed from any taint of sentimentality, almost terrifyingly down-to-earth in its bearing on human relationships. We who are Christians believe that in Jesus Christ there has been given a revelation of the nature of God in the Person of our Lord which is adequate for our need. "He who has seen me has seen the Father." "God, who commanded the light to shine out of darkness, has shined in our hearts, to give the light of the knowledge of the glory of God in the face of Jesus Christ." There is much in life which leaves us sorely puzzled. Question-marks abound and persist for the thinking man. But in Christ, the Word and Revelation of the Father, we have One to whom, in the fulness of our manhood and womanhood, we can respond in faith, in confidence and in hope; and in so doing find the fulfilment of the destiny for which we were made.

If I understand it rightly, one of the main tasks of the English-Speaking Union is to enable its members to create and strengthen personal bonds at all levels between peoples and organisations of all types, fostering human relationships worldwide. Experience shows very clearly that when such efforts are made on a purely human level they are very fragile—they have within them the seeds of disintegration. Something deeper and more solid is called for. I believe that an Old Testament prophet gave us a clue when he wrote, in words which most of you will remember: "What doth the Lord require of thee, but to do justly, and to love mercy, and to walk humbly with thy God?" The closing words of the quotation—"to walk humbly *with thy God*"—are the words least frequently heeded; but they are, of all the words, the most crucial.

Only as we learn to "walk with God", the God of justice and love revealed to us in Christ, shall we be able to "do justly and love mercy", and to make those positive relationships which are needed in a world whose trends in government are increasingly secular and totalitarian.

I believe that the greatest contribution which we in the English-Speaking Union can make to the welfare of our world—shrunken, frightened, divided, exciting—is to help men to realise who they are, made in the image of God and responsible to him; and to show them, by the example of ourselves as we "walk humbly with God" that, in that very response, we begin to find the road to justice and to peace.

A Battle to be Fought

THE SERVICE IN which we are joining this morning presents us with such a richness of historical allusion and of picturesque imagery that the preacher is hard put to it to decide on what aspect he should fasten in his address.

History is being made today, in that the Order is celebrating the 250th anniversary of its inception and is installing a new Grand Master—an installation which brings joy and satisfaction to us all. The name of the Order takes us back to the days when the Knights expressed their desire for purity in the actual taking of a bath when first they were installed. But in all the wealth of historical allusion and imagery one note has predominated—in the symbolism of installation both of Grand Master and of Knights, in the psalmody and in the Lesson. It is the note of the *service* of Crown and Nation and of the *defence* of the right against all adversaries. The ceremony has been saying, as clearly as any ritual can do, "There are certain things more precious than life itself, things which can easily be lost and must be defended. There is a battle to be fought, and a fight to be won. And if the fight be bloody, we will not complain."

Patriotism, that much misunderstood word, that muted concept, patriotism (the love of Crown and nation) is to the fore in the Oath which has been administered. It is put in very personal terms: "You shall love the Queen, your Sovereign Lady, and her and her right defend to your power." I would that we in this

The Order of the Bath, 28 May, 1975 (250th anniversary together with the installation as Grand Master of His Royal Highness, the Prince of Wales).

70

nation might recapture that note, and with it an interpretation of patriotism in terms of service. If down the long centuries of our history this nation has acquired traditions worth preserving, traditions of freedom of thought and expression, of reverence for life, of love of scholarship and beauty, then here is a treasure which we must share with all who will receive it. I could wish that, in the controversy about the referendum in which we shall vote next week, less had been heard about how we shall, or shall not, profit by maintaining our position in Europe, and more about what, in the goodness of God, we might be able to contribute to the European Economic Community. We shall maintain our spiritual treasures only by sharing them. Patriotism, thought of in terms of giving and of sharing, is nothing to be ashamed of. On the contrary, it is something to be recaptured and prized.

I said that today's service and ceremony have proclaimed very clearly that "there is a battle to be fought and a fight to be won". He would be a very blind man who did not see this today in England. To us in Britain in the late twentieth century the words "You shall defend maidens, widows and orphans in their rights" have an archaic ring about them. The Welfare State is doing its best to see that these rights are guarded—if you think in terms of money and housing and legal matters. We may thank God for that. But there are other perils than these, other dangers to be met, more subtle than the defencelessness of a maiden who must be rescued by the sword of a knight. What about the defencelessness of an unborn child helpless against the ravages of those who treat abortion as if it were little more than a minor surgical operation? What about the defencelessness of a youngster who is brought up in a home where there is no love, no family security, no discipline, no Christian example and teaching? What about the menace of that philosophy of life, which seeps into us like a dank fog, which assumes that more to be desired than anything else is the acquisition of stocks and shares, or of honours and the esteem of men, rather than the smile of God? What about the selfishness which puts personal gain before national welfare? Are not *these* the enemies at the gate—the gate of our national life and of our personal eternal welfare?

How pertinent, then, are the opening words of the Oath:

"You shall honour God above all things; you shall be steadfast in the Faith of Christ." *This comes first.* Neglect *that*, and the gates of national and personal life are open to the invasion of every kind of ill. Mark that well, live by it, embrace it as your own, and together "strong in the Lord and in the power of his might, we shall be able to stand against the wiles of the devil . . . we shall be able to withstand in the evil day, and, having done all, to stand." God grant it.

One Word of Truth

As I SPEAK to you today, I have in mind the speech which Alexander Solzhenitsyn made on receiving the Nobel Prize in 1970. The title of his speech was: "One word of truth"—words which he took from the Russian proverb: "One word of truth outweighs the whole world." The idea is old—*magna est veritas et praevalebit*—but is it true?

It was Solzhenitsyn's thesis that until recently people were guided by their experience of life within their own restricted locality. So it was possible for individuals to adopt some common scale of values—to decide what was criminal, what was deceitful, and so on. During recent decades, however, mankind has become united reassuringly *and* dangerously. In one minute the modern world learns of a given event—radio and press have united us. But they have not given us a yardstick of measurement or of judgement. Thus, an accident in my home town, just because it is near me, seems more important to me than a flood which drowns two hundred thousand people in China.

So Solzhenitsyn can speak of "this paralysis and lack of understanding of a stranger's distant grief". Such lack of understanding, he says, "threatens to bring a rapid and stormy end". "Who", he asks, "will explain to mankind what is truly terrible . . . and what only irritates our skin because it is near? Who will direct our anger against that which is truly terrible and not that which is merely near?"

Solzhenitsyn holds that art and literature can somewhat straighten the twisted paths of men's history. "Woe betide that

Parliamentary Press Gallery, Houses of Parliament, 19 February, 1975.

nation whose literature is interrupted by the interference of force. To wall up alive a creative literary genius is to threaten the whole nation." In these words, we hear the voice of his bitter experience.

He looks at his world. The same old primitive urges rend and sunder it—greed, envy, licence, mutual malevolence—though they now adopt euphemistic synonyms. "Violence strides bold and victorious through the world." He tilts at the older ones among us—we dare not argue with those who would break up law and order, lest we be thought "conservative". We are, as Dostoevsky said, "in bondage to advanced notions". We surrender to the lust for comfort at any price, to materialism as the main aim of our life on earth.

Solzhenitsyn's analysis is keen and sure. Where does he see hope? He sees it as being "within the powers of world literature . . . to help humanity to comprehend its own nature", to censure not only their inadequate leaders but also their own society. Violence cannot survive in isolation. It is inevitably bound up with "the lie". "Writers and artists can vanquish the lie. We are capable of helping the world in its agonised testing hour. We must not seek excuses on the ground that we lack weapons. We must not give ourselves over to a carefree life, we must go into battle."

Solzhenitsyn was thinking primarily of books of weight which were likely to take their place in the abiding literature of the world. Most of *our* work is more ephemeral—a leader, a sermon, an article, a radio talk, a television programme. But what is true of such works as he had in mind is to some extent true of the work of all of us who use words as our medium. We have in them a weapon of enormous potential, mightier than it was a few decades ago because it has its share in uniting the world for good or ill.

We *can* do something to right the distortion of truth by distance, to differentiate what is terrible from what irritates the skin. We *can* do something not merely to describe the outward manifestations of greed, envy, licence, but to point to their source. Perhaps you and I, joining hands and fostering the interplay of minds, can bring certain yardsticks of measurement and judgement to bear.

Recently I have spoken publicly of the need for a charter of human duties, "guidelines for a healthy society". Is there anything to this? I should value your judgement. If we find ourselves promoting certain values which might be called "conservative", we will not shrink from the taunts of those who, in abandoning those virtues, have bid fair to overthrow society lock, stock and barrel. We will not "be in bondage to advanced notions", if those notions break up all that history has told us is integral to the health of the world, nation, individual. But as Solzhenitsyn saw with blinding clarity, this means the end of a carefree life. It means going into battle.

As a Christian I find it significant that, when St John wanted to find the most expressive phrase by which to speak of Christ, he called him "the Word". He could have chosen other epithets, but he chose the epithet "Word" because a word expresses the mind, the heart, the will of him who utters it. Jesus expresses the mind of the eternal towards us men. He is what God has to say to men.

Those of us who are disciples of the Word and who use words as the stuff of our work find ourselves stimulated by this concept.

I note that in Scripture the word is sometimes spoken of as a sword—"with the sword of his mouth he shall slay the wicked", and so on. The word speaks of battle. He who wields a sword may fall in the battle. A sword pierced the side of the Word and he died in the fight. But he rose, and his word has gone out into all the world.

Perhaps the proverb *is* true: "one word of truth outweighs the whole world." Perhaps when we wield this sword we are on the winning side. Our sword is sharper than we think.

> Say not, the struggle naught availeth,
> The labour and the wounds are vain,
> The enemy faints not, nor faileth,
> And as things have been they remain.

Clough was right, and Churchill knew what he was doing when he quoted him in our darkest hour.

Light-bearers

IF OUR ROLES could be reversed this afternoon, and I could sit where you are sitting, while you entered this pulpit and gave the address, what would you say? What would you want to get across to the members of this great congregation and to the overflow meeting in St Margaret's Church? What would you want them to take back home with them—to remember and to live by, whatever part of this island or of the world they come from?

Well, I had to face that question as I prepared to come to you today. There were, of course, many possibilities open to me. I could have given you a history of the work done by the Mothers' Union over a hundred years and paid a well-deserved tribute to its founder and to its achievements here in England and throughout the whole Anglican Communion. Or I could have talked to you about *New Dimensions*, the new charter, and the new look of an organisation now moving into its second century. Again, I could have spoken about "the continuing importance of the family in the changing circumstances of Britain today", as I hope to do next week in introducing a debate in the House of Lords under those terms (see pp 80–89).

But I have decided to do none of these things. Rather, as I look out over this congregation, I want to speak to each one of you as if there were only one of you to speak to; to ask you to listen as if your life depended on it; and then to take the simple message I bring you back to your own area, for discussion and action.

Mothers' Union Centenary, Westminster Abbey, 10 June, 1976.

Let me begin with a picture. Many of you have travelled here by air. Most of you have, at one time or another, undertaken an air journey. I myself have travelled in the service of the Church, as our President has done in the service of the Mothers' Union, many thousands of miles by jet, or even by Concorde. I am still fascinated by air travel *at night*. As one flies over a town or city, making one's descent in the darkness of the night, one looks out at the town below and sees little pin-points of light. Most of the offices and factories, it may well be, are closed. These pin-points of light—each one represents a home, a family, its light penetrating the darkness, shining out into the gloom.

This is my parable. Our world today is pretty dark. In parts of it there are conflicts and open manifestations of tension and hatred. I think of Ireland, of parts of Africa and of the Middle East, and so on. In parts of it there are hunger and social conditions which beggar description. In other parts there has been such a loss of moral standards and such a lack of the teaching of Christ that the children grow up in a maze of moral uncertainty. "Darkness covers the land and gross darkness the people"—there is no doubt about that. But all over the world, from Arctic to Equator, from East to West, in countries where there is religious liberty and in communist-dominated lands, there are Christian homes where the light of Christ shines—and *here* is our hope. *These* are the pin-points of light which penetrate the surrounding darkness.

Now—what do I mean by Christian homes? I would find that hard to define, but I think I could *describe* it. Let me at least have a try. I look inside one of these homes, these centres of light, and this is what I see:

I see a man and woman who love one another with a deep and understanding love. This is the basis of the security and confidence which the children feel, as they go out from the home and mix with others who have no such privilege. It may be that in this home there are not the signs of such affluence as there are in other homes in the neighbourhood. But this man and woman know that there are more important things than television sets and spin-driers, convenient and pleasurable as these indeed are. The security of love, the confidence created by a deep harmony at home, is a treasure beyond all price.

I look again, and I think I can see in the living-room a copy of the New Testament, perhaps of the whole Bible. Not one of those gloomy-looking Bibles which some of us had as children, with small type and language three and a half centuries old, but an attractive book, well printed, in language which a modern youngster can grasp without undue difficulty. Here it is, available among the other books or papers in the room, easy of reach, read from time to time by the individuals in the home, and read pretty regularly by father or mother when they say to the children: "Let's kneel down and have a prayer together." For this little family, into whose home we are looking today, knows the truth of the old saying that "the family that prays together stays together". Bible and prayer—it is a good duet.

I look again—and here physical sight gives place to a more subtle "sensing" of things—and I see an allegiance to Jesus Christ on the part of the parents which is of such a kind that it is likely, if not now then later on in their lives, to lead the children to give to him an allegiance similar to that of their parents. To this mother and father, their religion has about it, not so much a sense of duty (though that element is not to be despised) as of glad response to the One who loved them and gave himself for them. This response, this allegiance, will issue, of course, in worship with the people of God in the neighbourhood, for discipleship needs the nurture and strength which can only be found in regular participation in the ministry of word and sacrament. It will issue also in a sensitiveness to social need and evangelistic outreach which is part and parcel of the meaning of being "good soldiers of Jesus Christ".

I look out over our world and I see these pin-points of light in the darkness. There are more of them than some of our backward-looking pessimists would think. "They that be with us are more than they that be with them." And anyway, whether our numbers be big or small, we derive our light from him who is the Light of the world, and *that* Light can never be extinguished. In him and through him we are on the victory side.

How I long that these pin-points of light, here in England or elsewhere in God's world, should as it were join up, till there is a flood of light irradiating the darkness. Why not? "That life", said St John, speaking about Jesus in the prologue to his Gospel, "that life was the light of men. The light shines on in the dark, and the darkness has never quenched it." No, thank God. Nor will it ever do so!

"I am the Light of the world," said our Lord.

"You are the light of the world," said our Lord.

Ours is a derived light, a reflected light, rather as the moon derives its light from the sun and reflects it. What more wonderful calling could anyone have than so to live that through him, through her, the light of Jesus should shine out, in the family, out from the family, into the street, into the neighbourhood, out into the world?

That is your calling—that your destiny. So—

> Forth in the peace of Christ you go;
> Christ to the world with joy you bring;
> Christ in your minds, Christ on your lips,
> Christ in your hearts, the world's true King.

Forth you go, and the Lord be with you, in peace, and joy and light, and may he make you, every one, a light-bearer.

The Importance of the Family

To draw attention to the continuing importance of the family in the changing circumstances of Britain today.

My Lords,

In venturing to draw your Lordships' attention to the continuing importance of the family, I do so—in the words of the motion before you—in the context of "the changing circumstances of Britain today". For many of these changing circumstances we can be profoundly thankful. It is possible that the *Morning Star* does not find its way with any regularity on to the breakfast table of the majority of your Lordships! I therefore quote from an article entitled *The Battle for a Healthy Society* which I wrote for that paper and which appeared in its issue of 29 May:

> Social conditions as I saw them in Manchester and in North London in the early and mid-1930's and as they are in Britain generally in the mid-1970's present a contrast that has to be seen to be believed. The people of Britain today are far better provided for than they were forty years ago; they have opportunities for a fuller life, in education, in provision for the elderly, in the care of the sick and in the realm of the arts, of which their parents knew all too little. Who would want to go back to the social conditions of four decades ago? No one who knew them at first hand!

House of Lords, 16 June, 1976.

Yes, from some points of view changing circumstances augur well for the family. There is less grinding poverty. There are fewer women worn out with child-bearing, since contraceptive knowledge and methods have been made available. Further, an understanding of the marriage relationship in terms of complementarity rather than of dominance of one member of the partnership over the other, of mutuality of relationship, of symmetry rather than of demand and response, of sharing both of goods and of responsibilities—all this has helped in the stabilisation and strengthening of family life. The striking advance during this century in the position of woman in society, the realisation that a smaller proportion of her life is given to the rearing of a family, and that it is quite possible and often highly desirable that she should have a profession of her own and an income of her own, this too has led, and will increasingly lead, to great changes in the pattern of social life and particularly of family life in Britain.

Some, indeed, would argue that the family as the basic social unit is finished, and that we should cease to regard it with that reverence and take it for granted with that assurance which we have accorded it in the past. This, I believe, would be a totally wrong reaction to the changing pattern of life which we see around us. It is deeply significant that some non-Christian cultures—Russia and Maoist China (to take two examples)—which have attempted to develop on collective principles opposed to Western patterns of marriage and family life, have turned their backs on these new patterns and returned in large measure to a reverence for the family, or at least to inter-personal relationships which approximate to the norms of Western society. It would seem to be difficult, perhaps impossible, to find any substitute. Social instability, juvenile delinquency, the experience that fragile and tenuous sexual relationships do not make for human happiness—all these things have led those who at first wished to abandon it to see that marriage as we know it, or something very similar to it, is necessary if there is to be a stable society in which to bring up a new generation. For security and continuity a micro-society is called for within the larger body corporate. Marriage provides economic, social and psychological support of a kind which is difficult to substitute, acts as a first line of defence in times of crisis or strain, and provides a small society in which human values are preserved against the pressures of mass living. An anti-family policy will not work.

An examination of such experiments as those I have mentioned might serve as a healthy warning to those who take lightly the rapidly rising figures of divorce in this country. I will not bore your Lordships with too many figures, but a few are necessary to make the picture clear. The divorce rate in England and Wales in 1975 was 320 per thousand marriages—120,000 divorces in 1975, i.e. three times as many as in 1967. (It had risen steadily from 8 per thousand in 1920, to 11.1 in 1930, to 16.5 in 1940, to 86.1 in 1950. In the succeeding quarter of a century it leapt from 86.1 to 320.) If we take the figure for 1975, i.e. 120,000 divorces, we can see that it is likely that some 200,000 children were involved. The effect on them, of course, cannot be calculated, either during the years of their childhood and adolescence, or on their attitude to marriage when their own time comes to found a home of their own. It must, further, be borne in mind that the figures for divorce do not indicate the total extent of marriage breakdown, for many couples, especially among the poorer sections of the population, simply separated without a divorce.

A modern writer and broadcaster, dealing with family life, describes it as "a closely knit environment in which a new generation can discover the meaning of life, and the values upon which life must be based. It is because of the small number of people involved, the intimacy of their relationship and the long period of time in which they are in close touch with each other, that the family has a greater educational influence than any other group in society. A handful of people, of varying ages, temperaments and interests have to learn how to face together the ups and downs, the joys and sorrows which life brings to them. It is a school for living which has no adequate substitute. For here, more than anywhere else, is learned that interdependence which gives meaning to life."

If, then, the family must be regarded as the bulwark of a stable society, we should do well to do two things: *first*, to ask what are the factors in our society which constitute a major menace to its continuing stability; and *secondly*, what action is called for in the strengthening of family life? The *first* may appear to be negative, but necessarily calls for mention. The *second* is wholly positive.

First, I mention certain things which need no elaboration but which do constitute serious setbacks in the establishing and maintaining of stable family life.

1. *Bad housing*. Many marriages get off to a bad start because the newly-married couple have no home of their own. Their accommodation is inadequate. The starting of a family has to be postponed, or the tension produced by young children in a house where grandfather and grandmother also live has to be contended with. Tensions are at once created, and the roots of bitterness are sown. For all that I said about improved social conditions in Britain today, it is still the case that there are grievously bad housing conditions in certain areas, conditions which so far from improving as years go by only worsen, and constitute a disgrace to our society. No bath or indoor sanitation—this is not right for a Britain in the late twentieth century! "Three million homes either unfit or lack standard amenities" was a heading in *The Times* on June 8 this year. It was a summary of the findings of the Building Research Establishment, published in its Report for 1975.

Further thought should also be given to the rightness or wrongness of rearing children in high-rise flats, where there is nowhere easily accessible for them to play; where mother is often cut off from friends and finds herself lonely and, as a result, bad-tempered; where any sense of community is almost non-existent; where a tree or a blade of grass is an unknown thing. Is this the right environment for a youngster? I doubt it.

2. *Too early marriage*. It is, I think, an undoubted fact that the proportion of divorces is greater among those who marry very early than among any other age-group. The fact seems to be clear. The reasons behind the fact are more complex. The earlier age of the onset of adolescence is one reason. The influence of the philosophy—if so it may be dignified!—which says: "I want it, therefore I must have it, and have it now; I will not, and I cannot, wait" is another. The fundamental falsehood lying behind much that leads to early marriage is the argument that, because a boy or girl is physically mature, he or she

therefore has the necessary maturity which is required for marriage. Nothing could be further from the truth. For marriage calls for a maturity of mind and spirit, of the total personality, which goes far beyond the maturity of the body. The lack of that frequently leads to rapid breakdown in the marriage relationship, and sometimes to that exasperation of spirit which leads to wife-battering or baby-battering. Wife-battering is a newly-recognised feature of our society; first estimates would point to a figure in the region of 25,000 a year. It constitutes a grave social problem in itself.

3. *Unemployment*, especially when it occurs among the young and the young marrieds, is a shattering experience. It seems to be part of a man's natural dignity that he should have work to do. It is not enough to say that, in the absence of work, the State will provide money more or less equivalent to what the man would earn if he were employed. That is to beg the question, even if the money were adequate. Work, particularly if it be of the kind that the worker can *see* to be worthwhile, provides an incentive for the keeping together of the family unit. The absence of it makes for breakdown. The head of a family deprived of work finds himself deprived of a dignity which he feels is his by right, and thereby senses a diminution of his authority.

4. Perhaps the factor above all others which leads to the breakdown of marriage and of the security of the home is that *trivialisation of the sexual* which is all too prevalent in our present society. I would not be so foolish as to compare our morals with those of a previous age to the detriment of our present society. The imponderables in any such comparison are too many to allow of valid conclusions. I am not one of those who would re-write the old hymn and have your Lordships sing:

> *Backward*, Christian soldiers
> Marching as to war,
> Yearning to recapture
> The "good old days" of yore!

That is a singularly useless exercise.

But I would engage in the profitable task of keeping one's eyes open to dangers around us and ahead of us.

When I use the phrase "the trivialisation of the sexual", I do so out of the conviction that sex is to be regarded as a gift of immense value and joy, to be treated with responsibility and reverence. The attitude of the Church in days gone by has not infrequently been negative, and sometimes oppressive. But he who charges the Church on that score today shows that he does not know what he is talking about and is badly out of date. Dr Jack Dominian recently wrote—and so rightly—"Sex should not be seen as something frightening, fearful and inhibiting, but as something from which the renewal of two people, as well as new life, comes. This is a great reversal of Christian thought, from considering marriage primarily as being for the benefit of children, to thinking of it primarily as a relationship of two spouses from whose love children benefit enormously." It is precisely because the Church appreciates the glory of the thing that it seeks to fence it around from harm. It is because we value human life that we have white lines down the middle of the roads and safety belts in the seats of our cars. They restrict our freedom a little, true enough; but they save our lives. Thus, to lower the age of consent, as some would have us do, would not be kindness to the young but an act of the greatest cruelty. Or again, to use the powerful media to stimulate the idea that to be "with it" you must throw over the wisdom of the ages, and that material things matter more than cultural and moral values, is to strike a blow for the undermining of the health of society. To hint that it is a small thing to start a human life, or a small thing to snuff it out by abortion; to teach that an abortion does little to the woman who undergoes it, and that it can be done with little more effect on her than a tonsillectomy or a tooth extraction; to suggest that a one-parent family is much the same as a two-parent family, when all the evidence goes to show that a child needs the support of both mother and father; to teach that any kind of sexual activity will do, and practically at any age; to suggest that acts of homosexuality can be engaged in with impunity by the young whose patterns of sexual activity are as yet undetermined and unformed; to encourage or allow the publication of pornographic literature which inflames instincts which on any reckoning take

some strength of character to control; to suggest that minds
cannot be polluted by such stuff as easily as bodies can be
infected by dirty water—these things, and like things that often
go with them, are the lies which damn, the fifth column that
betrays our national well-being and undermines the stability of
our homes.

So much, my Lords, for some of the factors in our society
which constitute a menace to the continuing stability of the
family.

I pass on to ask, secondly, what action is called for in the
strengthening of family life? Here I would be very positive, and
very brief, for others of your Lordships, far better qualified
than myself, will point the way forward for us.

1. I would plead for better education in marriage. I am not
referring to "sex education" in the schools, which, at its worst,
can be little more than the teaching of the physiological facts. I
am referring to that kind of educational work which helps to
shape the attitudes and expectations of young people to marriage and family life, long before the stage of getting married—
the kind of assumptions conveyed throughout childhood and
adolescence in such fields as relationships between the sexes,
commitment and freedom, sharing, the capacity to adapt, and
so on. Family life education may be a relatively new concern; it
is certainly one of great importance.

Others of your Lordships may, I hope, speak of the importance in this connection of religion in schools. I would only say
that we should bear in mind that courses of lessons on comparative religion can never take the place of the teaching of the facts
of the Christian religion and of their ethical relevance.

While I am speaking of education, I should mention the need
for the counselling of couples whose marriages are under stress.
The criticisms made at the time of the passing of the Divorce
Reform Act 1969 that it was wrong to leave reconciliation
efforts until instructions for divorce were given seem to be
justified. That stage is too late. Counselling is needed earlier,
and an expansion of the services will need to be undertaken.

When the cost of marriage breakdown, in sheer financial
terms, is recognised, it is not too much to ask that more money
should be spent on educational and counselling services.

2. I have already said enough about the effects of bad housing and of lack of play-facilities for the young on the stability of
family life. This, and the attempt to lower the figure of unemployment, should surely be very high on the list of government priorities when capital expenditure is being considered.

3. But my last plea for the consideration of your Lordships is
this: is it not time that thought were given to the appointment of
a *Minister for the Family*? In putting forward this idea—in
expressing this hope—I bear in mind the words of the noble
Lord, Lord Wells-Pestell, in his speech last January in this
House in the debate on sex education. He said:

> I think I must make it clear . . . that there are four Govern-
> ment Departments which have a particular interest in this
> subject. The Department of Education and Science in its
> responsibility for the education service including schools
> and colleges of further education has perhaps the major
> interest . . . The Department of Health and Social Secur-
> ity is also closely concerned because of its general responsi-
> bilities for sex education . . . The Scottish Home and
> Health Department and the Welsh Office have responsi-
> bility for these matters in Scotland and Wales.

Here is cause for encouragement, but here is also cause for
anxiety. There is always the possibility that, when a matter is
the concern of too many people, it becomes the concern of
none; it falls between two stools, or, in this case, between four!

The Prime Minister is reported in the *Sunday Times* of 2 May
this year as having said: "What is needed is more family responsibility and social cohesion. No government can legislate for it.
It can only be done by a moral approach." That, I believe, is
true in part. You cannot make people good by law. But you can
make them bad by bad law. And there is much that the Government *can* do. It can protect young parents and single parents
where the problems are basically those of housing and income.
And it can do the reverse. Here I illustrate. The Government
decision to abandon the Child Benefit Scheme which was due to
start in April 1977 is bewildering. The alternative offered, of £1
for family allowance for each first child, will be worth 30p to the

average family after tax and *less* for the poorer families who in many cases will lose more than £1 in the benefits they already get. There was a very wide consensus in favour of Child Benefits and it was accepted and supported by the TUC. More support was needed, and now, apparently, it is to be withdrawn in this particular area.

In fairness it should be said that the new Consultative Document from the Department of Health and Social Security provides for continual expansion, though at a lower rate than in the past five years. Slight increases are envisaged in capital and current expenditure for the mentally handicapped, the mentally ill and the elderly, and that is good, so far as it goes. But the point I am making holds good, viz. the need for a Minister whose task it would be constantly to keep abreast of the facts relating to the family, to study the impact of the Government's social and other policies, including regional employment policies, to ensure that in practice they do not work against the best interests of families, and to watch with an eagle eye the progress of legislation.

A Minister for the Family would find himself surveying the present Divorce law, and facing evidence which shows that not only does that law make divorce far too easy, but also that it often proves unfair on the husband who finds that, after his wife has walked out, he has to sell his house to provide for his children. Such a Minister would have to consider seriously the value of some kind of service for young people who would otherwise be unemployed. I refer not to military service but to something parallel to it, such as was employed by the Government of Iran in reducing their illiteracy rate—young people were allowed to spend the major part of the "military" service in educational work, to the great benefit of their country.

Such a Minister would cast a highly critical eye on the abortion laws, as they now obtain, and on the laws which govern the sale of pornographic literature or of the showing of films, the advertisements for which degrade our London streets and those of other cities.

Such a Minister would watch the legislation which affects the teaching of religion in schools, and he would do so fully aware of the inadequacies of much that has passed for this in recent years and also of the fact, which I have already mentioned, that lessons in comparative religion can never take the place of systematic and intelligent teaching of Christianity and of its ethical relevance to life.

And lastly, such a Minister would show himself aware of the ill-effects on society when its structure becomes two-tier rather than three-tier. By that I mean when society is so ordered that grandparents are separated from grandchildren and the only family influence on the young is that of their parents.

If, my Lords, I end by quoting an essay from an eight-year-old entitled *What a Grandmother is*, I do so, not only to provide a lighter element to a speech which has been over-heavy and over-long, but also because I believe the essay enshrines a truth which society neglects at its peril, viz. that a child if it is to be healthy (and hence if the family is to be healthy) needs to be given time-consuming attention by its seniors, and this can often be provided not by the next generation but by the next generation but one. This is what he wrote:

> A grandmother is a lady who has no children of her own, so she likes other people's little girls and boys. A grandfather is a man grandmother. He goes for walks with the boys and they talk about fishing and tractors.
>
> Grandmothers don't have to do anything but be there. They are old, so they shouldn't play hard or run. They should never say "hurry up". Usually they are fat, but not too fat to tie children's shoes.
>
> They wear glasses and funny underwear, and they can take their teeth and gums off.
>
> They don't have to be smart, only answer questions like why dogs hate cats and why God isn't married.
>
> They don't talk baby-talk like visitors. When they read to us, they don't skip bits, or mind if it is the same story over again.
>
> Everybody should have one, especially if you don't have television, because grandmothers are the only grown-ups who have time.

The point of that little essay is in the last sentence. My Lords, I beg to move the motion standing in my name.

On Dying and Dying Well

IT WAS IN December last year that I was first approached by Sir Gordon Wolstenholme as to the possibility of my giving the Edwin Stevens Lecture this year. Let me say at once how high a privilege I consider this to be, though I accept the honour with a considerable measure of diffidence due in part to the distinction of the audience which I address and in part to the immense difficulty of the subject which I have been given.

Since I was rash enough to accept the invitation, I have myself been a victim in the hands of the doctors—for me a rare experience and, as I discovered somewhat to my surprise, an enriching one. I will not succumb to the temptation, often yielded to by men of advancing years, to go into detail as to the nature of my complaint. Nothing could be less interesting. It was a matter of minor surgery, and I was out of the hospital some ten days after entering it. What I do feel constrained to say is this: I wrote to my daughter, who is a gynaecologist serving in Pakistan, and I said to my wife, who is the daughter of a surgeon, "I raise my hat to the medical profession."

Trying to analyse what it was that made a slightly painful experience so enriching a one, I recognise, of course, that there is an element of vanity in all of us and it is pleasant to be made a fuss of. I recognise, further, that even in a comparatively minor piece of surgery there is a combination of skills the operation of which gives great confidence to the man on whose behalf they are used. But I think the main reason which converted the bane

Edwin Stevens Lecture, Royal Society of Medicine, 13 December, 1976.

of this experience into the blessing that it undoubtedly has become was the skilled friendship—and I use adjective and noun advisedly—shown by the two doctors mainly involved.

I preface my lecture with these words, partly because I welcome the opportunity of paying a tiny tribute to a great profession and partly because I shall have occasion to revert to them, in a very different context, later on.

The subject which has been assigned to me is one of very great difficulty and complexity, and only a fool would approach it without the utmost diffidence. Those who have spoken before me this evening have touched on some of the related problems within their own particular spheres of learning. The title of this lecture was suggested by the title of a report (1975) of a working party set up by the Board for Social Responsibility of the Church of England which formed the subject of a debate in its General Synod in February 1976. I have given this title to this lecture because it seemed to me to sum up, perhaps better than any other form of words, what the President of the Royal Society of Medicine had in mind when he wrote to me a year ago.

I make what small contribution I can today out of the conviction that much hard thinking remains to be done on this subject, and that we shall only work our way towards positive and helpful principles in so far as practitioners in various departments of life and learning join their skills and marry their experiences in the give and take of open discussion. I speak as one who, unlike those who have spoken before me this evening, has no scientific or legal expertise, but as one who, in a ministry as priest and bishop extending well over forty years, has often come close to those who are dying and is deeply concerned that the act of dying should be as good an act as preparation and skill and love can make it. I speak as a Christian, with all the bearing that Christian belief and practice have on our subject. But I am convinced that the major part of what I shall say has relevance for those who do not hold the Christian faith, or only partially do so, and much of it for those who cannot even subscribe to that view of death which is summed up in the words (from the preface of the Mass of the Dead) *Vita mutatur, non tollitur*, "Life is changed, not taken away", by the incident of death.

It might be of help if, at the outset, I said a word about the limits to the doctor's responsibility to keep his patient alive, and what Christian moralists have to say on the subject. I refer first to some words contained in the Papal Allocution of Pope Pius XII to a congress of anaesthetists which met in November 1957, and I quote from the booklet *Decisions about Life and Death: A Problem in Modern Medicine* (Board for Social Responsibility of the Church of England 1965, pp 52–53):

The Pope was considering *inter alia* certain moral questions that may arise through the use of artificial respiration in cases of cerebral lesion. A patient has been plunged into unconsciousness by central paralysis, artificial respiration has been applied so as to maintain his breathing and circulation, but after several days of treatment there is no sign or prospect of any improvement in his condition. In such circumstances may the apparatus that is maintaining the circulation be removed, or ought it to be kept in operation until the circulation stops in spite of it?

The answer given in the allocution was based on the distinction, already drawn by Roman Catholic moralists, between "ordinary" and "extraordinary" medical or surgical procedures. "Ordinary" in this context does not mean what a medical man would regard as "normal" treatment: it means whatever a patient can obtain and undergo without thereby imposing an excessive burden on himself or others. Thus "extraordinary" treatment has been defined as "whatever here and now is very costly or very unusual or very painful or very difficult or very dangerous, or if the good effects that can be expected from its use are not proportionate to the difficulty and inconvenience that are entailed".

The point of the distinction is this. As a general rule a sick man is bound, as are those who have the care of him, to employ the appropriate available means of preserving his life and restoring his health. But there are obviously limits to this obligation. He is not bound to incur, or impose upon his family, an impoverishing expense; nor is he bound to submit to treatment which would cause him great distress and of which the benefits are problematical. In other words his strict obligation extends only to the "ordinary" means of preserving life and restoring health, and not to the "extraordinary" as defined above. He may accept "extraordinary" treatment if he thinks fit; but he is not bound to do so, unless he has some special obligation to stay alive. As for those who have the care of the patient, the doctor has neither right nor duty to insist on "extraordinary" treatment against the patient's will, nor is he bound to apply such treatment in cases where the patient cannot be consulted; and the patient's family is in much the same position.

Though there are obvious difficulties in the outworking of the principles enunciated in this allocution, there are marked similarities between them and the attitude reflected by the Anglican canon lawyer, Chancellor E. Garth Moore, when dealing with another aspect of the same problem, namely the legitimacy of action taken by a doctor which may lead to the shortening of the patient's life. The useful ethical distinction between a principal intention, or moral object, which is good, and indirect consequences, may throw light on the nature of the decision facing the doctor who wishes to give a pain-killing drug to a patient. Garth Moore writes:

> It would seem reasonably certain that the giving of a pain-killing drug to a patient *in extremis* can be justified, not only by the theologian's law of double effect, but also by the Common Law doctrine of necessity, even where one of the effects of the drug is the probable shortening of the patient's life. This is because the evil averted, namely the agony of the patient, is greater than the evil performed, namely an act leading to the probable shortening of his life . . . (Board for Social Responsibility of the Church of England 1965, p 50).

The first two *Conclusions* of the signatories of the report "On Dying Well" (to which allusion has already been made) also show marked similarity to the general conclusions both of Pope Pius XII and of Chancellor Garth Moore. They read:

> 1. In its narrow current sense, euthanasia implies killing, and it is misleading to extend it to cover decisions not to preserve life by artificial means when it would be better

for the patient to be allowed to die. Such decisions, coupled with a determination to give the patient as good a death as possible, may be quite legitimate.

2. Nor should it be used to cover the giving of drugs for the relief of pain and other distress in cases where there is a risk that they may marginally shorten the patient's life. This too we think legitimate (Board for Social Responsibility of the Church of England 1975, p 61).

This is in keeping with the point made by the Bishop of Truro in introducing the debate on the Report, when he said: "The demands that a patient *in extremis* should not be subjected to troublesome treatment which cannot restore him to health and that doctors may use drugs to control pain even at the risk of shortening life do not involve voluntary euthanasia at all and are not in question" (General Synod of the Church of England 1976).

In the light of these references, I need hardly emphasise that the view, held by many, that Christians believe that life must be artificially prolonged under all circumstances is not true. You will recall the case of the American girl, Karen Quinlan, which was widely reported in the press last year. I am informed that it was the doctors, not the priest, who gave the advice which led to the prolongation of her life. Probably all of us would agree in deploring the events which so fearfully prolonged the life—if life it can be called—of General Franco. A similar case of malpractice is described in a letter quoted by Hugh Trowell (1973, p 29) in his important and sensitive book *The Unfinished Debate on Euthanasia*. He rightly describes the letter as terrible."

Lord Edmund-Davies has already quoted Arthur Hugh Clough's words:

> Thou shalt not kill, but need'st not strive
> Officiously to keep alive.[1]

However great the difficulties in law of working out the implications of these oft-quoted lines, there would seem to be a wide consensus of Christian opinion in favour of the principles contained in them.

There is another matter, closely related to the one which we have just been considering, which must cause anxiety, and at times perhaps agony, to a doctor who has to weigh up his responsibility in making a choice. I refer to the choice between, on the one hand, making the most advanced techniques available to a few, and, on the other hand, improving the level of services available to many, and especially to those who have in the past been inadequately cared for. The resources of the national exchequer are not limitless (in the year 1975/76 the nation spent £4564 million on health and welfare, including local authority costs), and the prolongation of the life of one aged patient may in fact entail the deprivation of aid to others and even the shortening of their lives. Nor are beds in hospitals limitless; and the extension of the life of a terminal patient may necessarily involve the suffering or even death of those who, if speedily admitted to hospital treatment, might have many years of useful life ahead of them.

I realise that here I am treading on exceedingly dangerous ground. I am fully aware of the great dangers of legalised euthanasia. I bear in mind a passage in Sir Norman Anderson's recent book *Issues of Life and Death* in which he writes that, if voluntary euthanasia were to be made legal

. . . there would soon be a demand for further conces- sions. It would not be long before the argument would be heard that paralysed, incontinent or semi-comatose elderly persons would certainly sign the suitable form if only they were to have a sufficiently lucid interval; so why should not their relatives do for them what they would wish to do for themselves? "That agreed"—to quote a recent article by R. F. R. Gardener—"within a month someone would say, 'But to expect relatives to make this decision is to impose an impossible emotional burden; let us authorise an official to do this without distressing them.' Naturally parallel arguments would be advanced for the congenitally dam- aged neonates. It would then be suggested that the prob- lem of approval for the euthanasia of the conscious but incapacitated aged would be even more distressing, and therefore it would be vital to relieve relatives of any in- volvement in this and have it arranged by some distant office" (Anderson 1976).

Of all this I am vividly aware—one has not lived through the days of the Nazis without memories which are not easily blotted out.[2] But the awareness of these appalling abuses must not blind us to the realities of a situation the severity of which will not diminish but rather increase as the percentage of old people rises and, quite possibly, the extent of Government financial aid reaches a figure beyond which it cannot go.

The doctor has a responsibility—an accountability—to the patient and the patient's family under his immediate care. But he has also a responsibility to the other patients in the long waiting queue. He has a further responsibility—to the Government, or, to put it more personally but none the less accurately, to his fellow tax-payers who provide the resources to keep the National Health Service going. The question arises as to whether some kind of consensus—I had almost said some kind of ethic—can emerge on the distribution of resources as between one part of the Health Service and another. A free-for-all could be disastrous. (I understand that the DHSS has this year issued a Discussion Document on Priorities in the Health and Personal Social Services.)

In this connection, my attention has been drawn to a recent lecture by Dr David Millard of the Oxford University Department of Social and Administrative Studies. It was given in July this year to the Hospital Chaplains' Fellowship in Oxford. He writes:

> The life-time of the National Health Service has seen a burgeoning of such bodies as the National Association for the Welfare of Children in Hospital, the association to do with patients' rights to free visiting and indeed to staying in hospital with their sick children, the Patients' Association, of a more political role for MIND (formerly the NAMH), among many others. They seem to have grown up partly, at least, in response to a lack of accountability on the part of doctors for the wider implications of their work.

He continues:

> The administrative re-organisation of the NHS of 1974 seems to me to be another form of response to this situ-

ation—by increasing the power of the administration there has been introduced a greater requirement of account-ability of the medical profession. We are seeing, I suggest, a considerable national experiment in the relationship be-tween the professions and the public, in the replacement of accountability through the forces of the market by other forms of social control more consistent with citizenship principles. Some doctors would like to keep its account-ability within the profession—accountability to peers, or in terms of some form of medical audit. Now this is splendid, but it is not, in my view, enough. Neither, however, is it enough to make the professionals accountable simply to bureaucrats in medical administration, for bureaucracies themselves can be the opponents of the common good—especially when they become too large. So ultimately accountability needs to be to the recipients of the service—to the community on whose behalf the service exists. And the healthy way of managing our national medical service should maximise the participation of the consumer in the choices which are made about that service.

From a severely practical point of view, the main problem with which we are dealing, namely dying well, points to several urgent needs. One is the multiplication of such institutions as St Christopher's Hospice, over which Dr Cicely Saunders pre-sides with such distinction. Such institutions help to reverse the unfortunate trend of recent years to institutionalise medical care and dying. There is great need to enable those at home to offer the care that they can give and wish to give. These are institutions specially designed for terminal cases, where tech-nical skills are married to deep but non-sentimental compas-sion, and where arrangements are such that there is time for a loving relationship to be built up between patient and doctor and between patient and nurse. I have used two words here of great importance—relationship and time. You cannot have the one without the other. And there's the rub.

One of the main disadvantages of the National Health Service as it now operates is that so often a relationship of any depth and intimacy fails to exist between patient and doctor. The patient is passed from one doctor to another in such a way that little confidence of the one in the other has any opportunity of development. Nor is this the fault of the doctor. He is not callous. On the contrary, he longs for the development of such a relationship in depth. But this system makes this well-nigh impossible. If this is tragic in the case of ordinary patients, it is doubly tragic when the life of the patient is nearing its close. Even when the patient has relatives and friends, and when conditions are such that visits can be long and frequent, the need for a close relationship between doctor and patient, or nurse and patient, is paramount. When the patient has no relatives or friends—and there are many such cases in Britain today—and when conditions for visiting are difficult, the need is all the greater. But how can this exist in the big institutions for the aged and the dying which are to be found in many of our large cities?

As the percentage of aged in the population increases, pressure will have to be brought to bear on the Government not only for homes for the aged—these have increased in number in recent years—but for hospitals for terminal cases where the organisation is small enough to allow of the establishment and deepening of the trustful relationship which I now have in mind.[3] But there can be no doubt that this will involve very heavy expenditure. And the expenditure will not only be on bricks and mortar. It will extend also to the training of young doctors and nurses specifically for the manning of these small institutions; and for this a very special kind of expertise, and, one may add, of character will be called for. In this task there should be the closest cooperation between local priests or clergymen and doctors and nurses. Hence the need for careful training for the ordinand in the care of the dying, so that, wherever one of these small specialist institutions for the dying is set up, there should be a little team—doctor, nurse and priest—who will between them provide a little network of intimate caring for the dying man or woman.

Much is being done in groups linked to the Society for the Study of Medical Ethics. There are such medical groups in twenty-one British medical schools, And great attention is being given to teaching about death and clinical practice for the dying. But much—very much—waits to be done.

Dr Willem Berger is a Roman Catholic priest born in Holland

in 1919. He lectures at the University of Nijmegen on applied psychology of religion and pastoral psychology. He is one of a growing number of priests and psychologists who want more and better help for the dying. In a book (Berger 1974) entitled *The Last Achievement* (first published in Holland in 1973 and in England in 1974), he shares with his readers some of his thoughts on dying well. He is—rightly, as I think—distressed at the conspiracy of silence which so often surrounds death, a silence which isolates the person who is dying and who, just because of his condition, needs the consolation of understanding companionship. He writes of priests who are ill at ease and uncertain in the presence of death, of nurses who, almost without realising it, delay on their way to the dying person's bed. This kind of thing results in putting the dying person in emotional isolation, or in treating him as though he were a child unable to take responsibility on an adult level. He thus finds himself in loose touch with people who do not communicate with him naturally and who, because of their lack of ease in the presence of impending death, fail to fulfil their share of total responsibility.

Dr Berger, as a priest and a psychologist, of course recognises to the full the part to be played by the professional in the help of the sick person. But he argues that much of the work for the dying man should be done by the "layman" and that it is the task of the professional (the doctor, the priest and so on) to help the ordinary members of the family to help one another, and so to help the patient to come to terms with his own death and to die it with dignity.

We have largely overcome the conspiracy of silence which surrounded the subject of sex a few decades ago. Some would think we have so overcome it that we have become obsessed by the subject until a lovely thing has become a boring thing. Now there is a conspiracy of silence about death. Literature would seem to suggest that the Victorians were more open about it than we are—sometimes to the point of morbidness. But this can be said for them—that they did not dress it up, use euphemisms when referring to it, or think it necessary to indulge in the kind of excesses to which morticians on the other side of the Atlantic and elsewhere go. Is there not a need for those of us whose work brings us frequently into contact with death so to

come to terms with it ourselves that we co-operate in breaking
up the conspiracy of silence and helping more people to speak of
it naturally and react to it constructively?

The question to tell or not to tell is undoubtedly a difficult
one, and there is no one clear answer in all cases. I can well
conceive cases where to tell would be to depress and to ex-
tinguish co-operation between patient and doctor: the patient
would, like the sick Hezekiah (Isaiah 38:1–3), simply turn his
face to the wall and give up. But I suspect that in more cases
than we generally recognise the patient knows when he is
terminally ill, and immense relief would come to him if he knew
that those around him were not sharing in a kind of play-acting
to the effect that he was soon going to get better. How often
does a dying patient find himself an unwilling participant in a
kind of charade—a charade kindly meant, I have no doubt—
but one from which he would gladly be free, if he might find
himself upheld by the skill of experts and the love of friends
who would speak naturally with him of the coming event. As it
is, relatives and friends find themselves in the position so well
described by Hugh Trowell (1973, p 90);

> They must start the task of mourning, but this they
> must hide as far as possible from the loved one, for often he
> has as yet not realised his fate. This introduces an element
> of constraint into all their talk. *They meet but cannot talk;
> they talk but cannot meet* [italics mine].

Elisabeth Kübler-Ross, whose book *On Death and Dying* is
written against a background of research far more extensive
than that of most other writers on this and kindred subjects, put
this matter with real insight:

> I believe the question should not be stated, "Do I tell my
> patient?" but should be re-phrased as, "How do I share this
> knowledge with my patient?" The physician should first
> examine his own attitude towards malignancy and death so
> that he is able to talk about such grave matters without
> undue anxiety. He should listen for cues from the patient
> which enable him to elicit the patient's willingness to face
> the reality. The more people in the patient's environment

who know the diagnosis of a malignancy, the sooner the patient himself will realise the true state of affairs anyway, since few people are actors enough to maintain a believable mask of cheerfulness over a long period of time. Most if not all of the patients know anyway. They sense it by the changed attention, by the new and different approach that people take to them, by the lowering of voices or avoidance of rounds, by a tearful face of a relative or an ominous, smiling member of the family who cannot hide their true feelings. They will pretend not to know when the doctor or relative is unable to talk about their true condition, and they will welcome someone who is willing to talk about it but allows them to keep their defences as long as they have the need for them (Kübler-Ross 1969, pp 36–37).

One of the most sensitive articles I have read on this matter is a paper by J. Michael Wilson (1975) of the Department of Theology, University of Birmingham, entitled 'Communicating with the Dying'.

I feel this particularly strongly in the case of husband and wife who over a long period of years have shared every decision, every major event and every intimacy of life. Why, except in the most exceptional circumstances, should the last great event be un-shared? Why should there be the whispering behind closed doors, and not, rather, the openness of a healthy sharing? And if those concerned believe in the resurrection to life eternal, then why deprive them of the joy of shared anticipation?

A friend of mine who recently retired from a splendid career as a surgeon, a man of fine skill and deep compassion, recently shared with me some of his strongest convictions. I re-read them after I had written what I have just said, and I venture to quote in part what he wrote to me:

Some very elderly patients have no will to live, are tired of life and have no fear of death. We must let them die in peace and even quickly with our own medical skill. Those who are terrified of dying need spiritual help. Those who are frightened of pain must be relieved. However, even the old and sick and weary tend to cling to life.

Surely in all this we *must* have and give our patients

hope, never tell them lies even if we don't always tell them the full truth, or do so only in stages.

Everyone must see and feel that we care, never lose confidence in their doctor or nurse, never feel they are neglected or that full medical resources are not available for them.

I have had far more letters from patients expressing thanks for my kindness, my caring, my consideration, than ever for my medical skill or surgical expertise.

Today in the great State medicine of the NHS it is often the relatives or loving friends that are neglected rather than the patients. In intensive care units or post-operative recovery areas we may keep them out for reasons of sterility, but I'm sure we don't keep them fully informed or consult them enough about our reasons for and methods of prolongation of life.

It is interesting that in this letter the writer stresses not only the combination of compassion and skill but also the need to care for the relatives of the patients, thus indirectly underlining the need which I have already stressed for the multiplication of small units to which terminal patients can be sent and where visiting facilities are greater than they can be in the wards of our large hospitals. Incidentally, and relevant to this last point, those of us who have travelled in the Far East have often noted how well the patient is cared for by his relatives who surround him (even though at the same time we have been horrified at the lack of cleanliness which their presence often entails).

There is a loneliness about dying in our Western society which is not healthy. There is much we could learn, for example, from Africa. The Archbishop of Central Africa, Donald S. Arden (1976), writing of the distinction made by the African between natural death at full age and the accidental death of the young, says of the former:

The death of the old is quite different, and the domestic theology of the living-dead draws on a wisdom that the West has lost. In Swaziland I spent a night with the medical assistant of a government clinic, who was also the leader of a little Christian congregation. Another guest was his

father, a gentle, happy man in his late sixties, who lived
eighty miles away. On my next monthly round I was
shocked to be told by my friend that his father had just
died at the family home. I expressed surprise, since he had
seemed to be in excellent health, and asked of what he had
died. "Nothing, it was just his time. We are four children
in the family, so he came to stay with each of us for a week
and talk and play with all his grandchildren, and to say
good-bye. He reached home last week, and now he has
gone. It is good."

It is indeed good, and better than our complex way of
prolonging life in order to launch ourselves on disputations
about the rightness of shortening it again to its natural
span.

The Christian will see in this African approach to the dead an
adumbration of the doctrine of the communion of saints,
springing as that does from his conviction that Christ is Lord of
the living and the dead.

Ladislaus Boros (1965), in his book *The Moment of Truth*,
speaks of dying as the event which gives "man the opportunity
of posing his first completely personal act". How important,
then, that he should prepare, seriously and intelligently, for
this great act, the more so if he believes it to be the return of his
life to the God who gave it to him. But "completely personal"
though that act undoubtedly is, it should not be completely
lonely. Even Jesus, forsaken by God as he felt himself to be, had
his mother and young John by him as the end drew near. The
gist of what we have been saying is that a man as he comes to die
should have around him not only—not even primarily—the
apparatus of modern technical medicine designed to extend his
life a trifle or to ease his physical suffering, but also the unhurried companionship of people who are not frightened by the fact
of death and are prepared to go with the man concerned as far as
they may to the point of his departure.

Sigmund Freud maintained that the two central questions of
life were: how do you deal with your sexuality? and how do you
deal with your death? If a fraction of the care were given to the
second question that is given to the first, life would be robbed of
much of its fear and death itself would gain a measure of the

dignity which belongs to it. That is where—to revert to the matter to which I alluded at the beginning of this lecture—both skill and friendship are called for. Given the skill alone, however brilliant and sophisticated that skill may be, there can only be a clinical chill about the dying. Given friendship alone, however warm that friendship may be, there will be needless suffering and discomfort. Given both, you have the main ingredients which go to the helping of a man to die with dignity. Given a living faith, there can be added an element of triumph, for death is then viewed not as a terminus but as a junction. *Incipit vita nova.*

I have forborne in this lecture to ask you to follow me in detail down the path of discussion as to the rightness or wrongness of euthanasia, as that word is usually understood. Suffice it to say two things: first, I have little doubt that most of you have debated this with yourselves over many a long year and reached certain conclusions. Secondly, I have myself been influenced and largely persuaded by such books as Hugh Trowell's *The Unfinished Debate on Euthanasia*, Sir Norman Anderson's *Issues of Life and Death* and Professor G. R. Dunstan's *The Artifice of Ethics* (Dunstan 1974). The warnings given in those books, to mention no others, seem to me to be so weighty as to make the case very strong indeed for leaving the issues much as they now are in the hands of the doctors. And I note, not only in books such as these but also in the debate on Baroness Wootton's recent (and abortive) Incurable Patients Bill (February 1976) in the House of Lords, that it is, generally speaking, the doctors themselves who as much as anybody else—even *more* than others—resist the idea of any legislation which would define the limits within which euthanasia could be put into effect by doctors or nurses in hospitals or homes.

Rather, I have sought to show that there is a large measure of agreement among Christians of widely differing traditions as to the wrongness of prolonging the life of all those with terminal illnesses, just for the sake of doing so. Rather, leaving the duty of caring appropriately for their dying patients to the wisdom and skill of doctors and nurses who are in consultation with ministers of religion and with the relatives of the patients concerned, we should eschew the pursuit of legislation and let experience and wisdom decide.

Further, I have pleaded for such consultation between doctors and their colleagues, between representatives of the National Health Service, and between recipients of the service, as would lead towards some kind of consensus, or ethic, on the distribution of the resources provided by the taxpayer.

Again, I have urged the multiplication not only of such institutions as St Christopher's Hospice but also the provision of those conditions where a close relationship between the doctor and the terminally sick patient can be achieved. I have stressed the importance of the most careful training of doctors, nurses, clergy and others in the understanding of what it means to care for the dying; and I have underlined the point made by Dr Kübler-Ross that the right approach to our patients should be the sharing, on the part of as many as is reasonably possible, of the knowledge of the terminal nature of the illness of the patient concerned. The "completely personal" act of a dying man does not mean the total loneliness of that man.

Along such lines as these we may move forward—forward to a day when death will be regarded not as a sordid end but rather as an act of dignity on the part of a man "dying well", an act worthy of someone made in the image of God; an act which, it is true, ends one phase of his manhood, but which ushers in that new phase for which indeed he was created, the phase when— so the Christian believes—the vision of God, dimly seen here, is fulfilled in the bliss of life eternal.

Notes
[1] These lines of Arthur Hugh Clough are from *The Latest Decalogue*. They are frequently quoted, with some solemnity, in books and papers on euthanasia and kindred subjects. The author would, I think, have been amused, for Clough's *Decalogue* is satirical, one might almost say cynical. See, for example, the last of his "commandments".

> Thou shalt not covet, but tradition
> Approves all forms of competition.

[2] See also J. A. Baker (1970, pp 85ff), for a sensitive discussion of this subject.

[3] There is a list of Hospices in the United Kingdom and of Marie Curie Memorial Foundation Homes and Centres in *Care of the Dying* by Cicely Saunders (1976). This is a valuable collection of essays by an acknowledged expert.

References

Anderson N
(1976) *Issues of Life and Death.* Hodder & Stoughton, London; p 102
Arden D S
(1976) *Anglican Theological Review,* Supplementary Series, June, p 24
Baker J A
(1970) *The Foolishness of God.* Darton, Longman & Todd, London
Berger W
(1974) *The Last Achievement.* Grail (England) Publications, Pinner, Middlesex
Board for Social Responsibility of the Church of England
(1965) *Decisions about Life and Death: A Problem in Modern Medicine.* Church Information Office, London
(1975) *On Dying Well.* Report of a Working Party. Church Information Office, London
Boros L
(1965) *The Moment of Truth.* Burns & Oates, London
Dunstan G R
(1974) *The Artifice of Ethics* (Moorhouse Lectures). SCM Press, London
General Synod of the Church of England
(1976) *Report of Proceedings* 7, 506
Kübler-Ross E
(1969) *On Death and Dying.* Macmillan, New York
Saunders C
(1976) "Care of the Dying" *Nursing Times,* London
Trowell H
(1973) *The Unfinished Debate on Euthanasia.* SCM Press, London
Wilson J M
(1975) *Journal of Medical Ethics* 1, 18

Waste in the West

MR PRESIDENT, MY lords, ladies and gentlemen: it is a very great joy to me to be back in what for me is a very beloved country. For having spent seven happy years here, had two daughters born here and been back several times since, Canada has a place in my affections and indeed in those of my wife, far greater than any other country in the world apart from the little island where we were both born.

I am very grateful to you, Mr President, for the kind way in which you have introduced me today, and for the over-kind words with which you have written up my undistinguished life. I remember the story of the man who was introduced, perhaps over-flatteringly, when he was about to make a speech. When he got up to reply to the introduction, he said that he felt that he had to offer up two prayers for forgiveness: one, forgiveness for the man who introduced him because he told so many lies, and the second for himself because he enjoyed it so much. These things are very bad for one's pride, Mr President, and so we will pass on from these unimportant matters to what I want to speak to you about today at this combined meeting—and may I say how glad I am that the Canadian Club has joined with the Empire Club so that I have such a magnificent audience to which to speak.

I speak to you as men and women, all of whom occupy positions of strategic importance, and therefore if I speak with a measure of seriousness today you will understand that I do so

The Empire Club of Canada and The Canadian Club of Toronto. Royal York Hotel, 1 May, 1975.

because I believe you can convey anything of truth in what I am saying to your own circles of influence. I see this address as the dropping of a stone into a pool, and I hope that the circles may spread in ever widening influence.

If I may begin with a truism, it would be to say that our world has become a global village. The world is on our doorstep. I breakfasted yesterday in Lambeth by the Thames, I dined last night here after a leisurely journey to Toronto. But as I travel on my errands through the world, I am of course, as any of you must be who travel, appalled by the gap that yawns between luxury and poverty, appalled by the contrast between our world and what has come to be known as the Third World. So long as we in the West remain complacent about that kind of yawning gap, we sow the seeds of disaster which might come very quickly, the seeds of war, the seeds of hate, and the seeds for the spread of those creeds which we least want to see in our little world.

So it is that I take for my theme today the theme of waste in the West. I want to share with you a concern about this. I want to illustrate my theme from various aspects of our late twentieth-century life. I think, of course, of the waste that comes through the pollution of our world, of the air, the sea, the land; a pollution which is very often due to the fact that we are so rapacious that we cannot wait to think and plan. So we turn beautiful land into dust bowls, simply because we will not plan, we will not wait; we must get rich quick.

I think of the wastage of food. I suppose that an Indian village could keep going for several weeks on what we have thrown out from lunch today. I'm reminded of the fact that during the course of this year, some forty or fifty million people will die, in this global village, through starvation.

I think of the wastage of human life, not only through war but also through abortion laws that have gone wrong. This is one of the problems we are facing in England today, that we passed through Parliament an abortion law which has proved, I was going to say, abortive. It reminds me of a street car running down hill and the brakes have failed. We drafted it, I think, far too widely. The result is that the best gynaecologists and doctors are becoming extremely anxious about this. There is a stress on the consciences of the gynaecologists and some appalling jobs for the nurses. The thing has got out of control, because we have failed to have that reverence for life of which Schweitzer used to speak so much, and which indeed was the centre of his whole philosophical theology.

I think, again, of the way we are wasting some of our best youth.

Last month, in the London *Times*, there appeared an article headed "Ten Thousand Pounds a Day for Manchester Vandalism". The gist of that article is that those who perpetrate that vandalism, which wastes some three and a half million pounds per annum, are in the age groups between ten and twenty, and twenty and thirty. Now I am speaking here not simply of the waste of money, and of buildings that are desecrated, but of the wastage of youth who haven't got anything better to do. I ask whether perhaps that vandalism may be due to the fact that there is a passion to get rich quick which makes for dead-end jobs.

Before I start labelling the people who perpetrate that violence as thugs or what you will, I ask myself whether I might not have been among their number if I came from the kind of homes from which some of them do, and if I had the kind of boring job that they have. I don't excuse them, but I don't condemn them quite so readily until I've asked what it is that leads to those conditions.

I think again of the wastage in our universities. I don't know whether this applies to Canada, for I'm out of intimate touch with the life of this country. But in our own country of England, too many young people are sent up to the universities who are unsuitable for a university education, very often because the parents are so proud that they want to push little Johnny ahead and themselves get the glory. This means not only a waste of money to the State which has to support the student, but a waste of confidence in the students who don't make the grade. So they start off their career on the wrong foot.

I am very much wondering whether, with the earlier age of retirement into which we are now coming, we are not very often wasting the expertise and experience of people who retire in their late fifties or early sixties. It seems to me that we ought to give some rather hard thinking to the possibility of using what these men and women have gained down the years, even when they are not employed fully as before.

Now I realise that it is easy for me at a luncheon like this to speak about waste, waste of our sea and land and air, waste of our food, waste of our life, waste of our resources. It's very easy for me to do that and some will say, "Yes, Archbishop, physician heal thyself. How are you getting on in the Church?" Here I bow my head with a certain element of shame, for I have very real anxieties on that score. I think, for example, of how slow, how terribly slow we are in getting on with the job of Christian unity. The result of that slowness means that there is not only an appalling waste in our resources of money and of buildings, but also of man- and woman-power. It may very well be that the Almighty will make us get together, those of us who have been unable to do so on theological grounds, on economic grounds.

But let me be more practical. What can a group of men and women like this, all occupying positions of responsibility and influence, do in the face of this problem of waste in the West?

I'm going to suggest there are two things we can do.

First, we can make people aware of the problem which I have been sketching and which you yourselves could elaborate far more fully. We must do this, and bring to bear on the problem all the resources of science and common sense. What we need is long-term planning rather than immediate urgent action. Let me illustrate what I mean from recent disasters in Ethiopia.

I went to Addis Ababa two or three years ago to preside at a conference. I stayed in that city, a modern, beautiful city, and was entertained liberally. But I knew that if I were to move up country, even only a matter of a few miles, I should run into the most appalling problems of land disposition, land tenure, agriculture and communication, such conditions of travel that a woman, perhaps about to have a baby, might have to travel three days on donkeyback before she could get medical aid. Those were the conditions two or three years ago in Ethiopia.

Then tragedy struck. I don't suppose anybody quite knows how many tens or hundreds of thousands of people died through starvation. The hearts of the people in the West were touched. They always are, and rightly so, when there is some emergent disaster. We poured in our money and we did a healing operation.

But what was really called for was long-term international thinking to bring about proper communications, and pressure upon governments for proper land tenure and disposition. The money that we poured in was simply palliative. What was needed was international thinking and pressure for long-term remedies.

I was glad to know that one of our own cabinet ministers, Mrs Judith Hart, has put herself very strongly behind the formation of a disaster unit on an international basis, so that when there is some great international tragedy there can be at once international co-ordination so that the need may be met.

The second thing we can do is this. We must look to the basic questions that lie behind the problems of waste. We must do some far more radical thinking than most of us are prepared to do. *The Times*, that gave me my "text" for today in connection with that £10,000 a day vandalism waste in one city in the north of England, refers to this as part of a nation-wide malaise. It's so in every great nation; if you take that three and a half million per annum for one city in Britain, what must it be in the West alone?

What does *The Times* mean when it speaks of a nation-wide malaise, a sickness, behind this appalling waste? It makes me ask certain questions. For example, is there a connection between the vandalism of those young people in the age groups ten to twenty, twenty to thirty, a connection between that and the break-up of marriage? This is to say, if you have an unstable home where Mum and Dad don't get on, or live in two separate homes, or where a youngster has never known the discipline and the love of a father and mother but only one or the other, if you have that kind of situation is it that which produces your young vandal? I think it is, because the sheer figures show that in the courts, young people who come before the judge are predominantly those who come from broken homes.

The sooner we face that problem, the better.

These figures make me ask a second question. It's a question about education. Is the kind of education that we are giving to our young people today adequate to help them to meet the strains of adolescence, the strains that the media bring to bear on them, the strains of a highly technical and very sophisticated late twentieth century? If I may pinpoint that a little more closely, to those who are interested in the education of the young, is a mild dose of comparative religion in the schools an adequate substitute for what we used to know as religious education? I don't think it is. If your children come from homes in which God is hardly ever spoken of except in a swear word, where mother and father never go to church with them on any regular basis, where father and mother never say to the young-sters, "Let's kneel down and have a prayer together," and where the Bible is only referred to when you want a cross-word clue, can you blame those youngsters if they have no moral code, nothing to undergird them, and if they break out in violence against the society that hasn't given them any guidelines? Don't blame the youngsters. Blame the home situation and the educational situation. The two are inter-twined.

Now when you get on to that kind of thinking, the asking of those fundamental questions, you come to even deeper ques-tions that lie behind them. For example, what sort of person am I? What is man? Am I just a bunch of chemicals that would sell for about fifty cents? Yes, I am, from one point of view. Am I a hundred billion cells in some marvellous formation? Yes I am, from one point of view. Am I just the highest in a series of animal evolution? Yes I am, from one point of view. Am I just here today, and gone for ever? "When I die, I rot," said Bertrand Russell.

Or is it possible that I am God's vice-gerent in his world, responsible for the use and not the abuse of my world, which is God's world, so that I do my bit in *not* polluting it, responsible for my use of sexuality, responsible for my action in the creation of new life and the protection of the young? Am I, in other words, just the best in the line of the animal creation? Or am I someone who, quite literally, is responsible, answerable to a God who is at once Creator and Redeemer?

May I ask another question? This lies at the back of the fun-damental questions we are facing together. This mysterious person—what is his relationship to his fellows?

It can be one of hate. In my study, last Sunday afternoon, in Canterbury, I had a lady talking to me who hardly ever spoke to her husband though she lived in the same house with him. She didn't know, I think, that some weeks before I had had her husband telling me much the same thing! We laugh, but it's a terrible tragedy, a relationship of hate.

What's my relationship with my fellow? Is it simply one of competition—who will get to the top first? Or is it in fact a relationship of love, of respect for him as a person, destined with me for an eternity to be spent somewhere or other? Is the parable of the Good Samaritan just a pleasant story that Jesus told to entertain his hearers, or is it the only basis on which civilised life can exist?

These are the fundamental questions. So what began as a talk with a rather peculiar title, "Waste in the West", lands every one of us straight in the midst of theology and religion. But, of course, so do all the great questions—the issues of life, and death, and love and human destiny are fundamentally theological and religious questions.

There is a waste which is no waste. There was a woman, you remember, who had not very much, but she had a box of very precious ointment, and she went and broke it over the head of Jesus. Some said, "What a waste!" But he said, "What a lovely thing!"

It all depends on how you look at things and people and love and life. Do you measure by cash, or do you measure in the light of eternity? There you are—we're in the thick of theology and religion again. I guess it's the right place to be.

IV
CHURCH AND UNITY

A Great Door and Effectual

On 28 April, 1977 the great doors of St Paul's-within-the-Walls Anglican-Episcopal Church, Via Napoli at Via Nazionale, Rome, were dedicated.

They celebrate the historic dialogue between two great streams of Christianity, begun in Rome in 1960 when Pope John XXIII met with the Archbishop of Canterbury, Dr Geoffrey Fisher. The following year, the Rt Rev Arthur Lichtenberger, then Presiding Bishop of the Episcopal Church of the United States, visited Pope John. The dialogue has continued and deepened in succeeding years.

The doors are the work of Dimitri Hadzi, an internationally recognised sculptor of Macedonian origin and Greek Orthodox religious background. They symbolise the modern progression of Christendom from disintegration to integration.

THE FACT THAT I have the privilege of dedicating these doors may be taken as a symbol of the relationship of communion and brotherhood which exists between the Episcopal Church of the United States of America and the Church of England, as indeed it does between all the Churches of the Anglican Communion. That friendship is personified in the presence of Bishop Ervine Swift representing my dear friend the Presiding Bishop. The fact that His Eminence Cardinal Willebrands, representing His Holiness the Pope, presides at

St Paul's-within-the-Walls Anglican-Episcopal Church, Rome, 28 April, 1977.

this service together with me is a symbol of that growing understanding which exists between the Roman Catholic Church and the Anglican Communion throughout the world. In the name of that Anglican Communion I pay this visit to Rome, the third visit of an Archbishop of Canterbury, in the succession of Archbishop Geoffrey Fisher's visit in 1960 and that of Archbishop Michael Ramsey in 1966.

Let me congratulate those whose tenacity of purpose has seen this project through to completion; and let me congratulate the artists and craftsmen who have carried out the work.

What better text could I choose than that in the first Epistle to the Corinthians in which St Paul—we meet in St Paul's Church—speaks of a *door*. 1 Cor. 16:9: "A great door and effectual is opened unto me, and there are many adversaries." So runs the King James Version. "A great opportunity has opened for effective work, and there is much opposition." So runs the New English Bible translation.

What is the *context* of these words? It is quite straightforward. St Paul is planning a journey to Corinth—that evil city whose name gave birth to the verb "to Corinthianise", which meant to go to the dogs. It was not an easy place in which to establish a church, but that had been done. Bengel refers to that fact in a pregnant phrase—"the mighty paradox, the Church of *God* at *Corinth*". Now St Paul plans to visit it again, by way of Macedonia, and possibly to spend the whole winter in the city. But first he must pursue his work at Ephesus till Whitsuntide, "for a great opportunity has opened for effective work, and there is much opposition." That opposition is understandable, for Ephesus, standing as it did on the great East–West high road, was not only the centre of the worship of the great goddess Diana but was also the centre of every wind of strange doctrine which blew through that city of commerce and of intellectual discussion. If Corinth was a difficult centre in which to found a church, Ephesus was not much easier.

But the work of evangelism, of the preaching of the gospel and of the winning of men to its allegiance, must go on, not *in spite of* the difficulties but *because* of them. The greater the opposition and the more mountainous the barriers, the more urgent was the task. Ephesus, Corinth and the other great centres of the Graeco-Roman world must be stormed and won for the crucified-risen Lord. To that end St Paul dedicates himself, and sets about his task with a will, in the company of a band of men in every centre whose baptism had spoken to them of burial and resurrection with Christ, whose strength was found in a shared ministry of word and sacrament, and whose hearts were touched by the love of God which they experienced in the fellowship of Christ and his Church. The result of their dedication was seen in the rapid spread of the Christian faith from Jerusalem and Tarsus, through Asia Minor to Rome, and from this city throughout Europe to the West and to faraway India. A great door had opened, and St Paul and his friends entered it with a glad mind and a willing heart.

The world to which the Christian Church goes in the twentieth century is not unlike that to which the Church went in the first. Vast multitudes even today have never heard the name of Jesus. Many of those in the favoured lands where Christianity has existed for centuries only know that name as a swear-word; and others among them know so little of him as to make no sense of his religion. In the West there is a widespread disillusion with politics and, among the more thoughtful, with materialism, as in the first century there was disillusion with the "gods many and lords many" whose images were seen in every city and town. Their world was rightly described by St Paul as "without God and without hope". That would be a fair description of a large part of ours. This sheer sense of disillusion constitutes for the Christian "a great door", "a great opportunity for effective work", and they are very blind who cannot see it and very callous who would not enter it. Opposition? Yes—in plenty. But that is no cause for hesitation. Rather is it a summons to action.

The publication, in December 1975, of the Apostolic Exhortation *Evangelii Nuntiandi* by His Holiness Pope Paul VI on *Evangelisation in the Modern World*, is warmly to be welcomed. It has commanded the assent, in the main thrust of its argument, of millions not only of our Roman Catholic brethren but of members of the Anglican Communion and of others besides. Indebted as it is to such documents as those of the Second Vatican Ecumenical Council's Decree on the Church's Missionary Activity *Ad Gentes* and on the Dogmatic Constitution on the Church *Lumen Gentium*, it makes it crystal clear that "those

who sincerely accept the Good News . . . make up a community which is in its turn evangelising. The command to the
Twelve to go out and proclaim the Good News is also valid for
all Christians. . . Moreover, the Good News of the Kingdom
which is coming and which has begun is meant for all people of
all times. Those who have received the Good News and who
have been gathered by it into the community of salvation can
and must communicate and spread it" (para. 13). Such an
emphasis as this is music in the ears of those who, having read
the New Testament and having seen the need of the world for
the message of the Church, give priority to the task of evangelistic outreach.

What, then, is the situation of the Church in our world of the
late twentieth century—a world growing in population at a
terrifying rate and shrinking in size as the discoveries of science
draw us all closer together? It is this: we find ourselves faced
with an evangelistic task whose size escalates with the multi-
plying of the millions, and whose strength is debilitated by our
divisions. "Talk to us about reconciliation", says an unbeliev-
ing world, "when you yourselves are reconciled, and we will
listen." Who can blame the world for its scepticism? We have
been forced to listen to that word from the world outside the
Church and it has added urgency to our task of seeking full
unity. At the same time, many of have been discovering this
interesting fact: that, when Christians belonging to different
communions of the Church go out on evangelistic work
together, they discover, in the course of that work, a measure of
unity of which they had no inkling before. In other words, obey
the Lord of the Church and you will find that, in his infinite
mercy, he will give you, as a kind of reward for your obedience,
an experience of unity which will surprise you. Or, to put it
another way, joint evangelism is one of the most rewarding
roads to Christian unity. We need not—and in view of the
world's spiritual starvation we dare not—wait until we are fully
one before we give the Bread of the Christian message in which
as Christians we share to a hungry world and before we do that
giving *together*. I express the hope that the coming months and
years will see a great growth in joint evangelistic outreach to
those totally untouched, or only superficially touched, by the
gospel.

It is at this point that we come to a matter of great importance and, I believe, of great urgency. *Behind us* lies a task well done. The Anglican-Roman Catholic International Commission has done good work in producing the three Agreed Statements on the Eucharist, on Ministry and Ordination, and on Authority in the Church. It is to be hoped that these will be studied at the so-called grass-root level, lest there be too large a gap between the thinking of the theologians and that of the people in our pews. *Before us* lies a period of further exploration and study, in which we pursue the gains which we have already made and develop further the understanding of what we have in common and of the difficulties and differences which still perplex us. *Around us*, as we have already said, is a world of doubt and cynicism and, very frequently, of wistful searching. To this world the Lord of the Church sends us with his divine commission: "Go forth . . . make all nations my disciples; baptise . . . and teach . . . And be assured, I am with you always, to the end of time." These things being so, I ask this question: has not the time now arrived when we have reached such a measure of agreement on so many of the fundamentals of the gospel that a relationship of shared communion can be encouraged by the leadership of both our Churches? I would go further and ask whether our work of joint evangelisation will not be seriously weakened until we are able to go to that work strengthened by our joint participation in the Sacrament of Christ's Body and Blood? The day must come when together we kneel and receive from one another's hands the tokens of God's redeeming love and then directly go, again together, to the world which Christ came to redeem.

"The day must come," I said. In many places around the world, as those of us who travel know perfectly well, the day has already come. Without waiting for official sanction (indeed sometimes *with* local official sanction), Roman Catholics are receiving the Sacrament of Holy Communion at the hands of Anglican bishops and priests, and the reverse is also the case. This, I venture to believe, will increasingly take place, whether official sanction in the highest quarters be given or no. Has not the time, God's time, for such official sanction arrived? I think it has.

I am not asking for a blurring of the issues—and they are not inconsiderable—on which at present we cannot agree. Truth is not advanced by pretending not to see the divisions and disagreements which still exist. The search must go on; and the evangelistic task of the Church must go on. Both must go on together. But I believe both will be crowned with greater success when we say to one another: "We do not want indiscipline in the Church of God. We desire that all things be done decently and in order. We can no longer be separated at the sacrament of unity. We are all sinners in need of the forgiveness and strength of our Lord. We will kneel *together* to receive it."

Unity, Theology and Evangelism

IT IS A high privilege for my wife and myself to be invited to share, if only for a little while, in the deliberations of the General Assembly of the Church of Scotland, and I consider it an honour to be asked to address you. The privilege and honour are the greater in that our visit occurs during the celebration of the Silver Jubilee of the accession of our beloved Queen. Whatever differences of opinion there may be on such matters as devolution, we are at one in our loyalty to the Crown and to the royal Person who has graced the office of Sovereign for a quarter of a century.

I am particularly glad to address you just now, after a year in which you have had as your Moderator the very distinguished Professor, Tom Torrance. He and I must have known one another for some forty-five years. Though our paths have crossed but rarely, I have followed his researches, valued his books, and rejoiced in his leadership in Christ's Church. May he long continue to guide us, and, now that his *annus mirabilis* is at an end, may his pen resume its activity.

I bring the warm and affectionate greetings of the Church of England to this Assembly and our good wishes to the new Moderator as he begins his year of office.

I long for the closest possible unity between our two great Churches; pre-eminently because I believe this to be the will of the Lord of the Church, but also because of the need of a world which has something of a right to say: we will listen to you with your message of reconciliation when we see you reconciled among yourselves.

General Assembly of the Church of Scotland, 27 May, 1977.

123

There is cause for encouragement. Relations between our people at parish level are good and friendly. There is a good deal of assent to the Lund principle that we never do separately what we can do together, and this works out well, e.g. in joint activity in tackling social issues.

My recent visit to Geneva has underlined for me the importance of the full participation of both our Churches in the work which the British Council of Churches and the World Council of Churches are doing. We are an island—and in that we may still rejoice. But we must not succumb to the temptation of insularity. We are part of Europe, and the stretch of water which divides us from the mainland is very narrow. Further, we are part of a rapidly shrinking world. Africa in its need, Asia with its teeming millions (India adds twelve million and China fifteen million to their populations every year!), Latin America with its revolutions and *favellas*—these are on our doorstep. Full conciliar participation would seem to be incumbent on us all if we are to play our part in ministering to a world in need. If I may don my hat as President of the BCC for a moment, it would be to emphasise the value which we in London attach to Scottish participation in the work of the BCC. And if, doffing this hat, I may speak as one who has been at three world assemblies of the WCC—New Delhi, Uppsala and Nairobi—I would stress the welcome accorded by the World body to the distinctive contribution which Scotland makes to its deliberations.

If we have lost anything of that world-vision which was a characteristic of ours when we were at the heart of a great Empire, we should ask the Lord's forgiveness and seek to recapture that vision. For Papua New Guinea, the Sudan, Pakistan—to mention but three of the places which I have visited in recent months—still look with affection and hope to the islands in the West which brought them the Christian faith. Let them not look in vain. We must continue, in things spiritual as well as commercial, in personnel and in skills, to export our best. Here the economics of the gospel must constantly be borne in mind: he who saves his life will lose it; he who is willing to lose his life for the sake of the gospel will find it. Here the BCC and the Scottish Churches' Council must, and please God will, work in total complementarity.

But has it not been one of the weaknesses of the Christianity of these islands that we have found it easier to give than to receive? Receiving calls for humility, for an acknowledgement of weakness or at least of lack; and humility does not come easily to us, North or South of the border, who have so long a history behind us. What I am trying to say is this: we shall not go to the world with a full gospel until we have been ready, not only to receive (as between our two Churches) at one another's hands, but to receive from the younger Churches some of the riches with which God has graced them. We need not only to export but to *import*. My own diocese of Canterbury has recently been enriched beyond measure by having a presbyter of the Church of South India living with and moving among us for a year. I believe that our churches—which at times show a kind of spiritual arthritis due in part to old age—would be vastly invigorated by a willingness to invite Africans, Asians, Latin Americans, clergy and lay men and women, and to sit at their feet and to listen to the word of the Lord from their lips. Let us continue to give, and to give of our best; but let us also learn to receive.

Let me take up a phrase which I used a moment ago: "Going to the world with a full gospel." "Go into all the world"—the divine command has often been disobeyed and its challenge soft-pedalled. God forgive us that the urgency of the divine imperative has gone unheeded while we have occupied ourselves with lesser matters! I believe that, if together we addressed ourselves to obeying the Lord of the Church in the area of the evangelisation of our country and of the world, he would draw us closer together in unity.

I am not sure that the time has come for the recommencement of official joint negotiations for the union of our Churches. I believe the importance of that union is very great, and that we ought to be on the alert for the right moment. But is there not another way in? Or, perhaps, a two-way in?

I would like to see a little group of theologians, say three from Scotland and three from England, who would engage on very informal but very deep theological work together. I would like to see them become a closely-knit family who, at considerable cost of time and energy, would meet and live together periodically, engage in leisurely prayer and honest discussion, pressing back behind the controversies which have engaged us in recent centuries, back to the basic biblical documents and the writings of the early Church. I confess that, in putting this forward, I have in mind the kind of fellowship, the kind of depth of praying and theologising, which marked the members of the Anglican Roman-Catholic International Commission, and which issued in the publication of the three Agreed Statements. There would be little that was official about this body, at least at the beginning of their work. It might well be that, in the course of it, the members would come upon issues, or produce documents, which they would wish to bring to the notice of our official assemblies. They would see how the Spirit led them. But their labours would ensure that theology, sound and deep, was being done, and done jointly.

Meanwhile, and at the grass-root level, members of all the churches in these islands and particularly those of Presbyterian and Anglican allegiance, seeking together to be obedient to the command of their common Lord, would be working at the problems and responding to the challenge of evangelism in their vicinities. God knows it is needed! I cannot speak for Scotland—you know it as I never can. But I can speak for England. There are millions of children there to whom the name of Jesus Christ is little more than a swear-word; millions of young people who, coming from homes where worship is unknown and the Bible never read, see no reason why it should not be thought clever, rather than immoral, to steal or thoughtlessly to start a new life and almost as thoughtlessly to snuff it out; millions of middle-aged people to whom the verb to *have* is the dominant one, rather than the verb to *be*; millions of elderly people who have no hope of the life to come. But alongside of this, there is much to encourage—young people looking for a cause worthy of their dedication; with a concern for the underdog at home and abroad and a sense of social justice often lacking in their seniors; young people and older ones too, who at school got little in the way of a lively presentation of an intelligent Christian faith but who would grasp at it if it were offered them; middle-aged and older people who are disillusioned with many of the panaceas which are offered them and are ready for a gospel which embraces the needs of this life and the hope of a fulfilment hereafter. Cannot we, together, leaving the fastnesses of our church buildings, go to these people in the Name of our risen Lord, and, as agents of the Good Shepherd, lovingly, imaginatively, and intelligently seek them and win them? If we do not do this, and do it with an urgency and with a priority of attention which has been lacking among us in recent years, then we must not be surprised if the Lord of the Church removes our candlestick from its place.

Let these two activities go on side by side—the joint prayerful theologising of representatives of our Churches, echoed, as it were, locally by those capable of engaging in such an exercise; and united evangelistic activity on the part of members of our two Churches in their own localities—and I believe that, before very long, we should see forces at work among us which would compel us to face the reality of the sin of our divisions and would lead on to a measure of unity, to which hitherto we have been strangers.

Unity without Absorption

WE MEET, AS our service paper reminds us, on the seventieth anniversary of the first Week of Prayer for Unity. We thank God for those Roman Catholics and Anglicans who first conceived the idea, and for men like the Abbé Paul Couturier who gave it new direction and broadened its basis.

It is understandable if something of the "first, fine, careless rapture" of earlier weeks of prayer has been lost as the years have gone by. Until comparatively recent times, it was unusual to find Christians of different traditions worshipping and praying together. Now, thank God, this is a common experience. The novelty of the idea has passed away. It would be sad if the passionate desire for unity which gave birth to the idea of a week of prayer grew less. We must not rest content with what has already been achieved or with any concept of unity short of God's full will.

Two great longings burn in my heart as I address you tonight. Let me share them with you. The first is admirably summed up in the Apostolic Exhortation *Evangelii Nuntiandi*, which was quoted in the Common Declaration signed by His Holiness the Pope and myself when I visited Rome in April last year (see pp 314–317). The Exhortation and the Declaration spoke of a "greater common witness to Christ before the world in the work of evangelisation". In a letter addressed to me by the Pope in October last year, he referred to this again, and in a

Service of Prayer for Christian Unity, led jointly with HE Cardinal Basil Hume OSB, Archbishop of Westminster, Westminster Cathedral, 25 January, 1978.

message of Christmas greetings to the Pope I took the matter up again, in the light of the meteoric rise in world population and of the spread of materialistic philosophies of life in many parts of the world.

Such joint evangelistic work, such spreading of the light of Christ in the menacing darkness of our world, is not, and cannot be, brought about by resolutions agreed to by Church leaders. A decade ago, Cardinal Bea, writing to my predecessor, Archbishop Michael Ramsey, approved the recommendation of the Malta Report that there should be "periodical joint meetings in regions where both the Roman Catholic Church and the Anglican Communion have a hierarchy of either the whole or some considerable representation of the two hierarchies" and "consultations on pastoral problems of evangelisation in the modern world". That, I repeat, was ten years ago. I doubt not that a beginning has been made in the implementation of these recommendations. But the process is too slow, in view of the speed with which forces inimical to Christianity press on with their programmes. Nor must these consultations be confined to the members of the hierarchies. The whole people of God, in their own communities and areas, must together take counsel, *and act*, in being torch-bearers of the Light.

This, it seems to me, is a matter of mere obedience to the Lord of the Church; and obedience to this command is only weakened—I had almost said vitiated—if we go separately and dividedly.

Slowly but surely Christians in this country are coming to realise that the spreading of the good news of God's love in Christ and of his power to save and redeem men is not the task of a small coterie within the Church. It is incumbent on every baptised member of the Church. It is part of his discipleship, and it is his highest privilege. Evangelism comes second only to worship in the priorities of a man who would be faithful to his Lord. As this conviction deepens, we shall see, ever more clearly, the necessity of *united* action.

Already we have achieved a remarkable unity in the proclamation of the word of God. Only a few years ago, the societies whose first task it is to see that the Bible, in whole or in part, is available to as many people as possible in a language they understand and at a price they can afford, worked without the aid of their Roman Catholic brothers and sisters. Now they work together—all over the world—the hands of men of all the Churches mightily strengthened by their joint participation in spreading the word of life. This is a great and constructive achievement in an area of work which demands great skill and devotion, an advance for which we may all thank God and from which we may all take courage.

This leads me to the second longing which burns in my heart and which I would share with you tonight. Let me preface what I have to say about this by remarking that for many years it has been my great privilege to enjoy the friendship of my dear brother in Christ, Basil Hume. I have shared with him, as my friend and host, what I am saying to you in this address, and he has expressed himself happy that I should say it, even though he is unable to agree with me because of theological differences. Next week he will, I hope, speak to us with equal frankness when he is our guest at our General Synod.

I think it is a measure of the maturity which dialogue between us has reached, and, I would hope, a measure of the maturity of the dialogue between our two communions, that we can speak openly on matters on which as yet we are not fully agreed, one of which is the matter of our joint participation in the sacrament of the Eucharist. Such frank dialogue, undertaken in deep love, is, I believe, the most fruitful way forward to the goal we both long for.

We are united in our common baptism into the Triune Name. We are united in our love for the Lord who loved us and gave himself up for us. We are united in our membership of his Church, though there are still areas of theological interpretation in which we do not find agreement and which no doubt will continue to perplex us. We are united in our desire to be obedient to the Lord's commission to "go . . . make disciples . . . baptise . . . teach". We are united, as I have just said, in the ministry of spreading the printed word. This is a wonderful measure of unity. This is the result of the operation of the Holy Spirit. Thanks be to God. But, let us confess it, the impact that we make on a world which, like the Greeks in St John's Gospel, "would see Jesus", is pathetically feeble, the witness we bear is muted, the vision which we share is blurred. I ask: why is this so? Can the reason be that we are divided at the deepest point of unity, the sacrament of the Body and Blood of Christ? Is this God's judgement on us for failing to grasp this nettle? We recognise our unity in baptism; we persist in disunity at the Eucharist. So we go to our mission weak, where we should be strong and invigorated by joint participation in the Supper of the Lord.

We shelter behind differences of doctrine, of expression, of explanation. But is there, underlying it all, almost in our subconscious, a failure to repent of the way we have injured one another in the past? My attention has recently been drawn to a passage in Dean Church's essay on Lancelot Andrewes, where he says of the conflict in the reigns of Elizabeth and James I: "Controversy, never silent, and always truculent and unsparing, was but a light matter compared with the terrible hostilities carried on, not by word, but by deed. . . We may well be aghast at the horrors of the struggle. The deep hatreds and deep injuries of the political conflict gave to the theological controversy—the necessary theological controversy—an unfairness and virulence from which it has never recovered, and which have been a disgrace to Christendom, and fatal, not merely to unity, but in many ways to truth."

We are the heirs of those who shared in these terrible deeds. *Our* eyes, to a lesser or greater degree, have been blinded to the saving, healing truths of the gospel. We rejoice at the three agreed statements produced by the members of the Anglican/Roman Catholic International Commission. We rejoice at the recent dedication of the memorial in Westminster Abbey to the martyrs who "divided at the Reformation by different convictions laid down their lives for Christ and conscience sake". But should I not be asking—as indeed I now do—for the forgiveness of my Roman Catholic friends for the lingering attitudes of suspicion and coldness—even sometimes of contempt—which characterised us up to fifteen or twenty years ago, and sometimes do so still? And should not that confession of sin be sealed in joint participation in the sacrament of Holy Communion? Is not that the way forward to that "unity without absorption" of which Pope Paul, echoing a phrase first used in 1925, spoke when we met in Rome last year?

Throughout the world, men and women, ordained and lay,

in both our communions, are refusing to continue in disunity at what Christ intended to be the sacrament of unity, Roman Catholics receiving at Anglican hands the tokens of Christ's passion, and vice-versa. I have seen this happen, and taken part in it, and been deeply moved by it, in Australasia and in other places beyond these islands. Order within the Church matters, and encouragement must not be given to the breaking of rules. But I ask: is the Holy Spirit speaking to the leadership of our Churches through the voice of people who see, with a clarity sometimes hidden from our eyes, the scandal of disunity?

In the two famous passages in St Matthew's Gospel (16:19 and 18:18) about "binding" and "loosing", it is generally recognised that in Aramaic the terms to "bind" and to "loose" are academic language for the decision of the rabbis as to what was "forbidden" or "permitted". Among us in the past, more attention has been given to "binding" than to "loosing", to "forbidding" than to "permitting". I ask again: is the Spirit saying to the Church: "Ye that do truly and earnestly repent you of your sins, and are in love and charity with your neighbours, draw near with faith—draw near *together* with faith—and take this Holy Sacrament to your comfort"?

As I pondered on this matter last week, I listened again to those words of St Paul in which he spoke of the age-long barrier which separated Jews from Gentiles, Gentiles from Jews. He had been brought up under the old rules and regulations. Now they were annulled. The wall was down. The enmity was broken. Christ had done—was doing—his reconciling work. This is what he wrote:

> For he is himself our peace. Gentiles and Jews, he has made the two one, and in his own body of flesh and blood has broken down the enmity which stood like a dividing wall between them; for he annulled the law with its rules and regulations, so as to create out of the two a single new humanity in himself, thereby making peace. This was his purpose, to reconcile the two in a single body to God through the cross, on which he killed the enmity. (Ephesians 2:14–16, NEB)

Let that be our text tonight, and let that be our guide tomorrow.

There is a Lord to be obeyed.

There is a light to be passed on.

There is a world to be won.

We have talked about the pain of disunity long enough. Now let us act.

And in the strength of the Body broken and the Blood outpoured, we will walk in love, and we will go in peace.

Though we are many . . .

"I SHALL BE closed on December 28", said a friend to me just before Christmas. He owns a shop down the road a little way from here. "We shall be stock-taking." Wise man. Before the new year dawned, he wanted to know where he stood in his business—to assess the situation.

Let us begin tonight, at this ecumenical service, with a little stock-taking. How goes the business of Christian unity? Where do we now stand?

We have cause for thankfulness. Young people today find it hard to believe me when I tell them that I can remember the day when Roman Catholics in this country were not (officially) allowed to say the Lord's Prayer in public with those who did not belong to their Church. Those days, thank God, are gone. We pray, plan, work together, Anglicans, Roman Catholics, Orthodox, Free Churches; and great is the good for the nation and for ourselves that accrues from such co-operation. The wind of the Spirit has blown away a great many of the old cobwebs of disunity.

But there is no room for complacency. All is not well. I think I sense a certain tiredness in some ecumenical circles. Do you sense the same? We do not have to look abroad only to see the failure of certain schemes on which much prayer and labour had been spent. That is no doubt one reason for disillusionment. But a more subtle danger presents itself when we find Christians satisfied with things as they are—satisfied with a kind of happy camaraderie between Christians of varying traditions, a
Ecumenical Service, Canterbury Cathedral, 20 January, 1980.

camaraderie which does not press on to the full unity which Christ wills for his Church, and in particular to unity at the place where it most loudly cries out for expression, namely, at the sacrament of the Body and Blood of Christ. In our care for correct order in the Church and in our desire to prevent any possible anomaly in the progress toward unity, we sometimes forget that the supreme anomaly is disunity itself. "Though we are many", we Anglicans say in the Holy Communion service, "we are one body, for we all partake of the one bread." Sometimes I feel I want to beat my breast as I say these words.

All too easily we in England grow accustomed to the gross wastage of man-power (person-power, should I say?) and of money which results from our disunity, while we continue to prop up the structures of our denominations, organisationally and architecturally. I sometimes wonder whether the Lord of the Church will not soon say to us: "Dear silly children of mine, if you will not get together in any other way, I shall make you get together on the sheer grounds of economic necessity. I may even use the rod of my servant Sheik Yamani to this end!"

Of the iniquity of exporting our divisions to countries overseas I will say nothing, for if I did my language might not be suitable in so sacred a shrine as this beloved Cathedral!

I try to peer into the eighties. What do I see? I see at least the possibility of the people in the pews taking the law into their own hands if the clergy and the synods and the governing bodies of the Churches do not give a more courageous lead. I long to see a little more daring in the governing bodies of the Churches, an impatience which can rightly be called divine, and a persistence, in truth and in love, which continues with the pursuit of unity "until it be thoroughly finished".

I want to be very practical and very positive tonight. I ask what steps we can take in this big and urgent task of Christian re-union. I suggest four steps:

First, *prayer*. In 1933 Paul Couturier, a French Roman Catholic priest, introduced a three-day period of prayer for Church unity. This was followed in 1934 by an octave of prayer for the unity of all baptised Christians "as and how Christ wills". Who can say how great have been the results of these weeks of prayer? If they have lost something of their original power, that may be partly due to the fact that now, in contrast to those days, we frequently pray together—and not just in January! But it may also be due to the fact—the regrettable fact—that in these weeks there has been too much talking and too little praying, too little waiting on God. Let this be borne in mind in future!

Secondly, *thought*. The hard work of rigorous, honest, open theological dialogue must go on, with a respect for truth which dares to face the issues and to press behind old controversies to basic essentials. I think of this work going on in our universities and theological colleges and ecumenical commissions. But I also think of it going on, albeit in a less specialised way, in groups at local levels. "When he, the Spirit of truth, is come, he will guide you into all truth"—why should we not claim this for ourselves as, prayerfully and with open minds, we "speak the truth in love" one with another?

Thirdly, *joint evangelism*. The divine command to "go, make disciples, baptise and teach" has never been withdrawn. Mission is of the essence of the Church. Evangelism, together with worship, is the prime task of Christian men and women. Said a Christian leader in a letter to me the other day: "Sometimes I think that we forget that our main task is to offer Christ as Lord and Saviour . . . We talk so much about mission that we haven't time to get on with the job."

We do not need to wait to resolve all our differences before we can engage in joint evangelism. Obey Christ by proclaiming him together, and he will give you, as a bonus, a measure of unity which you have not experienced before when you have gone on in your separate ways.

The Nationwide Initiative in Evangelism seeks to help us all—yes, *all* who are disciples of Jesus—to turn our eyes from looking inward at the task of self-preservation (of ourselves or of our church-structures), to look at the world around us and beyond us in its desperate need of Christ. It is not concerned with the organisation of great campaigns. It *is* concerned with the study of evangelism within the particular social setting where we live and work, and with getting on with the actual business of offering Christ in a way that men and women can understand. If we can be the agents of a confrontation, a meeting, an encounter between our friends and our Lord, then we have done the essential part of our work, and it is up to those friends to do what they will with that encounter. It is over to them—and to the Holy Spirit who is the life-giver.

Fourthly and lastly, *holiness*. Please do not switch off because I have used that word. I define holiness as likeness to Jesus, and growth in that likeness is for every Christian. As we come closer to him we come closer to one another, as surely as the spokes of a wheel come closer to one another the nearer they get to the hub. If I have a burning love of Jesus, and you have a similar love, that will not resolve all our differences just like that, but it will mean that they are seen for what in fact they are—peripheral. At the centre we are one, for we both love him; we worship and adore him; we are determined to serve him, and to make him known in his love and beauty and power.

There are many excuses which we put up for our lack of unity. Some of them are valid. Some are not. But would it not be true to say that the *main* cause of our disunity is that our love of Jesus has burned low, that the fire is flickering rather than blazing? The message to the Church at Laodicea is the message to the Church of England and to the Churches in England: "You say, 'How rich I am! And how well I have done! I have everything I want.' In fact, though you do not know it, you are the most pitiful wretch, poor, blind and naked." Yes, that is true of us, if our love has gone lukewarm.

I have said enough. In a moment I shall ask you to kneel, that in silence we may ponder on what we have heard, then I shall say a prayer, and then we shall, if we dare, say that prayer together, line by line. Let us kneel.

"Here I stand, knocking at the door." It is the voice of Christ, not, in the context, to the pagan outsider, but to the members of a *Church*. "Here I stand, knocking at the door; if anyone hears my voice and opens the door, I will come in . . . Be on your mettle then, and repent . . ."

Come as flame, and like unto the wind, come from the heights of heaven, O God the Holy Ghost:

Touch thou our tongues, illuminate our minds, make our hearts strong, when we do need thee most.

Teach us to speak of thee; help us to worship thee.

May we lead souls to thee, O God the Holy Ghost.

Amen.

V
BIBLE AND WORLD

The Bible and Social Justice

I BEGIN THIS lecture with two quotations. The first is from Alan Ecclestone's new book *A Staircase for Silence* (Darton, Longman and Todd, 1977):

New and still newer features supplied every day to create a new world require us to look forward more than ever before, to travel more lightly unencumbered by our past, to be more alert to the signs of the times, and above all to be more expectant of God's help in the most unlooked for situations.[1]

The second is from Max Warren's *I Believe in the Great Commission* (Hodder and Stoughton, 1976):

We today are to be on the alert for the signs of God's working in our history, not just in the past, but in the present, with an eye alert to God's future. I believe that we can mark his footsteps, almost hear them, if we look around us and listen.[2]

These two quotations have much in common. In particular, there is the demand for *alertness*. Ecclestone bids us be "alert for the signs of the times". So does Warren, who bids us be "alert to the signs of God's working in our history" and to have an eye "alert to God's future".

The William Floyd Memorial Lecture, Holy Trinity Cathedral, Suva, 23 March, 1977.

These writers, I believe, strike the right note for this lecture. The title of the lecture has within it the words "The Bible . . .". That takes us into the past at once. The other part of this lecture's title is "Social Justice". Here is no relapse into the past! Here is a matter which cries out to us from every daily paper, from radio news-bulletin after radio news-bulletin. It cries out to us from the prison camps of Soviet Russia, from the detention centres of South Africa, from the hovels of Calcutta and the *favellas* of Latin America. The question which the title of the lecture poses lies in the conjunction—"The Bible *and* Social Justice". Is there an authentic link between the two? Has the Bible anything definite to say on the matter? Is there a word to which I, as a thinking modern man set in a world of howling injustice, should be "alert"?

Max Warren, we have noticed, believes that the alert man can mark God's footsteps—"almost hear them", he said—if he looks around him and listens. Warren sees the marks of God's activity, for example, in the birth of a "compassionate society", an awareness of human misery on the part of millions, and a desire to help. He sees the marks of God's activity in the search for belonging, in the search for unity, in the ecumenical move-ment—and so on. But he sees it very clearly in what he calls "the passion for justice"—"was there ever", he asks, "a time when that passion was blazing so like a forest fire as it is today?" And here he answers my question about the conjunction in the title of the lecture—"The Bible *and* Social Justice". "If you want the standard work on *justice* you will find it in the Old Testament."[3]

That is plain speaking—no beating about the bush there! Max Warren refers to the Old Testament only. My title refers to "the Bible" as a whole. My canvas is large, alarmingly large. The strokes of my brush must, therefore, be large, and detail must be eschewed.

Where am I to begin? "With the eighth-century prophets," you will say, "if you are beginning with the Old Testament." And rightly, if we want to get to the heart of the matter, to the main part of the picture in the full blaze of its glory. But wait a minute. Should we not do well to sketch in some background? Indeed we should.

We can begin at no other point than at the character of God as the Hebrews conceived it. Their concept of social justice *sprang* from that. "I am . . . therefore thou shalt." That the evolution of their concept of God went through a long period of development, that the revelation came "in fragmentary and varied fashion through the prophets"[4] and others, that there were crudities of concept which had to be abandoned and roughnesses which had to be smoothed, no student of the Old Testament would attempt to deny. But the fact of a God who made his ways known to men, sometimes mysteriously through the forces of Nature, sometimes through the events, hardly less mysterious, of history, sometimes through his particular dealings with a special people (Israel), sometimes through the giving of a special teaching (*Torah*)—this lies back, this is the *hintergrund* of the total biblical picture. "Verily thou art a God that hidest thyself."[5] Yes, there is the abyss of mystery in divinity. The Hebrews, though they would not have put it this way, had to learn that "all theology *exit in mysterium*". *But* the God of the Hebrews is not a silent God. He is the God who speaks. He is the God who makes his ways known.[6] Eventually, supremely, in the teaching of Jesus, he will be seen as the God who *seeks*—but that in its fullness is a later revelation.

"I am . . . thou shalt . . ."[7] The content, the character, of that "I am" will be clarified, purified, filled out as the centuries go on. But there he stands, the God who speaks, who wills to make himself known. "I am the Lord, I change not, therefore ye sons of Jacob are not consumed."[8] The content of the Decalogue may be predominantly negative; it may be little more than a fence put there to prevent a people from falling over the precipice into chaos and death. But it is there because it seeks to reflect the character of a God who cares for his people and desires their health ("salvation").

In the great poem in which Job finally surveys his case,[9] Job stoutly maintains not only his innocence but also his positive charity and beneficence. He was "eyes to the blind, and feet to the lame; . . . father to the needy" and so on.[10] He was straight in his dealings and pure in his sexual relationships.[11] He was kind to his employees and generous to the down-and-outs.[12] Why this right conduct? What basic convictions lay behind a life lived with such probity? Job is in no doubt as to what moved him so to conduct himself. It was the reality of *God*—"the terror of God was heavy upon me, and for fear of his majesty I could do none of these [evil] things."[13] "What shall I answer if he intervenes?"[14]—there is a righteous judge to be reckoned with. Further, this righteous judge is not only the one who creates *him* but the one who also created his slave and his slave-girl—"did not he who made me in the womb make them? Did not the same God create us in the belly?"[15] The fact of God, inscrutable and terribly puzzling as the ways of that God undoubtedly were, was the great restraining and constraining moral influence on the writer of this great poem. "I am—thou shalt" was a mighty moral force. We may regard the book of Job as being mainly the cry of an individual who feels himself unjustly done by—an individual's wrestling with the problem of injustice as it affects him. Or we may see it as a book "in which, as in a concave mirror, is gathered together very much of the trials meted out to Israel, and intensified into a superhuman suffering".[16] But the point is the same whichever interpretation we put on the book. There is a God. Moreover, this God has spoken, declaring enough of his character and enough of his interest in human affairs to make it incumbent on this individual, or on this nation, to behave in such and such a way. "He is . . . therefore I . . ."

"He has declared . . . his character and his interest in human affairs." So we have just said. It was Israel's conviction that the character of God was best seen in his interventions in human history and particularly in his shaping of the history of his people Israel. Not that this latter thing was to be thought of in terms of favouritism—so to interpret election was to make a travesty of it. God's intervention in his people's history was an intervention of sheer grace—"because he loved you".[17] Israel came to see, through its best and deepest thinkers, that election entailed service; choice was not to be thought of in terms of privilege or status but of bringing light to others.[18] God had intervened—through the call of an Abraham or the mission of a Moses or the deliverance at the Red Sea—and in those interventions had made known some facet of his character. Indeed these mighty acts of God are sometimes called "the righteous acts of the Lord".[19]

This leads us to a point of great importance in the Hebrew thinking about God. Righteousness is not a static concept at all, far less a negative one. This is not always easy for a Westerner to realise, for to us "righteousness" is all too easily thought of in these terms—the righteous man is the man of blameless character who does *not* commit murder or adultery or injure his neighbour. But when the Hebrews, and the prophets in particular, spoke of God as righteous, they meant that God, just because he had certain essential qualities, intervened in human affairs and acted in human history in accordance with those qualities. So the Psalmist,[20] when he says of God that his "right hand is full of righteousness", means that God takes action, exerts his power and authority, according to his righteous nature and the effects are seen among the children of men. It is a highly *dynamic* concept.

So it is that there is about this idea of righteousness a strong note of relationship. A man's righteousness, on the horizontal level, may be gauged by his relationship to his family, or to his clan, or to foreigners; and, on the vertical level, to the Lord. Nor can the horizontal and the vertical be separated; they are inextricably interwoven one with the other.

At this point the prophets, and particularly the eighth-century prophets, come into their own. To them were given insights into the nature of God clearer than any hitherto revealed, so far as we can tell. Amos, wrestling in the scrubland around Tekoa with issues far more demanding than the care of sheep and of sycomore-figs, sees with a kind of blinding clarity that God is *just*. Hosea, bruised and battered by the desertion and adultery of his wife, peers through the tragedy of his broken home-life and of his own broken heart and sees that God's heart is broken over the defection of his people. He did not write, as St John was to do late in the first century AD, "God is *love*",[21] but he got wonderfully near that truth. *Justice* and *love* — yes. But the prophets do not see these as abstract virtues which may be attributed to God, with a kind of shrug of the shoulders and a cry of "so what?" No—these are dynamic concepts. If God is just and loving, then his relationship with his people, a relationship of justice and love, must be responded to by them and must be reflected in their relationships with one another.

In parenthesis it should be added that the prophets' faith in a God of justice and love led to severe ethical problems. The higher your doctrine of God, the greater your ethical problems become. *If* God was such a God, then why did injustice so often seem to prosper, and hatred to reign in the affairs of men rather than goodwill? It just was not the case, as the Psalmist seemed too facilely to suggest,[22] that the godly would be snatched away "from fowler's snare or raging tempest", or that "the pestilence that stalks in darkness or the plague raging at noonday" would by-pass the godly and fall only on those who turned their backs on the Lord. The facts of life did not support such a theory. Others of the Psalms are full of cries of outrage against the injustices of life which—like the sunshine!—fall on godly and ungodly alike.[23] The cries almost reach the point of blasphemy, were it not for their total sincerity. God seems to have dropped off to sleep—when will he wake up and do something about the iniquities and inequities of life as it actually is?[24] It was very largely this attempt to find a solution to the problem of life's injustice and at the same time to hold fast to a belief in the justice and love of God which led to the growth of that large body of writings, often garish in their colouring and sometimes crude in their expression, which goes by the name of apocalyptic, the most outstanding Old Testament example of which we find in the Book of Daniel, and in the New Testament in the Revelation of St John. Apocalypse is an attempt at theodicy. But that is a story into which we cannot enter in detail here.

We return to the point that God's relationship with his people, a relationship of justice and love, must be reflected in their relationships with one another. This fundamental principle does not apply only to the people of Israel. When Israel's thinkers came to see that Yahweh was the God not only of Israel but of the whole earth, they realised that God had certain expectations of *all* the nations. Thus, Amos in the opening chapter of his prophecy announces the judgement of God on Israel's neighbours[25] for the atrocities which they have committed—Damascus, Gaza, Tyre, Edom, Ammon, Moab, all come under the divine judgement. Only then does the prophet turn his gaze to Judah and Israel.[26] And if we ask what it is in Israel's neighbours which calls forth God's judgement, we find that it is not anything to do with the form of their worship, but it is to do with their attitudes and actions towards other human beings. The direction is horizontal. Thus, Gaza and Tyre are rebuked for deporting people, Edom for "hunting their kinsmen down, stifling their natural affections", and Ammon for greed in acquiring farmlands. Here are social issues. Here are social injustices. And Yahweh, just because he is the God of justice as well as of love, "interferes" in the affairs of men with a word of judgement through his spokesman, Amos.

It was this deep and passionate conviction of the inter-relationship of the vertical and the horizontal which led the prophets to inveigh, often in terms of scorching wrath and burning indignation, against worship divorced from morality, against the performance of cult activities, religious ceremonies, which did not issue in conduct which reflected the justice and love of the God in whose name and in whose sanctuary those religious "services" were held.

Amos, the man of the justice of God, denounces alike the senseless luxury of many of his contemporaries[27] and the rotten-ness of a nation which, while carrying on religious practices, is careless of the demands of social justice. Listen to this for sarcasm:

Come to Bethel—and rebel!
Come to Gilgal—and rebel the more!
Bring your sacrifices for the morning,
your tithes within three days.
Burn your thank-offering without leaven;
announce, proclaim your freewill offerings;
for you love to do what is proper, you men of Israel!
        This is the very word of the Lord God.[28]

Or this:

I hate, I spurn your pilgrim-feasts;
I will not delight in your sacred ceremonies.
When you present your sacrifices and offerings
I will not accept them,
nor look on the buffaloes of your shared-offerings.
Spare me the sound of your songs;
I cannot endure the music of your lutes.
Let justice roll on like a river
and righteousness like an ever-flowing stream.[29]

This latter passage has its parallel, only worked out in greater detail, in the prophecy of Isaiah:

> Hear the word of the Lord, you rulers of Sodom;
> attend, you people of Gomorrah, to the instruction of our God:
> Your countless sacrifices, what are they to me?
> says the Lord.
> I am sated with whole-offerings of rams
> and the fat of buffaloes;
> I have no desire for the blood of bulls,
> of sheep and he-goats.
> Whenever you come to enter my presence—
> who asked you for this?
> No more shall you trample my courts.
> The offer of your gifts is useless,
> the reek of sacrifice is abhorrent to me.
> New moons and sabbaths and assemblies,
> sacred seasons and ceremonies, I cannot endure.
> I cannot tolerate your new moons and your festivals;
> they have become a burden to me,
> and I can put up with them no longer.
> When you lift your hands outspread in prayer,
> I will hide my eyes from you.
> Though you offer countless prayers,
> I will not listen.
> There is blood on your hands;
> wash yourselves and be clean.
> Put away the evil of your deeds,
> away out of my sight.
> Cease to do evil and learn to do right,
> pursue justice and champion the oppressed;
> give the orphan his rights, plead the widow's cause.[30]

This passage, in turn, is paralleled in the Psalms, especially in one which strikes a deeper and more tender note than did Amos and Isaiah in the passages I have quoted. They use the language of denunciation and of sarcasm. The Psalmist points to penitence:

Thou hast no delight in sacrifice;
if I brought thee an offering, thou wouldst not accept it.
My sacrifice, O God, is a broken spirit;
a wounded heart, O God, thou wilt not despise.[31]

I have chosen only a very few of the passages, though they are some of the most vivid, which speak of the demands which belief in a just and loving God makes, in practical affairs, on those who worship him. There are, in many of the Old Testament writings, strong hints that such practical religion is the basis on which a healthy national life can be built. I give but one example, and will make no comment on it:

Deliverance is near to those who worship him,
so that glory may dwell in our land.
Love and fidelity have come together;
justice and peace join hands.
Fidelity springs up from earth
and justice looks down from heaven.
The Lord will add prosperity,
and our land shall yield its harvest.
Justice shall go in front of him
and the path before his feet shall be peace.[32]

On the morning on which I wrote this part of this lecture I received a postcard—anonymous, as are many of these communications!—protesting against something which I had said, or which the writer thought I had said, about race relations. "Please stick to religious ideas," said the postcard. I wonder what Amos or Isaiah would have replied, if he could have found the address of my correspondent. The Epistle of Amos to the Anonymous would have set the pillar box on fire!

It was because Karl Barth had worked his theological way through to a powerful doctrine of God and his righteousness, especially as he had seen this in St Paul's Epistle to the Romans, that he was able, in the hour of crisis, to utter his great *Nein* to the theories and the threatenings of the Nazis.[33] What was true of him was true of other great opponents of the régime, such as Dietrich Bonhoeffer and Martin Niemöller.

It was because Geoffrey Clayton, Archbishop of Cape Town,

believed certain things about the character of God as revealed in the prophets, and supremely in Christ, that he felt himself compelled to take the stand which he did against racial oppression in South Africa—a stand reflected with great clarity in the charges which he delivered to Diocesan and Provincial Synods during the years 1948–57.[34] The same can be said of Beyers Naudé and his brave colleagues, some of whom are today languishing in gaol for their beliefs and actions.

"Here, Sir, don't you know you're on private property?" says Colonel Blimp in Low's cartoon to Archbishop Temple as, taking his stand on "economic fields" he points to the notice "Trespassers will be prosecuted".[35] But Temple, clutching his papers entitled "The Christian Aim", stands firm.

"Here I stand. I can no other." The words were Martin Luther's. The principle abides.

All too briefly, we must turn from Old Testament to New. There is a very close link between them in the matter which we are considering. It would be a deeply interesting theme to pursue the development of apocalyptic and eschatology from their beginnings in the Old Testament through the inter-Testament period to their stage of further development in the New Testament period. If that were possible—and time does not allow—we should have to give careful consideration not only to the Book of the Revelation but also to such passages as St Mark 13 and 2 Thessalonians 2. And we should have to linger over the closing section of St Matthew 25[36] where, in the parable of the sheep and the goats, judgement is meted out to *nations* on the grounds of whether or not they acted with probity and generosity to those in need, to the under-privileged, or, as we should say today, to the depressed classes and to the Third World. But all that we must by-pass, with little more than a nod and the hope of a more careful look anon, and the reminder, withal, that we saw the same principles at work in the writings of Amos.

When we come to the teaching of Jesus, we see that his main teaching about God was given under the two headings of "God as King" and "God as Father". We might put this in the terms which we have been using in our study of the Old Testament—"God as righteous" and "God as loving"; for the ideal king is a figure of righteousness, exercising his power in holy justice, and the ideal father is a figure of love, looking for a loving response from his children. This is the God whom Jesus worshipped and obeyed. This is the God of whom he taught and preached.

How did he teach? He might have given, as did many in the rabbinic schools of his day, an explication of the laws of the Old Testament in terms of an elaborate casuistry. He might have given specific directions as to what particular people should do under particular circumstances, and what they should not do. But, judging by the records in the Gospels, Jesus seems to have refused to take this line of action. He gave no elaborate, clearly defined code of ethics. Rather, he preferred to give direction than directions; to describe the truly happy man, as in the Beatitudes;[37] to give thumb-nail sketches of the ideal community, as in the parables; to throw out broad principles and leave us to work them out as they apply in the circumstances of everyday life and work. This is all very annoying for those who like to be told exactly what to do at any particular moment of decision. But for those who are prepared to think, to wrestle, to apply, this is the kind of teaching which instils principles, which reveals the mind of God to his children, and which is applicable in situations far bigger than the particular one which elicited the teaching or drew forth the parable in the first case. To teach by the parable method is to cast yeast into the dough of life, and once that is done, no one can forecast what the resulting ferment will mean in terms of the individual or in terms of social, economic or national life. No wonder that Jesus used the metaphors of leaven and of new wine bursting old wine-skins![38]

When we turn to the Epistles, and especially to the Pauline Epistles, we find an ethic which emerges from a doctrine. Sometimes the Epistles are constructed in such a way as to make this clearly apparent. For example, in the magisterial Epistle to the Romans the first eleven chapters are predominantly doctrinal—in them the Apostle works out the great doctrines which emerge from God's announcement of his gospel in the person of his Son,[39] his mighty act in the death and resurrection of Jesus, and the results of that act for the individual and for the whole creation. But when we come to the section of the Epistle which begins with chapter 12 and goes on to the end of the letter, we find a long passage which in the New English Bible is rightly headed "Christian Behaviour". This is not a kind of second letter which has no connection with the first part. Rather, it is a description of the kind of behaviour which is to be expected from those for whom the mighty acts of God have, through the activity of the Spirit in the Body of Christ, become a dynamic reality.

How does the method of teaching of the Apostle compare with that of Jesus? It is true that there is a certain "laying down of the law" in regard to certain specific issues which a Christian will have to face in society. For example, a Christian's duty to the State is outlined in some detail[40]—Jesus had gone so far as to say that his followers should pay their taxes.[41] But on the whole, the ethical teaching partakes of the nature of direction rather than directions. For example, when it comes to matters of vegetarianism or of "sabbath observance", St Paul lays down no clearly defined rules which a man must obey or disobey. Instead he lays down the underlying principle of care for the "weaker brothers"[42] and of the fact that none of us lives to himself—he lives to (is responsible to) the Lord.[43]

When we come to the Epistles to the Corinthians, we find a less clear demarcation between doctrine and ethics than we do in the Epistle to the Romans—there is more of an "admixture" in these letters. That, perhaps, is scarcely to be wondered at, for the church that was in Corinth presented a number of grievous moral problems due at least in part to the very nature of Corinth itself. These required—partly by reason of the "infantile" state of the Corinthian's discipleship[44]—some elementary answers to elementary questions; and these drew from the Apostle certain directions (for example, about wearing hats in church) which may have been locally wise but are not universally binding.[45] Nevertheless, the ethical guidance and injunctions which are given in these letters clearly emerge from the overriding, ever-present reality of God's revelation of himself in Christ crucified and risen who has called the readers of the letters to his service and who, in the Church which is his Body, feeds them in the Supper of the Lord.

Much the same can be said of the other Pauline letters—they elaborate, from varying angles, the intervention of God in Christ and, in the light of that intervention, sketch the character which should emerge as a result of the harvest of the Spirit[46] in the lives of those who are followers of "The Way".

The Pastoral Epistles (1 and 2 Timothy and Titus) are concerned primarily with church order and with the character of Christian ministers, and the Epistle of St James, apart from three verses,[47] could have come from the pen of an Old Testament prophet.

Reviewing very broadly, then, the New Testament as a whole, we may be surprised to find that, apart from the Epistle of St James, there is a strange failure on the part of the writers to deal specifically with some of the issues which concern *us* most, some at least of which must have been burning issues in the days when these letters were written, and some of which had concerned the Old Testament prophets and moved them to heated and even violent utterance.

Take, for example, the issue of *slavery*. There can be little doubt that the position of many slaves in the first-century world was a happy one and sometimes one of dignity. For example, in a very big household the doctor was numbered among the "slaves" but was probably none the worse for that. There must have been many beneficent employers who exercised a kindly paternalism. But the system as a whole laid itself open to abuse, and the cruelties which obtained under it were often appalling. One would have thought, then, that we should have found in the pages of the New Testament violent outcries against the iniquity of the system, outcries such as those which the Old Testament prophets gave in relation to the wrongs of their day. But such is not the case. We look in vain for any over-all denunciation of the system. Rather, its presence and presumably its continuance are assumed. What precisely the Epistles say about this issue we shall see in a moment, but the point we have just made holds.

Or again, take the issue of *race* or of *colour*—in our generation one of the most grievous of our problems and one which generates more heated feeling and speaking than almost any other. Again, we look in vain in the New Testament for any passage where this issue is specifically held up to the light, and where discrimination on the grounds of race or colour is pilloried or denounced. Much the same may be said in relation to the matter of class-privilege; the nearest we get to direct denunciation of the rich is a passage in the Epistle of St James,[48] but we have already noted that the author of this Epistle stands in the succession of the Old Testament prophets and that his book, apart from two or three verses, could almost have been included in the Old Testament canon.

But all this having been noted, perhaps to our surprise, we must at once go on to say that from the Gospels and Epistles there emerge certain basic, fundamental principles which are totally relevant to the issues we have mentioned. Take, for example, the sentence of St Paul in one of his earliest letters:[49] "There is no such thing as Jew and Greek, slave and free-man, male and female; for you are all one person in Christ Jesus." If this be true, we have a principle which, as it were at one thrust, deals a blow at race- or colour-discrimination (Jew and Greek); at class-discrimination (slave and free-man); and at sex-discrimination (male and female). These were three of the main issues, perhaps we should say the three main issues, which faced the world of the first century, and a good case could be made out for saying that they are three of the main issues of *our* world. In this tremendous saying, there are no *directions* as to how to work out the implications of this dynamic principle. But there can be little doubt about the *direction* in which our thinking should go and our action be taken.

Look again at the issue of slavery. We must bear in mind that, at the time when the Epistles were written, Christians could not be numbered in hundreds of millions as they can today, but consisted of tiny groups, mostly of socially insignificant people, scattered widely over the Graeco-Roman world. For these tiny groups to go about waving "No slavery" banners would have been utterly useless, in fact worse than useless. What they did, or, rather, what some of their leaders whose writings are preserved in the New Testament did, was to enunciate certain universally valid principles which, if obeyed, would eventually break up the whole system. Thus, for example, the author of the Epistle of the Ephesians, faced by the fact of a system built on master and slave relationships, lays down the principle that "God has no favourites" and that all, master and slave alike, have "the same Master in Heaven",[50] to whom they are finally responsible. In other words, the ground on which all ranks stand is, so far as God is concerned, level.

The Christian slave does his work conscientiously, with his eye not merely to his earthly master, but to Christ, seeking whole-heartedly to do the will of God.[51] But the same principle applies also to the *master*.[52] If both slave and master have the same Lord, slaves cannot be inefficient, or masters threatening. All are under the judgement of God.

The principle of no-favouritism with God applies also in the sphere of what we should now call race-relations. There is a remarkable passage in the Gospel according to St Luke[53] in which he tells the story of our Lord's first sermon, after his temptation, in the synagogue of his home-town, Nazareth. He took as his text a passage from Isaiah 61 and used it as the manifesto of his forthcoming ministry. It was to be a ministry directed to the poor, the prisoners, the blind, the broken victims; to them he would "proclaim the year of the Lord's favour".[54] A sigh of delight went up from the congregation—they had never heard such gracious words before. But when the preacher began to apply the words, the atmosphere changed, and it was not long before "the whole congregation were infuriated. They leapt up, threw him out of the town, and took him to the brow of the hill on which it was built, meaning to hurl him over the edge".[55] Why this sudden change from admiration to hate? The reason is clear: Jesus had dared to point out that with God there are no racial favourites. If Israel, the people chosen to bring God's light to the world, will not listen, then God will go elsewhere—to Sidon or to Syria. The prophets had said as much—God can and will use a pagan Cyrus[56] as his Messiah, if need be. Race—colour—are immaterial to him.[57]

If we turn from issues of slavery and race to that of wealth, again we find a principle laid down to which we are bidden to give careful, even painful, heed. The accumulation of wealth, so far from creating a privileged class, is in the divine economy to be regarded as a matter not only of responsibility but of potentially grave danger. God's economics are profoundly disturbing: look at the parable of Dives and Lazarus,[58] or at the parable of the Rich Fool,[59] or at that uncomfortable saying about it being easier for a camel to go through the eye of a needle than for a rich man to enter the kingdom of heaven,[60] (and I don't mind if you tell me that instead of "a camel" we should read "a rope", the two words being very similar in Aramaic: the principle is the same!).

"The Bible and Social Justice." We have only touched the outskirts of the subject. But we have, I think, seen enough to persuade us that social justice is at the very heart of the concerns of this library of books. The power of what it has to say results from its theological basis—in the Old Testament, the power deriving from the basic concept of God as One who is just and loving; in the New Testament from the concept of God who is King (just) and Father (loving) and who has revealed himself uniquely in the Person, in the teaching, in the dying and the rising of his Son, the Word, the disclosed mind and heart of himself.

If it be objected that the dynamite of the biblical ethic has been slow in taking effect in our society; if, for example, it be pointed out that it was many centuries before Wilberforce and his colleagues were able to stab awake the consciences of enough people to make them heed the biblical principles on the subject of slavery and so break up the diabolical system; then one can only say that successive generations have proved toughly resistant to the insight of biblical ethics, or, to put it differently, have been resolutely opposed to the detonating of the biblical dynamite. And if we find ourselves shaking our heads in self-righteous condemnation of the slowness of our forebears in obeying the biblical principles about slavery, let us ask ourselves whether we, in this generation, have not been almost equally timid in applying those principles where sex-discrimination is concerned.

References

1 p 5. Alan Ecclestone is the author of *Yes to God* which was awarded the Collins Religious Book Award for 1974–76
2 p 139
3 op. cit. p 141
4 Hebrews 1:1
5 Isaiah 45:15
6 Psalm 103:7
7 Exodus 20:2ff
8 Malachi 3:6
9 Job 29–31
10 Job 29:15ff
11 Job 31:5ff
12 Job 31:13ff

13 Job 31:23
14 Job 31:14
15 Job 31:15
16 Gerhard von Rad, *Old Testament Theology*, Vol. I, p 408
17 Deuteronomy 7:7–8
18 See, for example, Isaiah 42:6; 49:6; 60:1–3
19 Examples of "the righteousness" of the Lord being used in the sense of his saving actions in history may be found in Judges 5:11 (NEB "the *victories* of the Lord"), 1 Samuel 12:7 ("recite all the *victories* which he has won for you and for your fathers"), Micah 6:5 ("consider the journey from Shittim to Gilgal, in order that you may know the *triumph* of the Lord"), etc.
20 Psalm 48:10
21 1 St John 4:8, 16
22 Psalm 91:3ff
23 E.g. Psalm 74
   The book of Job, surely the *least* "patient" of all biblical writers, is one great protest against the injustices which have befallen a godly man, viz. himself!
24 See, for example, Psalm 35:23; 44:23; 77:5–10
25 Amos 1:3ff
26 Amos 2:4ff
27 Amos 4:1ff; 6:1ff
28 Amos 4:4–5
29 Amos 5:21–24
30 Isaiah 1:10–17
31 Psalm 51:16–17. It is an open question as to whether v. 19 is part and parcel of the Psalm or is, rather, an addition by a writer who felt that vv. 16–17 might lead to the abandonment of sacrificial worship, a course which he himself would regret.
32 Psalm 85:9–13
33 See, e.g., Eberhard Busch: *Karl Barth: His life from letters and autobiographical texts* (S.C.M. Press, 1976).
34 See, for the charges, *Where We Stand* (OUP., 1960); also *Apartheid and the Archbishop: the Life and Times of Geoffrey Clayton*, by Alan Paton (David Philip, 1973).
35 See F.A. Iremonger: *William Temple*, opp. p 577 (OUP., 1948)
36 St Matthew 25:31–46
37 St Matthew 5:3–12
38 St Matthew 13:33; 9:17
39 Romans 1:1ff
40 Romans 13:1–8
41 St Matthew 22:21; cf. 17:24–27
42 Romans 14:1ff and 20ff and cf. 1 Corinthians 8
43 Romans 14:7ff
44 1 Corinthians 3:1–4
45 1 Corinthians 11:2ff; cf., as I would hold, 14:34–35
46 See, e.g. Galatians 5:22–25
47 St James 1:1; 2:1; 5:7 (and even this last reference need not necessarily refer to Christ specifically).
48 St James 5: 1ff
49 Galatians 3:28
50 Ephesians 6:9

51 Ephesians 6:5–8
52 Ephesians 6:9
53 St Luke 4
54 St Luke 4:18–19
55 St Luke 4:28–29
56 Isaiah 45:1
57 cf. St Matthew 8:10–12
58 St Luke 16:19ff
59 St Luke 12:13ff
60 St Matthew 19:24

Two Men and a Book

Acts 8:30–31
*Philip . . . asked: "Do you understand what you
are reading?". And he [the Ethiopian] said:
"How can I, unless someone guides me?"*

"DEAR DR LUKE", as St Paul called his friend
and colleague, loved a good story; and what an expert he was in
telling it! We see him at his best in the tale he tells of how
Christianity first came to Africa. It's the story of two men and a
book. That's all—humanly speaking.

The first of the two men was a court official, a man of very
considerable importance at the Ethiopian palace, a kind of
treasurer-cum-chief-attendant on the queen of the Ethio-
pians—no less! He was a deeply religious man, dissatisfied, like
so many of his contemporaries of many nations, with his own
religion, and on the look-out for a religion which went deeper
and could satisfy the mind and heart of a highly civilised human
being. Almost all the world knew that at Jerusalem there was a
temple unlike the other temples with which the world of the
first century was bestrewn—it had no image, no idol, in it.
Strange, that! The God proclaimed within that temple claimed
to be the *only* God—a fantastic claim in a world where, to put it
mildly, there were "gods many and lords many". This God, so
his representatives maintained, was a God of justice and of love,
who entered into agreements with those who followed him and
who could be relied on to keep his word. Though some of the
Scripture Union Centenary, St Paul's Cathedral, 31 March, 1979.

habits of his people were distinctly off-putting to many men of other races—their food laws, and their insistence on circumcision, to take but two examples—yet they had an ethic and an approach to life which were rapidly becoming the envy of the best thinkers of the nations of the world. The wealthier among them took the opportunity of making the long journey to Jerusalem—to see, and to listen at first hand, and, perhaps, to buy (at great cost, for each bit had to be written out by hand) a copy of part of Israel's sacred writings. This is precisely what our Ethiopian friend had done. It had been a long journey probably in an ox-waggon (even though he had the luxury of a chauffeur!). The bit of Isaiah which he had bought had proved very expensive; but it was worth it—or was it? For while it was undeniably beautiful, it was extraordinarily perplexing.

Well, that's the first of the two men. Now for the second. He can be more briefly described. He was a man in touch with God, open to his direction and ready to obey it. He felt an inner compulsion to take to the road which led from Jerusalem southwards. He had not gone far when he knew why he had been directed there. Along came the chariot, with its swarthy occupant engaged, between bumps, in reading a scroll. Greatly daring, and hardly knowing why, Philip climbed into the chariot, sat down by the reader, noticed he was reading from Isaiah about one who was "led like a sheep to the slaughter . . . his life taken from the earth", and then put the pointed question: "Do you understand what you are reading?" Clearly the answer was "Yes", for the man in the chariot knew Greek or he would not have bought the scroll. But the deeper answer was "No", for he hadn't a clue as to the person to whom the words referred—not till Philip told him and pointed him to Jesus.

"Two men and a book", that's what we have called the story. But there is much more to it than this. Unseen, but powerfully present, was the Holy Spirit, directing Philip, illuminating the mind and stirring the conscience of the Ethiopian. We must surely re-name the story—"*The Holy Spirit*, two men and a book". *That's* what led to the courtier's baptism. *That's* what led, I imagine, to the founding of the Church of God in Ethiopia. The Spirit had material to work on—a man sensitive to God, and a book which spoke of Christ. Anything can happen when these constituents are present!

"Do you understand what you are reading?" It is not enough to translate the Bible into languages which people can read, as the Hebrew of Isaiah had been translated into the Greek which the Ethiopian read. I am profoundly thankful for the work of the Bible Societies which translate, and print, and publish, and disseminate the Scriptures in cheap and attractive form. They are the handmaids of the Church which has always gone to the world with a book in its hand. But more than this is needed. "How can I understand, unless someone guides me?" The book is basic, but a guide is needed. That Guide is provided by God in the Person of the Holy Spirit. If Jesus is the Way, then the Holy Spirit is the Guide on the Way. If Jesus is the Truth, then the Holy Spirit is the Illuminator of the Truth. If Jesus is the Life, then the Holy Spirit is the Lord and Life-Giver.

The function of the Holy Spirit is to annihilate the distance of time and space which separates the Jesus of first-century Palestine from the Jesus of twentieth-century London, and to make him my contemporary—

> nearer than breathing,
> closer than hands and feet.

Just as, in Holy Communion, the Holy Spirit takes ordinary things, bread and wine, and makes them vehicles of the grace and strength of Jesus, so he takes words, the things we daily use in ordinary intercourse, the words of an ancient book, and makes them the vehicles of the grace and strength of Jesus.

> The Spirit breathes upon the word,
> And brings the truth to light.

But, in the mystery of God's plan, even more than this is needed. *Philips* are needed, human agents sensitive to his touch, obedient to his call, percipient of his plan, eager to tell the good news of Jesus, right-hand men and women of the Spirit.

This is why the work of the Scripture Union, now celebrating its centenary, is such glorious work. This is why, thankful though we are for what has happened in the past through the movement, we are much more interested in what God is calling us to do in the future. We are only touching the fringe of what waits to be done. There are multitudes who do not understand what they read when a Bible is put in their hands—nor will they, till somebody guides them, himself a right-hand man of the Spirit. And there are vaster multitudes who have not got a Bible, nor even a bit of the Bible, and who have never heard the Name which is above every name. Till they have heard that Name, till they can read that book, till they can understand what they read, and hear the good news of Jesus, and be baptised in His Church, your task, our task, is unfinished.

Go to it, then, in your second century, with all your might, as colleagues of the Holy Spirit, and may the joy of the Lord be your strength!

VI
HISTORIC
OCCASIONS

Service and Faith

The Queen's Free Chapel of St George within her Castle of Windsor is a Royal Peculiar, that is to say, it is exempt from diocesan and provincial jurisdiction. Founded by Edward III in 1348, it is a self-governing secular community of priests and laymen. Its first duty is to celebrate Divine Service daily on behalf of the Sovereign, the Royal House and the Order of the Garter.

Its present Chapel was founded by Edward IV in honour of Our Lady, St George and St Edward in 1475. A service was held on 23 April 1975 to celebrate the five hundredth anniversary of this event.

St Matthew 4:10
Jesus said: "You shall worship the Lord your God and him only shall you serve"

HE WOULD BE a very brave man who attempted to analyse with any measure of accuracy the motives which led King Edward IV to plan the building of this glorious chapel five centuries ago. All of us are men of mixed motives, and there was about the King a taste for splendour which bordered on the luxurious and the extravagant. That matters little to us who have been fortunate enough to be the heirs of his munificence. What does matter is what this chapel has stood for during the years and what it stands for today. I suggest two things.

First, it stands for the truth that *service and faith go together.*
St George's Chapel, Windsor, 23 April, 1975.

165

The Choir was designed and built to contain an equal number of knights and clerks, that is to say of laymen doing God's work in the world and of men ordained to sustain that work in prayer. Service and faith were to walk hand in hand.

That did not mean that the men who went out to work were not themselves to be men of prayer. Of course not. Nor did it mean that the ordained men were to lead a soft life of inactivity. But it did mean that only where work and prayer went together, inextricably interlocked, could life be seen in its proper context and work itself be truly fruitful. That needed saying in the fifteenth century. It needs re-emphasising in our materialistic age today.

Secondly, this chapel stands for the truth that *knowledge alone will not give men the clue they need to the meaning of their life and destiny.*

When first this building was conceived, the Middle Ages were nearing their close and a new age was coming to birth. That great trio of humanists, Colet, Erasmus and More, were growing into manhood. Caxton was about to set up his printing press at Westminster. All was set for the dissemination of new knowledge. The Renaissance was almost in sight. Many must have thought that an increase in knowledge would lead to a cure of those ills which afflicted the world of Edward IV and his subjects.

The centuries which have intervened between then and now have seen a vast increase of knowledge, and for it we should be profoundly thankful. Science has leapt forward, the universities have opened up new spheres of exploration, and governments have made their discoveries available to all.

One might think that such changes, such increase of knowledge, such softening of the rough edges of life, would have ushered in a golden age. That has not proved to be the case. We in the twentieth century are aware of sinister forces within ourselves, within our nation, and abroad in the world, forces with which increased knowledge by itself is unable to deal. Knowledge alone will not cure hate nor bridge the gulfs made by colour or intolerance. Knowledge alone will not answer our deepest questions as to the nature of our own manhood or womanhood, the meaning of life here, or the destiny towards which we move when this little life is through.

More than this is called for. If I am to live as a son of the most
high God, a creature of eternity made in the likeness of God and
destined to see his glory and live in communion with him, I
need his mercy to deal with my sinfulness, his truth to guide my
feet, his presence with me daily and in the valley of the shadow
of death.

This chapel has been down five centuries, and is today, a
glorious and powerful reminder of these never-changing truths.
Without them, however sophisticated we may be, we are in
bondage. When they are central to our thinking and formative
to our acting, we are free.

If we had to sum up in one word what this chapel stands for it
would be the word "worship", for that wonderful word epito-
mises service and faith walking hand in hand. If you ask me
what I mean by worship, I can find no better way of defining it
than by using the words of William Temple:

> To worship is to quicken the conscience by the holiness of
> God, to nourish the mind with the truth of God, to purify
> the imagination by the beauty of God, to open the heart to
> the love of God, and to surrender the will to the purpose of
> God.

The man who thus lives his life, thus worships God, and thus
serves him alone, finds a measure of freedom which apart from
worship he is unable to conceive. The central paradox of Christianity—that to *serve* God is to *reign*—becomes a reality, and he
finds himself at liberty to attend to the needs and agonies of
those less fortunate than himself.

To remind men of this central truth of the Christian faith, to
point them to Christ who is himself the Way, the Truth and the
Life, and to nourish them with Word and Sacrament, this has
been—and is—the work of this great chapel. Here men are
equipped and strengthened to fight the good fight of faith, clad
like St George in the whole armour of God.

To think through the meaning of the Christian revelation and
its application to life in these islands and beyond, this is the
work of St George's House, and it has proved abundantly
worthwhile in the years since its inception.

So faith and action continue to walk hand in hand, and the life of our nation is purified and strengthened.

We pray that the influence of this chapel and of St George's House may grow deeper and more powerful, to the glory of God and the welfare of his people.

Penitence, Dedication and Thanksgiving

The Silver Jubilee of the Accession of Her Majesty Queen Elizabeth II to the throne was marked by great rejoicing throughout the Commonwealth and beyond in 1977. The Queen undertook long and strenuous journeys at home and abroad in the course of the year.

Nowhere was there greater enthusiasm than in London, where a service of thanksgiving was held on 7 June in St Paul's Cathedral. This was followed by a "walk-about", leading up to a luncheon in Guildhall.

St Matthew 7:24
Every one that heareth these sayings of mine and doeth them, I will liken him unto a wise man which built his house upon a rock.

WE LISTENED TO these words of Jesus a few moments ago. How right he was! Foundations matter. Watch any good team of builders at work in this or any other city, and note what care goes into the basic structure. It is useless building on shallow or shifting foundations. That way lies disaster. Long, patient, skilled work must be put in, down in the depths, before ever a brick or a stone can be seen above ground. Given that, we need not fear, whatever the strains and stresses put upon the building.

We meet today in this Cathedral, joined by millions all over the world who are rejoicing with us by means of radio and television, to thank Almighty God for a building which has

St Paul's Cathedral, 7 June, 1977.

stood the test of years because its foundations are strong. This is no material building which can be seen by the eye or touched with the hand. Rather, it is something at the heart of our national life of incalculable value—a spirit of devotion to duty and of service to others which has found its focus in a family and in a person. King George VI and his beloved Queen in days of war and of post-war stress taught us afresh what duty means. The years that followed that reign have not been easy, but the foundation then laid has proved strong enough for another sovereign to build upon; and this she has done.

Our nation and Commonwealth have been blessed beyond measure by having at their heart an example of service un-tiringly done, of duty faithfully fulfilled, and of a home-life stable and wonderfully happy. For this we thank God. From this we take courage.

The next twenty-five years will take us into a new millennium. None of us can foretell what those years will bring. Pray God they will be years free from war. Doubtless they will see developments in the realm of the physical sciences which will surprise us. Knowledge will increase. The superstructure of society will change—possibly almost beyond recognition. But what about the foundations? Will there be an increase in wisdom as well as in knowledge—for the two are by no means the same? "The fear of the Lord is the beginning of wisdom", said an Old Testament writer, and in saying so he laid down a principle which we neglect at our peril.

Many today are seeing through the hollowness of a way of life which seeks to build on a basis of materialism, of each for himself, or each for his sectional interest, and which forgets the good of the whole. Many are seeing the supreme need for reconciliation and understanding at the heart of a people, where rivalry or suspicion could so easily lead to open conflict. This is all to the good—so far as it goes. But by itself it does not provide a foundation strong enough to resist the storms which assail it in personal, family or national life. *That* requires a listening to the sayings of Jesus, and then carrying them out into action. And that takes some doing!

For what was the essence of the words, the sayings, the principles of Jesus? He taught that no man could live life to the full without the willing recognition of God as his Father, to be loved, and as his King, to be obeyed. He taught that, as God loved each individual, however insignificant in human eyes he might be, so should we; and that we should treat him with respect and dignity. He taught that the only way to build a society worthy of sons of the Most High was to build on a willingness to give and not to grab, and to lose our lives for Christ's sake and the gospel's. He not only taught that by word of mouth. He died to prove it, and to carry the sin of men and women who were too blind to see it.

My words today will reach the ears of millions who care deeply for our nation and Commonwealth and for the welfare of our wider world. Those who have joined in this service will remember it as an occasion of great splendour and joy. That is right and good. But if this service is to leave a mark of permanence on the lives of those who, near and far, have shared in it, it must lead to an act of *penitence* for all that has made our life as a nation or as individuals tawdry and unworthy; an act of *dedication* to the God who calls us to give ourselves to him and to our peoples in self-surrender and service; and an act of *thanksgiving* for the way God has guided us and the leadership which he has given us in our Royal House.

Penitence, dedication and *thanksgiving*. This is what matters. We listen again to the words of Jesus; we build again the foundations which have been broken down by our neglect; and we create, by the grace of God, a society which will be unshakeable in that it is built on our response to the living God.

Let my last word today, then, be one of thanksgiving—and in it I ask you to join—thanksgiving

for twenty-five years of service faithfully given;

for God's goodness and loving-kindness to us down those
years;

but above all for God's inestimable love, in the redemption
of the world by our Lord Jesus Christ;

for the means of grace, and for the hope of glory.

With full hearts and with deep thanksgiving, we sing: "Praise, my soul, the King of heaven."

Whatsoever things are true . . .

When Her Majesty Queen Elizabeth the Queen Mother was installed as Lord Warden of the Cinque Ports on 1 August, 1979, she referred to that office as one "which has one of the longest and proudest traditions in English history". She added: "It has been continuous since the reign of William the Conqueror, perhaps even before, and has been held by a succession of illustrious men, not least my two immediate predecessors, Sir Winston Churchill and Sir Robert Menzies."

Her Majesty was the first lady to hold this ancient office.

In the Middle Ages, the fifty-seven ships provided by the Cinque Ports constituted the largest element of our naval defence.

"WHATSOEVER THINGS ARE true . . . honest . . . pure . . . lovely . . . of good report . . . think on these things."

So we heard in the Lesson. We British are surrounded by such things, if only we have eyes to see them and minds to value them.

Last Saturday was one of those golden days of high summer. How lovely Kent looked, as we motored through its countryside in the early morning! And at night, in Canterbury Cathedral—surely one of Europe's most beautiful buildings—Beethoven, Sibelius and Brahms were played in all their glory! It was a lovely day. Nature and music spoke of God, the author of all beauty. "Pure, lovely, of good report . . ."

1 August, 1979.

Today we delight in something else which is dear to British hearts—a bit of tradition going back to days before the Norman Conquest. The Cinque Ports are a reminder of a time when coastal defence was a very different matter from what it is today, but none the less needed for that. Now those duties are fulfilled by others, but the offices of the Barons survive, and at their head that of the Lord Warden.

That office has been held by men of great distinction, the last two of whom have been Winston Churchill and Robert Menzies. Never before has there been a lady as Lord Warden. Today we are about to install one who is universally loved and respected, one to whom this nation and Commonwealth owe more than they can ever repay—Queen Elizabeth The Queen Mother. We have prayed together that God would bless "her life and ministry", and the prayer came from the hearts of us all. Life at its best *is* ministry, *is* service, done first to God and then, for his sake, to others. Queen Elizabeth has helped to teach us that lesson, for she has served her people down the years, in war and in peace, and she delights to do so still. Long may she continue to serve, and may the office of Lord Warden provide many an occasion for those of us who live in Kent to welcome her here.

Today is a happy day, a day of rejoicing in one of those things that we can call, in the words of our Lesson, "just, pure and lovely". It is right that in the midst of all our traditions, indeed at the heart of them, should be this half-hour of recollection, of dedication, and of prayer. Tradition, apart from such recollection and dedication, can be a barren thing, merely a bit of antiquarianism. But if, in a spirit of prayer, we use it, not only to look back with interest, but forward to further service, and upward to the God of all grace who equips us to fulfil that service—if we do that, then our celebrations together today will have been abundantly worthwhile.

So may God bless our Lord Warden in her going out and in her coming in; and may he unite us all in service to Queen and country, and above all to him who is King of kings and Lord of lords—to whom be praise and glory, today and ever.

Leadership

On 23 November, 1979, in the presence of Her Majesty the Queen, a service was held in St Paul's Cathedral to commemorate ten great military leaders of World War II and to dedicate individual plaques to each of them. These memorials are now on the walls of the Crypt chamber in which the sarcophagus of the first Duke of Wellington stands.

The ten generals thus commemorated are: Field Marshals Viscount Alanbrooke, Earl Alexander of Tunis, Sir Charles Auchinleck, Sir John Dill, Viscount Gort, Lord Ironside, Viscount Montgomery of Alamein, Viscount Slim, Earl Wavell, and Lord Wilson.

The dedicatory plaque reads: "The ten memorials on the walls of the Chamber commemorate the Field Marshals who were leaders of the Military Forces of the British Commonwealth of Nations in the Second World War 1939–45. They represent, as well, a tribute to those who served with these leaders in the victorious armies."

THE OUTSTANDING NOTE of this service of dedication is the note of *thanksgiving*. We are thankful to God for giving us in our hour of need ten great and good men who served king and country and indeed helped materially to save the free world. And we think today, with equal thankfulness, of the tens of thousands of men, many of whom proved faithful unto death, who served under them.

I note that all ten Field Marshals served King George VI who, with his Queen, our beloved Queen Elizabeth The Queen
St Paul's Cathedral, 23 November, 1979.

174

Mother, themselves set so fine an example of steadfastness in the hour of peril.

I note that they all were veterans of World War I and therefore shared a deep desire to avoid the terrible slaughter that was a mark of that long-drawn-out struggle.

I believe that history will show that these ten men were largely responsible for creating the pattern of our present Army which in recent years has acted, and at the present time is acting, as a peace-keeping force in many places, often at the specific request of nations in distress.

What were the qualities that made these men what they were and which enabled them to accomplish what they did? I mention four:

1. *Moral courage.* A leader in war must have physical courage, but in these men we see something even rarer than this. Moral courage is integrity—obedience to what a man knows to be right even when that obedience means loss to himself.

2. *Self-discipline.* No leader can expect to win the respect of others if he has not first learnt to discipline himself. At lower levels of command men have the help of discipline which is imposed from above. But at the higher levels the discipline must come from within.

3. *Unselfishness.* There can be no place for personal vanity or for personal disappointment in truly great leadership. How well this is seen in the lives of these ten men! Brooke learned that, despite the promise he had been given, he was not to command the invasion of Normandy—for he was needed most at Churchill's side. Wavell and Auchinleck successively had the Middle-East Command taken from them in circumstances which they must have found it hard to understand. Alexander slipped quietly into Rome, which his armies had captured, in a jeep, when lesser men would have been tempted to stage a triumphal entry.

4. *Vision.* This is the attribute which, perhaps above all else, is the distinguishing mark of the great leader. It is a highly creative gift—the ability to see not one but two or three steps ahead and to do the unexpected thing when this is right. In war

this is seen in the brilliant strategist—Slim's battle in central Burma, Montgomery's out-flanking of the Mareth Line, and Alexander's final stages in both Tunisia and Italy.

The men we commemorate today had these four qualities in differing proportions, but all in some measure. Their possession enabled them to develop that capacity which is the very essence of leadership—the ability to inspire people to give more than they know they have, and to persuade ordinary people to do extraordinary things.

Thirty-four years have gone by since the end of the war which called out the devotion of these ten men to the service of freedom. Today our nation is faced not with the serried ranks of Nazi hordes but with perils none the less dangerous for their being less visible.

To a young man growing up today it might seem that there is no great cause for which to fight, for which if need be to give his life. But how wrong he would be if he thought that way! The enemy is here—rampant and ready to devour—the enemy that makes men cry "Each for himself and who cares for the community?"; the enemy that makes a man put his rights before his duties; the enemy that makes us invert the divine order and put self first, others next and God last; the enemy that puts the acquisition of things before the building of a Christ-like character; the enemy of insularity which makes us forget a world in need. If ever leadership was called for to battle with such foes, it is called for today.

We need men and women of moral courage, unafraid to stand alone, and willing to say: "I believe and therefore will I speak."

We need men and women of self-discipline who know what it is to pray to God:

> Make me a captive, Lord, and then I shall be free,
> Force me to render up my sword, and I shall
>   conqueror be.

We need men and women of unselfishness, ready to "give and not to count the cost, to fight and not to heed the wounds".

We need men and women of vision who have caught a glimpse of what is right, seen the power of a God-guided life, and are prepared to venture and to dare in his service for his world.

When things were at their very blackest, in December 1939, King George VI made a broadcast which was to become historic. The King warned his listeners of "the dark times ahead of us". Then he said: "I feel that we may all find a message of encouragement in the lines which, in my closing words, I would like to say to you:

> I said to the man who stood at the Gate of the Year, 'Give me a light that I may tread safely into the unknown.' And he replied, 'Go out into the darkness, and put your hand into the hand of God. That shall be to you better than light, and safer than a known way.'

May that Almighty Hand guide and uphold us all."

We have dedicated the Memorial. Now there awaits us the more demanding task of dedicating ourselves, our hands in the Hand of God, resolved to stand fast in his faith, seeking the help of his Spirit, and doing battle for his perfect kingdom.

Please God, we will not fail.

VII
CHURCH AND
MINISTRY

Master, Men and Ministry

IN THE GREAT prayer of St John chapter 17, we are intended to see our Lord reviewing the work that he has done during his earthly ministry and praying for his men as they undertake the task of continuing it. We watch him at prayer—prophet, priest, pastor, servant-king.

There are four phrases which stand out with a certain similarity. They are:

> The work which thou gavest me to do (v 4)
> The men whom thou gavest me out of the world (v 6)
> The words which thou gavest me (v 8)
> The glory which thou gavest me (v 22)

We shall examine each briefly, bearing in mind the character and work of the parish priest.

1. *"The work which thou gavest me to do"* (v 4). The Bible represents God as the great worker. "In the beginning God created . . . And God saw everything that he had made, and, behold, it was very good" (Genesis 1:1, 31). In one of the creation stories, man is put into the garden to dress it and to keep it. This is not envisaged as a punishment for sin. This is pre-Fall. It is part of man's bliss to have work to do. Work makes character. Fortunate the people (for example, clergy) who have fulfilling, creative work to do, especially work closely involving people. One of the curses of modern civilisation is the proliferation of work which is so repetitive and mechanical that

few demands are made on a man's creative capacities. "God is essentially and unchangeably creative" (C. K. Barrett).

The picture of God as the great creator in Genesis 1 is picked up by St John—"My father has never yet ceased his work, and I am working too" (5:17). Jesus in the fourth Gospel calls his miracles "works" because they are a continuation of the creative and redemptive work on which God has been engaged from the beginning.

St Matthew succinctly summarises the work which the Father gave the Son to do as teaching, preaching and healing (9:35).

Teaching. When Jesus saw a crowd, his heart went out to them because they were like lost sheep. What did he do? St Mark says that "he had much to *teach* them" (6:34). There was their need. There was the provision he made. There is no substitute for a *teaching* ministry.

Preaching. St Matthew in this passage uses a word which means "heralding". A herald is "a messenger vested with public authority who conveyed the official messages of kings, magistrates, princes, military commanders, or who gave a public summons or demand" (Grimm-Thayer: *Lexicon of the New Testament*). His office is that of one who "partakes of the character of an ambassador . . . an honourable office in early times" (Liddell and Scott: *Greek-English Lexicon*).

Such was the work of Jesus. Such is the work of his men. It is elaborated by St Paul in 2 Corinthians 4:5, first *negatively*—"we preach not ourselves"; and then *positively*—"[we preach] Christ Jesus as Lord and ourselves as your slaves because of Jesus" (because of what he was, because of what he is, because he was, above all else, himself a servant).

Healing. The concern of Jesus for the whole man was seen in his care for men's bodies and minds–hence the amount of space in the Gospel narratives given to his healing ministry. The revival of praying groups, of the ministry of unction, of the co-operation of clergy and medical experts is one of the signs of lively Christianity in many parts of the Church today.

This threefold ministry of teaching, preaching and healing is a glorious task. In the exercise of it, the encroaching forces of ignorance, sin and disease are pushed back. As we watch our Lord at it in the Gospels, we see him unhurried, unflurried, reflecting St Augustine's description of the Creator God, *"semper agens, semper quietus"*.

What matters supremely is that, when our earthly ministry reaches its close, we shall be able to say, in some small way as our Lord said, "I have finished the work which thou gavest me to do", even as it is recorded that he said on the Cross, "It is finished", completed, brought to a perfect end.

2. *"The men whom thou gavest me out of the world"* (v 6).
Hoskyns points out that this work of Jesus, which we have been considering, "is not defined as a general proclamation of the Fatherhood of God and the Brotherhood of man, but rather as the creation of the Church, the Ecclesia of God, consisting of men of flesh and blood extracted from the world to which they had hitherto belonged—by the power of God" (*Fourth Gospel*, p 591). This is true, and gives us the right approach to verse 6.

As he looked on the Twelve, Jesus must often have been assailed by the temptation to complain, "If only I had had better material to work on! If only they showed greater stability of character, quicker apprehension of truth, firmer determination in discipleship!"

In truth, they were a mixed group—*Peter*, with his gift of incipient leadership, his startlingly clear insights (St Matthew 16:16) but with obtuseness (St Matthew 16:22) and with cowardice (St Matthew 26:69ff); *Thomas*, with his splendid courage (St John 11:16) and his gnawing doubt (St John 20:24ff); *Philip* with his heart obviously warmed by his discovery of Jesus (St John 1:43—46),but so slow to grasp the essence of what knowing Christ meant (St John 14:9). Then there was *Judas*. What are we to make of him? I do not know. Here is the mystery of apparently unanswered prayer, for the prayers of Jesus must often have been burdened with his name. Here is the mystery of iniquity at work. Jesus knew the bitterness of frustrated hopes and pastoral disaster. Often the failures of *our* pastoral work are due to our prayerlessness or spiritual blindness. But it is not always so. There are forces of spiritual wickedness at work which we do not understand. Jesus met them in the case of Judas. He knows, for he knew; and his heart nearly broke over Judas.

This, then, was the kind of material on which Jesus had to work in the training of the Twelve. It was recalcitrant material, but he set to work on it, and out of it came "the glorious company of the apostles".

They were given to him "out of the world"—a strange phrase. "The world" is that which is transitory; the world of glitter and tinsel and show, which the natural man thinks is of great importance, but which—in the dismissive phrase of St John—"passeth away" (1 St John 2:17). Yet the same word is used for the world which God so loved that he gave his Son for it (St John 3:16)!

Christ's men are still "in the world", with responsibilities to be discharged to Caesar as well as to God. They must not contract out into a false isolationism, for they are men of the Incarnation. At the same time, they are "out of the world", sitting loose to its glamour and its standard of values. There is a dividing line here which must be observed, if the witness of the Church is not to be impaired. Our Lord worked with this tension, plunging into the world and its affairs, going to the wedding party, mixing with the disreputables, dying between two ruffians. Yet he was "separate from sinners" (Hebrews 7:26), undefiled, untouched by any breath of scandal, utterly pure.

3. *"The words which thou gavest me I have given them"* (v 8). Christ is here seen as the *receiver* of the divine principles of life and truth—"thou gavest me". He is also seen as the *deliverer* of those principles—"I have given them".

Jesus is the perfect receiver. His will being one with that of the Father—and that is the unity, a unity of will and desire, mainly envisaged in St John 17—there is no barrier to reception of the divine message. As they say in the world of radio and television, there is no "interference."

This is not so with us. There, precisely, is our dilemma and our point of need. In the third of the Servant Songs of Isaiah (50:4ff), the Servant is depicted as the Servant of the *word*.

> The Lord Yahweh has given me
> a disciple's tongue.
> So that I may know how to reply to the learned

he provides me with speech.
Each morning he wakes me to hear,
to listen like a disciple.
The Lord Yahweh has opened my ear

Jerusalem Bible

"Has opened"—the literal meaning is "has bored through". We are hard of hearing. There are many reasons for such deafness. Sometimes it is plain sin, a wrong relationship, perhaps. Sometimes it is because we have grown accustomed to the miracle of Christianity or to the privilege of priesthood and ministry—no longer are we surprised that to us, "the least of all saints, is this grace given" (Ephesians 3:8). Sometimes the cause of deafness is "the sickness that destroyeth at the noon day" of life; sometimes it is sheer laziness—we will not get up in the morning "to hear, to listen like a disciple". Sometimes it is sheer busy-ness—we are trapped by our activism.

Only when we have learned to listen shall we be God's middlemen.

Let St John 17:8 be our test at the end of a Sunday's work. Has my preaching been an exposure of the word of God, a revealing of those principles of life and truth which God has given his Church to expound? Let this be our test when we periodically review our preaching and teaching work. Let this be our test when we lay down the reins of our ministry and look back over the parishes where we have served—"the words which thou gavest me I have given them".

4. *"The glory which thou gavest me I have given them"* (v 22). "Glory" is a major theme in St John's Gospel. We find the note first struck in chapter 1, verse 14: "The Word was made flesh . . . and we beheld his glory." St John would say to us that, if we want to understand the meaning of glory, we look not at the trappings of kings and grandees but at a manger, a carpenter's bench, a cross. *There* we see his glory. His "lifting up" is crucifixion (3:14).

This precisely is the glory which Christ gives to his men. "As he is, so are we in the world"—this is the unity of work and purpose of which the latter part of verse 22 speaks.

Nor is this Johannine doctrine only. It is Pauline also. Look at the great series of verbs in Romans 8:30. It begins with the mysterious election of God—"he marked us out". Then, when we were conscious and able to respond, "he called". Then "he put us right", so that we could look into the face of God and laugh for joy. Then—the consummation of it all—"he glorified" us. This is not a future tense, describing an experience to be enjoyed in heaven. This is present, earthly experience. "The curse of religion is the habit of translating into a vague future tense what Christ offers us now" (Dora Greenwell, quoted by J. S. Stewart in *Wind of the Spirit*, p 163).

The glory offered is the image of God which man has lost by the Fall (Romans 3:23). But when man is justified, the lost image is restored, and the process of "glorifying" has begun. "There is anticipated glory wrought in the Christians by the Holy Spirit as an earnest or foretaste of the glory to come". (A. M. Ramsey, *The Glory of God and the Transfiguration of Christ*, p 51.)

So St Paul can write to the Thessalonians: "It is for this that he called you . . . *so that you might possess for your own the splendour of our Lord Jesus Christ*" (2 Thessalonians 2:14).

> If thus, good Lord, thy grace be given,
> Our glory meets us *ere* we die;
> Before we upward pass to heaven
> We taste our immortality.

The Reinicker Lectures

I

Grace

IT IS A high privilege to be allowed to give the Reinicker Lectures in this Theological Seminary.

I shall not attempt to engage in abstruse discussion of a severely academic kind. For one thing, that would be a foolish endeavour on the part of one who, for the best part of a quarter of a century, has been engaged in the heavy task of a bishop's life and in the rough and tumble of diocesan work. But secondly, that would be a wrong approach, for I am fully conscious of the fact that I am addressing those who are today, or will be tomorrow, themselves in the thick of parochial, pastoral and evangelistic work, and who therefore need something which will not only nourish the mind but will also stimulate the spirit and nerve the whole man for action.

Let me venture a personal word to begin with, and then you can forget the lecturer and concentrate on the content of what he is trying to say. I have had some forty-five years in the ordained ministry of Christ's Church, glorious years and very strenuous ones. Three of them were spent in parochial work in London, in the days before there was a Welfare State, when the unemployment figures and the overcrowding were high, when the old age pension was about a dollar a week and the children's toes stuck out of the ill-fitting boots which had come to them as

The Protestant Episcopal Theological Seminary in Virginia, 15–17 October, 1979.

cast-offs from someone more affluent than they. Those years in the thirties taught one a great deal. They were followed by seven years of theological teaching in Canada, and by a dozen more in England as head of a theological college. Those nineteen years gave one a very close association with the parish clergy and their people—the academic and the pastoral interest went hand in hand.

Then followed five and a half years as bishop of a diocese in the north of England whose see city was the centre of the wool industry of the country. Those years were in turn succeeded by thirteen and a half as Archbishop of York, and they by nearly five as Archbishop of Canterbury. Those last two posts involved a good deal of world travel, of ecumenical work, of wrestling with world problems. But all the time there was close and intimate connection with the parishes of the dioceses over which one had been appointed chief pastor. One was never far from the problems of parochial life and the pressures which bear down on the clergy and their families. One was constantly in their churches and in their houses, celebrating the Holy Communion, preaching the word, sharing the joys and sorrows of clergy and laity, seeking to relate the everlasting gospel to contemporary needs. It was these contacts, together with constant visits to universities and schools, to prisons and hospitals, to factories and mines, to the Forces of the Crown, and so on, which did at least something to keep one from being a desk administrator only.

It is against that background of a long and deep care for the ministers of Christ's Church and for the people whom they serve that I venture to give these three lectures. In my hand, much of the time, will be a Bible. In my mind's eye, all of the time, will be the rectory (or manse), the church building, the altar, the pulpit, and—beyond—the hungry sheep.

Winter will soon once again be upon us. But cast your mind back only a few weeks and you will recall that your garden—if you are lucky enough to own one—was a scene of immense activity. Sun, rain, wind, soil had all combined to create a situation out of which beauty could come, vegetables grow, fruit be borne. If you had time to stop for a minute and consider, you realised that you were faced with a very interesting situation. On the one hand there was the *givenness* of

Nature—sun, rain, wind, soil were all there before ever you first put your spade in. I know you groused sometimes—too much (or, more likely, too little) sun, too much (or too little) rain, too much (or possibly too little) wind, too poor (or, conceivably, for certain things, too rich) soil. And you had to do something about these difficulties. You had to provide shelter from the sun (or glass to magnify its power); you had to store the rain-water, or provide gulleys to dispose of it; you had to plant a hedge to provide protection from the wind, and you had to enrich the soil with fertiliser. Granted. But there they were—sun, rain, wind and soil; free, gratis and for nothing, examples of Nature's bounty. All laid on. *Given*—that on the one hand.

On the other hand there was the *grind* of a garden! Don't you remember the back-ache? That too luxurious growth? That subduing of a field until it became a lawn? That battle with the weeds? That pruning of the trees?

What is the difference between that garden of yours and the Sahara Desert? Both had the *given*, but only the first had the *grind*. Both had the sun, the rain, the wind, the soil. One had care, the other neglect.

Take another example. Look at the miracle of the creation of a human life. A man and a woman love one another—and a child is born, a new life created. As he lies in his cradle discovering himself and beginning to correlate his faculties of seeing and hearing, of touching and smelling, the baby is (though he will not be able to see this for a long while yet) a superb example of the given-ness of which we have already spoken. He did not ask to be born. He was *given* life with all the attendant marvels which go to the make-up of a human being. We rightly say: "She *gave* birth to a child." What a marvellous gift! But, as any mother will tell you, there is the *grind* side to the rearing of a person—the battle against dirt and disease, literally a matter of life and death; and the battle for character—that baby there might be a Hitler or a Schweitzer, a Farouk or a William Temple; it depends, at least in large measure, on the grind which goes into the building of character.

In giving these two illustrations—of what I am calling the given-ness and the grind—I believe I am taking you very close to the centre of the Christian faith. Let me try to expound this a little more fully.

First, the *given-ness*, the *datum*; call it the *static* if you will. To begin with the most obvious aspect of this, we may note the proverb quoted in St John 4:37: "One sows, another reaps." This no doubt was originally a bitter reflection on the unfairness of life, but in the context Jesus gives the saying a new turn; he makes it a saying of *joy*—we are all engaged in God's great mission *together*. We in this generation stand, as it were, on the shoulders of the generations which have preceded us. How rich we are! What an inheritance is ours! Illustrations spring readily to mind (especially if one occupies the kind of position which I am called to do!).

Israel was very conscious of such an inheritance, and their writers constantly referred to it. To be the heirs of a history such as theirs carried with it the obligation to hand on the inheritance unimpaired. It was a *datum* not to be selfishly hugged but to be faithfully transmitted.

Listen, for example, to this:

> Listen to this Law, my people,
> pay attention to what I say;
> I am going to speak to you in parable
> and expound the mysteries of our past.

> What we have heard and known for ourselves,
> and what our ancestors have told us,
> must not be witheld from their descendants,
> but be handed on by us to the next generation;

> that is: the titles of Yahweh, his power
> and the miracles he has done.
> When he issued the decrees for Jacob
> and instituted a Law in Israel,

> he gave our ancestors strict orders
> to teach it to their children;
> the next generation was to learn it,
> the children still to be born,

> and these in their turn were to tell their own children
> so that they too would put their confidence in God,

never forgetting God's achievements,
and always keeping his commandments,

and not becoming, like their ancestors,
a stubborn and unruly generation,
a generation with no sincerity of heart,
in spirit unfaithful to God.

Psalm 78:1–8, Jerusalem Bible

To do this means to have a sure and firm base from which to operate. When Jeremiah bids his hearers: "Stand ye in the ways, and see, and ask for the old paths, where is the good way, and walk therein" (Jeremiah 6:16), he is not encouraging them to stay put where they are, still less to get stuck in a groove, but rather to be faithful to the riches which, without their ever having laboured for them, are part of the given-ness of their inheritance.

The writer of the Pastoral Epistles (1 and 2 Timothy) has a special word to express, in a Christian context, what we are speaking about—a word used nowhere else in the New Testament (it occurs in 1 Timothy 6:20 and 2 Timothy 1:12 and 14). It is *parathēkē*. James Moffatt translates it "the deposit", the Jerusalem Bible "all that has been entrusted to you" (1 Timothy 6:20). In the second letter (1:12) the writer is speaking of the gospel of which he is, by divine appointment, herald, apostle and teacher. He knows, he says, who it is in whom he has trusted, and is confident of his power to keep safe what he has put into his charge. So the New English Bible translates *parathēkē*. (It can equally well mean what *he*, the Apostle, has entrusted to *God*. The context must decide it. NEB is probably right—God and his Apostle are, as it were, co-trustees of the treasure of the Gospel.)

C. H. Dodd, whose *Life* has been written by F. W. Dillistone (Hodder and Stoughton, 1977), will go down in the history of New Testament scholarship for many things, especially for his great works on the Fourth Gospel and for his writings on "realised eschatology". Of the many books which came from his pen, one of the most influential was *The Apostolic Preaching and its Developments* (1936). Dillistone summarises the core of Dodd's thinking, as disclosed in that book, in this way:

> Dodd, rather like a musical composer, found a dominant theme, a recurring sequence, to which he delighted to return again and again and around which he created innumerable variations. This theme he found in its earliest and simplest form in 1 Corinthians 15:1–3. The gospel (or, using the Greek word denoting the proclamation made by a herald or public announcer, the *Kerygma*) there defined ran as follows:

> > Christ died for our sins according to the Scriptures.
> > He was buried;
> > He rose again the third day according to the Scriptures,
> > He was seen by Cephas.

> Comparing this formulation with other examples of evangelical proclamation recorded in the New Testament, Dodd came to the conclusion that a regulative pattern of first-century gospel-preaching could be discerned.
> Whatever the nature of subsequent exposition or elaboration or refinement might be, the basic theme remained firm and determinative. It could be expressed in these terms:

> > The prophecies are fulfilled, and the new Age is inaugurated by the coming of Christ.
> > He was born of the seed of David.
> > He died, according to the Scriptures,
> > to deliver us out of the present evil age.
> > He was buried.
> > He rose on the third day, according to the Scriptures.
> > He is exalted at the right hand of God, as Son of God and Lord of quick and dead.
> > He will come again as Judge and Saviour of men.

Put in a sentence, and in the words of John S. Whale, "the most amazing fact in the world, if it is really true, is the redeeming pardon of God" (*Christian Doctrine*, p 65). This Karl

Barth called "a sheerly new thing, an absolute datum". "Forgiveness of sins", said Martin Luther, "ought to make thee rejoice; this is the very heart of Christianity." This coming of God to meet man in his sin, this searching of God for man before ever he showed signs of seeking for him, this is the miracle, the heart of the gospel, the glorious *datum*, the centre of the *parathēkē*. This is gift, this it is to which nothing can be added, for it is grace, sheer grace straight from the heart of God.

The Church of England has a wonderfully dramatic way of giving expression to this truth, and I am constantly reminded of it when I take part in the ordination of deacons and priests and in the consecration of bishops. In these services, and at their most solemn moments, I give the candidates a present. I give the deacon a New Testament, the priest and the bishop a Bible. If it fell to my lot to enthrone a new monarch—which pray God it will not—I or some other minister would give him or her the same book, and with these words: "Here is wisdom. This is the royal law. These are the lively oracles of God." Why is *this* book given, and not some more modern book on how to influence people and be popular? The answer is that in this book, as nowhere else, is the record of the *datum*, of the acts of God for us men and for our salvation, adumbrated in the Old Testament, revealed in all their splendour in the Word made flesh. "Full, perfect and sufficient", they stand for all time as a demonstration of the heart and mind of the eternal God revealed in human history for all to see.

Let us recapitulate for a moment. We have been looking at the *datum*, the given; the *kerygma*, that which is announced and which is to be preached; the *parathēkē*, the sacred deposit entrusted to us. What lies behind all this? What is its source? It rests in the very heart of God. It springs from his very nature. It is best expressed by the word *charis*, grace, which itself is a regnant biblical theme. I say 'biblical' and not only 'New Testament', because the full flower of the New Testament doctrine springs from Old Testament roots. "The Lord did not set his love upon you nor choose you because ye were more in number than any people; for ye were the fewest of all people. But because the Lord loved you and because he would keep the oath which he had sworn unto your fathers, hath the Lord brought you out with a mighty hand and redeemed you . . ." (Deuteronomy 7:7–8).

The Old Testament antecedent of the New Testament *charis* is *chesed*—a word not easy to translate in such a way as to get its full flavour. "Loving-kindness" does not represent sufficiently the idea of strength and persistence which is involved. Sir George Adam Smith, that great expositor of the prophets, used to render it by the words "leal-love", but he was a Scot, and we English do not often use the word "leal". But it is a good word, because it means 'loyal'. *Chesed* is loyal-love, the attitude which each party to a covenant ought to maintain towards the other. "The word *chesed* stands for God's steady, persistent love for the Israel of his choice. It is the love that will not let us go, the love that not all man's weakness and sinfulness and stubbornness can destroy" (Norman Snaith: *Mercy and Sacrifice*, p 80). Hence the force of Hosea's use of the word, when he speaks of God's *chesed* under the deeply moving analogy of Yahweh's marriage-relationship with Israel: "I will betroth you to myself for ever, betroth you in lawful wedlock with unfailing devotion and love; I will betroth you to myself to have and to hold, and you shall know the Lord" (Hosea 2:19–20). Israel may go a-whoring after other gods and break the marriage-covenant, but *God* will be loyal to his word and to his covenant. "If it had not been for God's *chesed*, the story of God's people would have ceased before it had begun" (op. cit., p 82).

The idea of grace, the strong, loyal love of God, the outgoing, undeserved goodness of God, adumbrated in the Old Testament word *chesed*, comes into its own in the New. The word which in classical Greek can be used in a purely "secular" sense of loveliness of persons (e.g. by Aeschylus) takes on a deeper and more theological significance. (Perhaps the use of the word in St Luke 4:22 (cf. 2:52) hovers between the classical and the theological. Jesus had been preaching in the synagogue at Nazareth, and a kind of sigh of glad surprise went up that he could make religion, sometimes forbidding or even sour, so lovely a thing. His hearers "were surprised that words of such *grace*", such winsomeness, such attractiveness, "should fall from his lips". Or is there a deeper meaning to the word even here—his words exhibited something of the grace of God who was concerned with the poor, the prisoners, the blind . . .?)

Elsewhere in the Gospels there is no doubt about its specifically ethical and theological content. In the parable of the two debtors (Luke 7:42), the verb is used of "gracing away", forgiving, a debt which both debtors were equally unable to meet from their own resources. (Here St Luke is getting very near St Paul in his handling of this central theme.) St John uses the noun in the deepest theological sense in chapter 1, verse 14. He considers the Word made flesh, "the Word yet unable to speak a word" (as Lancelot Andrewes movingly put it), the babe, the boy, the young man taking up his temporary abode among us in an obscure corner of an unheeding world, and there, precisely there, he sees the condescension of an outgoing love; he sees not only the truth of God but also the *grace* of God.

When we come to St Paul, there is one passage of special significance to us who are entrusted with a share in the ministry. I refer to the opening verses of Ephesians 3. In verse 1 the writer is about to begin a prayer when the mention of the Gentiles on whose behalf he is a prisoner makes him break off—and we have to wait until verse 14 for the content of the prayer! The "interruptive" verses (2–13) are theological and autobiographical. The theological part has to do with the *mysterion*, the one-time secret now disclosed, namely that Gentiles are, as it were, on the level with Jews at the receiving end of God's mercy shown in Christ Jesus. At the cross the ground is level. There is no race-discrimination there. The autobiographical part of the passage comes at its start, verse 2. A grace-gift, a totally undeserved privilege, has been accorded to the writer. Noun (grace) and verb (given) are repeated in verse 8—verse 8 *resumes* verse 2. What is this grace-gift, this undeserved privilege given to the least of all God's people? It is the "privilege of proclaiming to the Gentiles the good news of the unfathomable riches of Christ". It is as if a man had been given the key to a store-house, access to which would bring wealth and satisfaction to starving multitudes. God's is the store-house. Paul's is the key. The nations are the beneficiaries. Through this passage there breathes the sense of an awed surprise, an astonishment that to such a one as him this grace-gift has been accorded.

There is a somewhat similar pasage to this in one of the Pastoral Epistles. I refer to 2 Timothy 1:11–14. The passage again is autobiographical. Again there is a sense of awed surprise and privilege. The word *charis* is not used, nor the verb *given* (though both occur in verse 9). Here, rather, is the word

parathēkē (in verses 12 and 14), which we have already considered—a treasure which God has put into the writer's charge,
to guard as a sacred thing, "with the help of the Holy Spirit
dwelling within us".

The writer of the Acts of the Apostles, in his record of St
Paul's final charge at Miletus to the elders of the Church at
Ephesus, makes a similar emphasis. His ministry at Ephesus
had been an unusually long one. Now it was over. St Paul was
en route to Jerusalem, not knowing what awaited him there but
with a strong anticipation of bonds and afflictions. But he was
singularly care-free. He had "guarded the deposit"—he does
not use the actual phrase; rather, he says that he had "kept back
nothing", but had "disclosed to you the whole purpose of God"
(Acts 20:27). It comes to the same thing. Now he has but one
consuming ambition: it is "to finish the race, and to complete
the task which the Lord Jesus had assigned" him (verse 24).

From these different New Testament strands—Ephesians,
2 Timothy, Acts—we draw the same sense of a grace-gift of
infinite privilege, to one undeserving of it, namely the sharing
of the treasure of the gospel.

It is enough to make one tremble. Indeed, I often tell ordinands that the only man about whom I am in doubt is the
ordinand who, on the eve of his ordination, does *not* tremble. (Is
not this one of the main purposes of a cassock—to hide the
trembling knees?) And yet, we may be quietly confident, even
joyfully so. There are what the hymn-writer, Thomas Binney,
called "a Holy Spirit's energies". There is, as 2 Timothy 1:14
reminds us, "the help of the Holy Spirit dwelling within us".
How right is the Anglican Ordinal (1662) which makes the
Bishop say to "every one that receiveth the Order of Priesthood
. . . *Receive the Holy Ghost* for the office and work of a Priest in
the Church of God", and which makes the Archbishop say, as
he lays his hands on the head of the Bishop-elect, "*Receive the
Holy Ghost* for the office and work of a Bishop in the Church of
God . . . and remember that thou stir up the *grace* of God which
is *given* thee by this imposition of our hands . . ."

We are back again at that great noun *grace*. We are back again
at that great verb *given*. We dare not move from them.

I take.

He undertakes.

2

Grind

I spoke yesterday of grace, of the given-ness of the gospel, of the *datum*, of *paradosis*, of *parathēkē*, of *kerygma*, of the *static*! I illustrated from the given-ness of Nature—sun, rain, wind and soil; from the given-ness of human life itself.

But we noticed that given-ness without grind was of little use—as, for example, in a garden untended or a baby left to itself. We noticed—and passed on, because grace gave us quite enough to think about in one lecture. Today we come back to look more closely at what I call the *grind* side of the matter. (Though I am not satisfied with the word, it will have to do for the moment.) We come to the *dynamic*, in its interplay with the static.

Here I turn at once to the figure of our Lord and ask you to consider with me his method of teaching divine truth. It was a method quite distinct from that of the other teachers of his day. There was about it an element which caused great surprise—as St Mark makes very clear at the beginning of his Gospel. "What is this?" said our Lord's listeners. "A new kind of teaching! He speaks with authority" (1:27). The "authoritative" teachers of the day were the men brought up in the Rabbinic schools of Shammai and Hillel and so on. To authenticate their authority, they would quote the decisions and the dicta of the teachers who had gone before them—the greater the array of teachers who could thus be quoted, the greater the authority which they could claim for their views. Not so with the teaching of Jesus. "He taught with authority, yes but not as the scribes" (St Matthew 7:29—the *kai* which I have translated as "yes but" can well be considered as an instance of what the grammarians call *kai adversative*). Sometimes he even dared to set up his authority in contrast to what had been said by the ancients (see, for example, St Matthew 5:21ff.—"You have learned that our forefathers were told . . . But what I tell you is this . . .").

It was, however, above all else in the *method* of the teaching of Jesus that his authority was most clearly seen, and in the demands which that method made upon his hearers that the dynamic of its content was most fully realised. He treated his hearers as adults, with minds of their own to think with, and wills of their own to decide with. They were not children to be dictated to, still less automata to be manipulated. That is why so often Jesus refused to give a straight answer to a straight question—all very annoying if you want to have your thinking done for you and your decisions made for you; but all very stimulating if you want to grow in mind and character. Let me give you an illustration—you will find it in St Luke 12:13ff. Father had died. The will had been read. It was patently unfair—or so, at least, it appeared to be to one of the two sons concerned. The one who felt himself wronged called upon Jesus to adjudicate— after all, he was widely acknowledged as a man of wisdom and fairness. But this is precisely what Jesus refused to do. It would have been easy to say: "This is clearly a case of injustice; x dollars should go to you, y dollars to your brother; that's that." But that would have been to deal with the superficial, and to leave the basic issues undealt with. Behind the question lay deep issues of a spiritual nature, issues which affected the character, even the eternal destiny, of the questioner. Avarice, the attitude to *things*, to the questioner's brother, to God, to eternity—these were the great, deep issues which really mattered. And so Jesus, instead of giving a straight answer in terms of money, gave the parable of the Rich Fool. All very annoying! Dynamic teaching! Some grinding hard work—of thinking and of deciding, of mind and of will—was called for; and the life of the questioner hung on whether or not he did that thinking and on how he decided. "Even when a man has more than enough, his wealth does not give him *life*" (v 15).

(A study of the phrase *ti soi dokei*, or similar use of *dokei*, as, e.g., in St Matthew 17:25; 18:12; 21:28; 22:17, would seem to indicate that Jesus put the onus of thinking on his hearers— "how does this seem to you? What sort of appeal does it make to your mind and will?")

The illustration of the "grind" element in the teaching of Jesus which I have just given (the story of the Rich Fool) introduces us to our Lord's favourite method of teaching. I refer to the *parable*. This method consisted of many different forms, from a one-sentence "analogy" ("God's reign is like the yeast a woman took and mixed with three measures of flour till it was leavened all through", St Matthew 13:33), to a full story, like that of the Prodigal Son (St Luke 15:11–32), better described as the Parable of the Two Lost Boys, or, alternatively, the Parable of the Prodigal Father. But the principle behind the method is clear. Jesus, if I may put it crudely (and you will see the reason behind my language in a moment), throws a story at his hearers, throws it at them to think through. "What do you make of *that?*" he says. You have minds to think with; use them. You have wills to use; exercise them according to the dictates of your conscience when that conscience has been stabbed awake by the story. You are responsible beings. The ball is in your court.

"He throws it at them . . . The ball is in your court." I have used this language because I wanted to bring out for you the meaning of the -*ble* part of parable. It is, of course, a Greek word. The *para* part of it is a prefix. The -*ble* part of it comes from *ballō* which fundamentally means to throw—we get our word *ball* from it.

The crisis for the hearer of a parable, a saying of Jesus, comes precisely when he finds the ball in his court. He can get out of the "grind" of decision and action by saying "What a pretty ball! What an entertaining story!" and leave it at that. That is often done. A preacher burdened with a word from the Lord delivers himself of that burden, and men say: "Wasn't that nice!" or "What a lovely voice he has!", or, if you are preaching in North America, "Didn't you *adore* his English accent—it was *just too cute!*" Ezekiel had similar heart-breaking disappointments. "As far as they are concerned, you are like a love-song beautifully sung to music. They listen to your words, but no one puts them into practice" (Ezekiel 33:32). On the other hand, and in glorious contrast, the "ball" of God's message may be received for what in truth it is—a word of judgement, or of grace, or of summons to action. And the interesting thing is—such is the kaleidoscopic richness of God's grace—that one and the same parable may call forth a wide variety of response from different people; one will hear *this* from the parable, another *that*, for it touches mind and heart and will at different points, depending on the position of the hearer at any given moment. What it says to me may be quite different from what it says to you. That is all right—it is of the nature of parabolic truth that it should be so. Parabolic truth is dynamic truth; and you can never be quite sure how dynamite will explode! After all, the Holy Spirit is the *dunamis* of God, "dividing" the truth of God to different people just as he chooses (1 Corinthians 12:11).

Granted, then, these two elements at the heart of the Christian gospel (the "given-ness", the datum, the static on the one hand, and the "grind", the dynamic, on the other), how does it all work out in Christian discipleship and ministry? St Paul puts it with incomparable clarity in Philippians 2:12. He has, in the words of St Augustine, just been writing of "the humility of the Lord our God descending to our pride". He has written of Christ who, though the divine nature was his from the first, made himself nothing, assumed the nature of a slave, humbled himself and in obedience accepted even death on a cross. Now God has raised him. One day every tongue will confess him— "Jesus Christ is Lord"—to the glory of the Father. There, as nowhere else, God was at work. And there, in you Christians at Philippi, God is at work. The static, the mighty acts of God in history, at Bethlehem, at Calvary, at the empty tomb, are, by the operation of the Spirit, dynamic. *Therefore*—therefore *what*? "You must work out, work *at*, your own salvation in fear and trembling." No pretty thing, this, to be dismissed with a patronising smile or a passing remark, "how nice!". But something immense, awe-inspiring, wonderful, to be worked at— the ball is in your court! God is at work in you—you work away with him—your hand in his!

It is this concept of our "working away" with God that calls for steady endurance. Here I would invite you to join me in a brief study of a major theme in the New Testament, though, generally speaking, it has not been given the consideration and the study which it deserves. The word is *hypomonē*.

Hypomonē is generally translated by some such word as "patience" or "endurance". "Patience" is certainly quite inadequate for what the New Testament means by the word. "Endurance" all too often has about it something of what the word "Stoicism" has come to mean from the sixteenth century onwards, viz. the repression of emotion, indifference to pleasure or pain, patience under trial (see Oxford English Dictionary).

But *hypomonē* means much more than this. According to the

New Testament, it grows out of hard and stony soil. According to Romans 5:3, it is tribulation, suffering, which produces *hypomonē*. According to James 1:3, it is the testing of our faith which produces it, and we only become mature and complete characters when *hypomonē* is allowed to have its full effect (v 4). In the New Testament, *hypomonē* keeps distinguished company. In 1 Timothy 6:11, it is surrounded by "justice, piety, fidelity, love . . . and gentleness"; in 2 Timothy 3:10, by "doctrine, . . . faith, patience, love and"—here we are reminded of Romans 5:3 (see above)—"persecutions and sufferings".

Hypomonē was a mark of *Job*, so James 5:11 tells us. Not indeed the (proverbial) *patience* of Job (is there in the whole of the Old Testament a more *im*patient figure than Job who constantly cries out against the apparent injustice of life?); but the steady *endurance* of Job, who never gave up, who never finally cursed God, who endured till he was vindicated.

Hypomonē is a mark of the *saints*. Twice in the book of the Revelation comes the refrain: "Here is the fortitude (and faithfulness) of the saints" (13:10 and 14:12). Small wonder that *hypomonē* occurs seven times in the Book of the Revelation, for that book was a tract written for a persecuted Church whose prime task it was to stick it out, to *endure* (cf. 2:2,3,19 and 3:10).

Hypomonē is a mark of *Christ*. In 2 Thessalonians 3:5, there is no reference to the second advent (as AV would make us think—"direct your hearts into the love of God, and into the patient waiting for Christ"). On the contrary, it is a plain reference to a characteristic of Christ—to his steadfastness (Phillips, his "patient suffering"). This is powerfully brought out in Hebrews 12:2-3 (where the *verb* is used): "He endured the cross . . . he endured opposition, hostility, from sinners."

Hypomonē is a mark of *God Himself*. In Romans 15:5, what does "the God of *hypomonē*" mean? "The God who inspires men to endure" (as Phillips)? "God, the source of all fortitude" (as NEB)? Or the God, one of whose most characteristic marks is endurance—for has he not shown endless endurance in putting up so long with a wayward race? It is a mark of *love* that "there is no limit to its *endurance*" (1 Corinthians 13:7, NEB); and God *is* love.

Hypomonē is a word with eschatological dimensions—"He who endures to the end, it is he who shall be saved" (Matthew 10:22; 24:13; Mark 13:13). "Through your endurance you will win your lives", i.e. you will participate in eternal life (so I. Howard Marshall, on Luke 21:19). And, according to the early hymn quoted in 2 Timothy 2:12, "if we endure, we shall also reign with him".

There is nothing coldly stoic about this word, no mere "repression of emotion", no mere "indifference to pleasure or pain". Here, rather, is something positive and creative, with a touch of eternity about it.

It is a noble word. *Hypomonē* takes what God, in the immensity of his grace, throws into our court, and works at it steadily. It is that which manifests itself as—forgive the word!—"stickability"; if you are a man of *hypomonē*, you don't look to the Bishop to move you to a less impossible parish more worthy of your undoubted but unrecognised gifts the moment the members of your Vestry start to get nasty! It is grit. It is stamina. It is character moulded by the Spirit and tested in the fires. It is staying power.

It is at this point that "Our Father Below", as C. S. Lewis liked to call our adversary the devil, gets busy among us and tempts us. Is it all worth the candle? Aren't we taking things a bit too seriously? As the old hymn had it:

> Christian, dost thou hear them,
> How they speak thee fair?
> "Always fast and vigil?
> Always watch and prayer?"

Sloth pokes its ugly face round the rectory door, for *hypomonē* is too stern and too creative a word for our adversary's liking.

We clergy and church workers have very special temptations in this area where sloth comes in. Many of us work alone. How fortunate are those who work in a team, the members of which keep one another up to scratch in the things of the Spirit, such as prayer, meditation and study! The weakness, the danger, of the position of most of us is that we have no mentor. If we are in bed in the morning when we should be on our knees, there is no one to see, or to rebuke, or to challenge, or to recall us from our slackness. So sloth wins, and we cover the nakedness of a prayerless condition by a relapse into a hectic activism—and wonder why nothing of eternal value happens in the parish. Did I say, "There is no one to see"? I was wrong. St Matthew, thrice in his record of the Sermon on the Mount (6:4; 6:18), uses the phrase "your Father which seeth in secret", "your Father who sees what you do in private". The phrase is an arresting one, even a solemn one. It is not meant to convey the impression of a celestial spy. Far from it, for this is a *Father* who sees, and even earthly fathers don't *spy* on their children. No; this is One who is deeply concerned for the spiritual development, the total welfare, of his children, as well as for the development of their ministry in depth and power. *He* sees. *He* knows.

The businessman is answerable to his boss. In that sense, most of us have no boss to answer to. We are answerable alone to him who sees what we do in private, yes, and what we do *not* do in private, at prayer-desk or in study. Would it sound unutterably old-fashioned to you if I said that the old habit of the parson tolling the church bell early every morning still has much to be said for it, not only because it tells John Smith as he goes to catch the 7.45 train that his parson is up and at his prayers, but also because it is a help to that same parson himself, a reminder not to default from the most important part of the work to which he was ordained?

I always have a feeling of dis-ease when I hear the word "profession" used in connection with the Christian ministry. There is something in me which registers a protest—prophets and priests are not members of a profession; they are people who have been, and are, obedient to a call. Their work is a calling, not a profession. "No man taketh this honour unto himself" (Hebrews 5:4). And yet that is not quite all that there is to the matter. There is a sense—a limited sense, if you will—in which our calling *is* a profession, the noblest and greatest of them all. And in that sense it calls for a professionalism of the very highest kind, a professionalism which makes demands in the big things and in the little ones—meticulousness in the way we wear our uniform, the way we keep our churches, the way we write our letters, the speed with which we pay our bills. And while we are talking of professionalism, what are we to say of the priest who says, "Of course, I'm no theologian"? Are you not, my dear brother? Why not? Suppose that, suffering from some physical trouble, I went at last to my doctor, explained my worry, and received the reply: "Of course, I'm no good at medicine, but we might as well open you up and have a look." I should rapidly go elsewhere! My illustration is obviously a very faulty one. There is more to our ministry than theology. I am not a gnostic. You *could* be a theologian and be dead towards God. Religion has dimensions which theology has not. But religion without sound theology can easily lead to sentimentality or superficiality or aridity, and we do well to take note.

Let me take this a little further. Perhaps our greatest need is for a big and constant supply of spiritual directors. I am not using the phrase in a restricted sense, nor in a male sense only. I am thinking of pastoral counsellors. And, using that phrase, I do not mean only those to whom people go who are in some desperate plight. *All* of us are in need of spiritual help. *All* of us are on the road, and if we are to arrive at journey's end in the kind of condition God wants us to, most of us (all of us) will only make it with help. That's what the Church is about. That is the meaning of spiritual counselling. That's our job, our calling, our supreme privilege—pastoral caring which is not only physically therapeutic but is concerned with a man's total well-being.

Kenneth Leech, in his book *Soul Friend*, points out that there is a search on, in the hearts of many, not least of the young, in many parts of the world and in a wide variety of strata of society, a search for what he calls the inner world. He writes: "There is a search for the inner world, for meditation, silence and contemplative prayer. Secondly, there is a sense of the need for power, for direct experience of the Spirit, and for personal love of Jesus. Thirdly, there is an increasing sense of the need to see the search for justice as an integral element in the gospel. Certainly a contemporary spirituality which does not include these elements will be inadequate" (p 29). Later in the book, he delineates the marks of the spiritual director, the man or woman who can meet this search, in this way: "He must be a man possessed by the Spirit (i.e. a man who lives close to God), a man of experience who has struggled with the realities of prayer and life, a man of learning, a man of discernment, and a man who gives way to the Holy Spirit" (pp 88–89).

Do you ask why I bring all this in under the heading of "sloth"? I do so because this kind of ministry makes enormous demands on those who exercise it. It is recorded of the Suffering Servant of Isaiah 53 that he "poured out his soul unto death" (v 12). It is recorded of our Lord that, after one of his healings, he knew that virtue had gone out of him (St Luke 8:46). It is said by St Paul that Jesus "emptied himself" (Philippians 2:7). Most of you know something of what that means. It is not just that we refuse to allow to seep in, even to our subconscious, the merest suggestion that our hours are absurdly long as compared with those of our businessman neighbour or of our teacher-friend, or even, sometimes, of our doctor-colleague. It is that in this kind of ministry we begin to learn what it means "to give and not to count the cost", the cost of the hours of prayer and study as well as of individual sharing, counselling, "directing" away from the trivialities of life, yes, and from the trivialities of religion, directing men's feet into the path of peace, "directing" men to the Prince of Peace himself.

3

Glory

In the first lecture, we looked at one of the immensities of the gospel—*grace*, that divine initiative which springs from the very Being of God, his "leal-love" which can never go back on his covenant with his people, and which is manifested at its clearest in "the grace of our Lord Jesus Christ who, though he was rich, yet for our sakes became poor, that we through his poverty might become rich" (2 Corinthians 8:9).

In the second lecture, we looked at the more human side of the divine-human encounter, though sure enough it is itself a divine gift—what we called *grind*, stamina, spiritual staying-power, endurance. Perhaps we came down to earth with a bump at the end of that lecture. But is that altogether blameworthy—for us who are followers of the incarnate Lord? Did not he

> come down to earth from heaven,
> Who is God and Lord of all?

In this third and last lecture, we look together at the subject of *glory*, a major concept in the Bible and in Christian experience.

There is a wide variety of words in the Old Testament which are translated in the Septuagint by the word *doxa*. The most common of the four is a word (*kabhod*) whose root meaning has to do with being heavy, with weight. That concept is not foreign to us, for we speak of a man of distinction, a man of character or of achievement, as a *weighty* person. We might say of a member of a legislative body that his speeches always carry weight. So in, for example Isaiah 17:4, "the *glory* of Jacob shall be made thin" clearly means that not much of his *wealth and prosperity* will be left; and when, in Genesis 45:13, Joseph tells his brothers of the position he had reached in Egypt, he orders them to go back to their old father and tell him "of all my *glory*", he means to say, as Knox translates it, "of all these honours I enjoy". He had become a man of weight.

When the Old Testament writers speak of the glory of God, they often do so in terms of light, radiance, and splendour. Glory is the majesty, power and love of God as manifested to men. Very often there was an element of the terrifying about it. For example, in the Exodus stories (especially in chapters 19 and 24) the people of Israel are warned not to go too near the mountain upon which God will descend; they must not touch even the edge of it. "There were peals of thunder and flashes of lightning, dense cloud on the mountain and a loud trumpet blast; the people in the camp were all terrified" (19:16). Eventually Moses, Aaron, Nadab and Abihu and seventy of the elders of Israel are allowed to ascend the mountain and see the God of Israel in his kingly majesty (24:10). "They stayed before God" (or, "they saw God"); "they ate and they drank", says the writer with obvious surprise, for such vision might well have been thought to be fatal. The elders are then left behind, and apparently Aaron, Nadab and Abihu also. Moses and Joshua alone go on, and Joshua is then left behind. In awful loneliness Moses goes up into the mountain, "and a cloud covered the mount. And the glory of the Lord abode upon Mount Sinai, and the cloud covered it six days" (vv 15–16), and on the seventh day Moses received his summons, "and went into the midst of the cloud and went up the mountain", there to meet with God face to face. "The sight of the glory of the Lord was like devouring fire . . ." (v 17). Cloud and devouring fire; distance and holiness; "otherness" and awful majesty—here is the numinous element in religion which we, in our familiarity with God, so often forget—but to our infinite loss. It is the antiseptic element in religion which saves it from lapsing into sentimentality. We moderns are not very good at taking our shoes off on holy ground before the presence of the glorious God! We might look at these Exodus stories again, for "our God is a consuming fire" (Hebrews 12:29). That is a *New* Testament utterance, from the writings of a man who had, more than most other writers, much to say about boldness in approaching God. I could wish we always held *both* these truths in tension.

Holiness is an essential part of the glory of the Lord. Nowhere does this come out more clearly than in the story of young Isaiah as recorded in Isaiah 6. The background of that chapter is a sombre one. King Uzziah had just died. His reign had been one of almost unbroken success and prosperity (see 2 Chronicles 26). For more than half a century he had succeeded in battle and had built up his people's fortunes. Then, nearing the end of his reign, he had presumed to attempt to burn incense at the censing-altar. Resisted by the high priest Azariah and by eighty priests, and commanded by them to leave, the king turned on them and threatened them. But not for long. As he threatened, a leprous mark appeared in his forehead and "he hasted to go out". He died apart, alone. Against the background of that pitiable tragedy, young Isaiah, pondering on his hero's downfall, felt his nation one with its king in their sinfulness, and felt himself one with his people. All alike were tainted. Then he saw another King in all the majesty of utter holiness, attended in his courts by seraphs who cried, "Holy, holy, holy is the Lord of hosts; His glory is the fulness of the whole earth". That vision of glory threw into bold relief the sin of his late king, of his people, and of himself. Only when, after the purging of his sin, he hears the words, "Whom shall I send and who will go for us?", is he in a position to realise something of the divine grace which can take such a man, from the midst of such a people, and use him as a prophet. He had had a vision of the glory of the Lord which had been cathartic to his soul. Now he must be the spokesman who shall show a dull and unreceptive people something of the glory of the Lord, his divine purpose for the nation and for the world.

This brings us to another aspect of the glory of the Lord in the Old Testament, an aspect which flowers in the New into a major doctrine. God might indeed manifest something of his character to his people by means of cloud and fire. But the normal means of his self-revelation to the world was to be through his own people. It was his purpose that they should "incarnate" in themselves something of what he stood for, something of his love and holiness. When other nations looked at Israel, they should be able to see something of what the glory of the Lord meant in terms of actual life. That was the ideal, though the Old Testament is largely a record of how Israel failed to rise to it.

In the seventy-eighth Psalm (v 61) there is a phrase which summarises this with almost startling brevity. The seventy-eighth is one of those Psalms, in which the Hebrews delighted, which passed in review God's dealings with his people in the long course of their history. The passage with which we are particularly concerned is recording how "they provoked him to anger with their high places", and it tells of the wrath of God which ensued, so that he forsook the tabernacle, "and delivered his *strength* into captivity and his *glory* into the enemy's hand". Israel as the strength and glory of the Lord! That was the divine plan; and no failure on Israel's part to live up to that plan must spoil for us the splendour of its conception.

St Paul takes up and develops the idea in his letters. Writing to the Corinthians of certain Christian brethren, he refers to them as "the glory of Christ" (2 Corinthians 8:23). In the Epistle to the Ephesians, where his doctrine of the Church reaches its height, he prays that his readers may have the eyes of their hearts so enlightened that they may know three things: *first*, what is the hope to which they have been called; *second*, what are the riches of the glory of his inheritance in the saints; *third*, what is the exceeding greatness of his power towards us who believe (1:18). It is the second item which concerns us here, and we do well to mark it carefully. St Paul does not pray that we may understand how rich we are in knowing him. He prays that we may understand how rich he is in his inheritance of the Church! Yes, those scattered little communities in Asia Minor, to which this circular letter was addressed, were the glory of Christ, his inheritance, the reflection to men of his purity and majesty and love. In the great ascription of praise in chapter 3:21, he asserts that glory will come to God *in the Church* by Christ Jesus. He is not far from the words of the great prayer in St John 17:10: "I am glorified *in them*." Nor should we, in our study of this doctrine of Ephesians, miss the reference in chapter 5:27. The Apostle has been writing of Christ's love of the Church, of his handing over of himself on her behalf, "that he might consecrate her . . . that he might present the Church to himself *glorious*, not having spot or wrinkle or any such thing, but that it might be holy and without blemish". That is his high and holy purpose for the Church. The language is, of course, the language of Old Testament sacrifice—the animal that was offered to the Lord had to be in every way a perfect specimen. So, if the Church is to "incarnate" in the world something of the majesty, power, and love of God and manifest them to men, she must be ready for death, for sacrifice to the limit; she must be un-marred by any kind of blemish if she is to be presented to the Lord "glorious". God "is glorified", wrote A. B. Davidson, "when by revealing his goodness he attracts men unto himself, and his own goodness is reproduced in them, and they are created anew in his image." So the Church, the glory of Christ, goes on.

We come now to the very heart of the concept of glory in the biblical revelation. I have just said that "if the Church is to 'incarnate' in the world something of the majesty, power and love of God and manifest them to men, she must be ready for death, for sacrifice to the limit". This insight into truth is drawn directly from the life and teaching, and supremely from the self-offering of himself in death, of Christ our Lord. The glory of God is seen—such is the divine paradox!—at a manger among the stench of the cattle and at a cross where man's hatred and malice burst into open flame. It was as the aged Simeon took up in his arms "a little baby thing which made a woman

210 Sure Foundation

cry" that he saw deliverance for the nations, revelation for the heathen, and "*glory* for thy people Israel" (St Luke 2:32). Truly "divine weakness is stronger than man's strength" (1 Corinthians 1:25)!

St Luke recurs to the same theme when he tells the story of the transfiguration of Jesus (9:28ff). Here is glory all right! The dividing line between "that" world and "this" is so thin that the divine presence breaks into this world-order in a unique manifestation of glory. *But* that manifestation of glory is set firmly in the context of passion. The heavenly visitors, Moses representing the law and Elijah the prophets, "who appeared in glory", spoke of the *exodus* which he was to fulfil in Jerusalem (verse 31). This is an extraordinary phrase. The exodus spoke to any Jew of that deliverance from Egypt which came through the agency of Moses to a captive people. Jesus was about to effect a greater deliverance for his captive people, but to do it *at Jerusalem*, at the cost of his life-blood on the cross. This "glory" passage has at its heart the sombre reality of the passion. Indeed, St Luke would insist that the supreme glory of Jesus is to be seen in the context of the cross, in his self-giving to the uttermost. St John, years later, was to put it thus: "The Word became flesh . . . and we beheld his glory." It is the glory of the Son of God to be abased, to humble himself even to the death of the cross (see also Philippians 2:5–11).

We must pause for a moment at that prologue to St John's Gospel. If only we were not so accustomed to it! If only our ears had not, over the years, become so attuned to it! "The *Word* became *flesh.*" Philo, the first-century Jewish philosopher of Alexandria, had an elaborate, and in some ways noble, doctrine of the Logos. But that doctrine hovered uncertainly between personality and non-personality. Never did he dream of saying: "The Word became flesh." Thus St John anchors the Eternal in history. "The highest," said Goethe in a memorable sentence, "the highest cannot be spoken; it can only be acted." So God, on the plane of human history, at a given moment, in a given (and insignificant) little town, *acted out* what was in his mind and heart, and "the Word became flesh". Would to God that the veil of familiarity, of accustomed-ness, could be torn from our eyes, and the marvel of the Incarnation could dawn afresh!

"The Word became flesh and *dwelt* among us." Tabernacled,

lived his life in the body as in a tent—it is a "a natural and effective symbol for the transitory character of human life" (E. C. Hoskyns). If *we* had been meditating on that, how should we have completed the sentence? Surely we should have written: "and we beheld his humiliation, his utter abasement." Not so St John. "We beheld his—*glory.*" Here is paradox, if ever there was paradox. "Flesh—glory"—such is the divine economy.

And the paradox is central to the whole of the Fourth Gospel. It would take a long lecture fully to elaborate this. Here I can only mention chapter 12, where the strong note of the impending passion is struck at the beginning in the reference to the Passover festival (v 1) and the story of Mary's anointing the feet of Jesus "against the day of his burying" (v 7). Greeks come to Jesus—his world-wide mission is in view; and he exultantly breaks out: "The hour has come for the Son of Man to be *glorified*" (v 23). But what does he mean by that? We are left in no doubt. Immediately he speaks not in the world's terms of triumphant paraphernalia but of a grain of wheat falling into the ground and dying; it is the only way to fruit-bearing. Here, once again, is the paradox of glory.

So it is when we come to the great high-priestly prayer (chapter 17). "Father, the hour has come"—the fearful hour of betrayal, of passion, of death on a cross. "*Glorify* thy Son, that the Son may glorify thee" (v 1). The crucifixion itself is an "exaltation"—the word has a significance far more profound than the spatial (12:32–33; cf. 3:14 and 8:28).

Having touched on the theme of glory in St John, we must pause briefly to look at St Paul's writings, for with him, as with St John, the theme of glory is important. Let us confine ourselves to the Epistle to the Romans. "All have missed the mark, and all constantly fall short of the *glory* of God" (3:23); that is to say, they fall short of the image of his likeness which God intended his creatures to bear. St Paul is looking back to the Genesis stories of creation, where man is described as being made in God's image, after his likeness. That was lost at "the Fall". But in the new creation which takes place when a man comes to be "in Christ", there takes place the miracle of a restored glory. This is a present reality, and in it St Paul rejoices—as may we all who are in Christ. But it is a future hope

as well, for there is an eschatological aspect to his use of the
word. "We exult in hope of the glory of God" (5:2). That is to
say, we exult in the sure confidence that what has been begun in
us will, by the grace of God, come to its fulfilment on "that
Day". God is working his purpose out, "shaping us to the
likeness of his Son" (8:29). No wonder that the Pauline letters
are shot through with *dox*ologies, glory songs! Personally and
cosmically the glory-process is at work through the operation of
the Lord, the Life-giver.

Clearly, I have only touched on this major biblical theme.
Perhaps I have said enough to get you going on a study of your
own; all you need for it is your working Bible, a lexicon, plenty
of paper for jottings, and prayer to the Illuminator Spirit.

We have noticed how in the Bible glory is often spoken of in
terms of light and radiance. As, in natural life, the radiance of
the sun can be dimmed by cloud or the brilliance of silver by
tarnishing, so in the operation of God's Spirit "in bringing
many sons to glory" (Hebrews 2:10) there are many things
which can hinder, or even stop, the process of glorifying. I
think, of course, in these lectures especially of those of us who
are engaged in what is usually called "the ministry of the
Church", and I mention two things which I find tarnish the
process. I mention them quite as much as a warning to myself as
to you.

First, I refer to the danger of *activism*. There are too many
breakdowns, or near-breakdowns, in the kind of homes from
which you and I come—physical breakdowns, nervous breakdowns, moral breakdowns, marriage breakdowns. I have no
easy, overall explanation for this phenomenon nor easy panacea
for this evil. The factors which lead to these breakdowns are
often complex, as any doctor or psychiatrist would tell us. "I
don't know whether I'm coming or going", said a Canadian
priest to a friend of mine and to me some time ago. The sermon
which I had just listened to from him only proved the truth of
his words. It is easy to say and hard to work out in practice, but
the word "hectic" should not occupy a place in our vocabulary
so far as a description of our ministry is concerned.

The cause of our trouble, of our driving ourselves to the point
of breakdown or even literally to the point of death, is sometimes a deeply theological one. We do not believe, really

believe, in the truth of justification by faith. We preach it—
does not one of our Articles, No. 11, put it most pointedly?:

> We are accounted righteous before God, only for the merit
> of our Lord and Saviour Jesus Christ by Faith, and not for
> our own works or deservings: Wherefore, that we are
> justified by Faith only is a most wholesome Doctrine, and
> very full of comfort.

But we do not believe it sufficiently deeply to live by it. We
preach justification by faith. We *live* justification by works.
These things ought not so to be.

Perhaps our best cure would be to study once again, in deep
humility, the first eight chapters of the Epistle to the Romans—
to study them not in preparation for sermons to others, but as
food for our very lives. As a kind of commentary on them, we
might think about these two extracts. The first is from Dr
Frank Lake's monumental *Clinical Theology: A Theological and
Psychiatric Basis to Clinical Pastoral Care*, pp 75–6:

> In Christ his Son, the Holy God receives sinners. Not
> reformed sinners; it is broken sinners in their sin with
> whom Christ is united in his redemptive work. All Christ-
> ian ethical motive arises in gratitude for these events in
> those who derive their very Being from them. We are no
> longer related to God by obedience to the law's require-
> ments. The law of holiness seems to serve only to break our
> pride in the attempt to fulfil it. We are now related to God
> by the obedience of faith, that is by the acceptance of the
> fact that the work of re-relating us to himself is his own
> work, that it must be so, and that he has achieved it in his
> Son our Saviour.
>
> It is fundamental to all pastoral ministry that the men
> who undertake it should be living by this gospel. This is
> the greatest resource of the Christian physician of souls.
> To be a stranger to the dynamics of justification by faith in
> the gracious reception of God to sinners through the
> mediation of his Son, is a difficulty quite fatal to the
> pastoral task.

The second is from Evelyn Underhill's *Anthology of the Love of God*, quoted by Kenneth Leech in an important section of his book *Soul Friend* (p 32) to which I referred in my second lecture:

> A shallow religiousness, the tendency to be content with a bright ethical piety wrongly called practical Christianity . . . seems to be one of the defects of institutional religion at the present time . . . and that is a type of religion which does not wear well. It does little for the soul in those awful moments when the pain and mystery of life are most deeply felt.

What did Jesus mean when he told us by clear implication to love ourselves? "Love your neighbour as you do yourself" (St Matthew 19:19). Did he mean to say, "You are a person in your own right. You are made in the image of God. You are destined, as St Paul was to say, to 'be shaped to the likeness of God's Son' (Romans 8:29). Don't wreck that destiny, don't destroy that pattern, don't destroy your*self* by an activism that runs riot with you. Respect yourself, recognising what you are in the mind of the God who made you."

1 Kings 19 is a chapter deserving of our study. Elijah and the prophets of Baal—what a story that is in chapter 18! Now it is all over, and the prophet is totally exhausted and totally self-pitying. "It's too much, Lord," he prayed, "take away my life; I might as well be dead" (19:4). (Here is a clerical Monday morning with a vengeance! Or the end of Lent—"how on earth can I face Easter?".) What does God do for his servant? What would you have done? Sent him off to a convention, or to a charismatic renewal meeting, or to the Diocesan Retreat House, according to your ecclesiastical taste? God does none of these things. Before any kind of "spiritual" treatment is given him, God sees to it that he gets food and sleep. He is exhausted, and *that* is what he needs. How very unspiritual—or is it? How very earthy! But our religion is *just that*. Only after sleep and food and plenty of both, only then can there be the correction of his self-pity (vv 10ff), and "the soft whisper of [the divine] voice" (v 12), and the commission to further service (vv 15ff).

You know the verse of the hymn:

Bringing all my burdens,
Sorrow, sin, and care,
At thy feet I lay them,
And I leave them there?

That is not to be sung just at evangelistic services. It is to be put on your desk, or over the kitchen sink, and to be lived by, especially the last line. It is the road along which release from tension and brittleness is to be found. It is the beginning of the end of that sweating activism which leads to a dead-end in any ministry worthy of the name. It might well be the answer to many a breakdown.

Secondly, I refer to the danger of *a lack of expectancy*. One of the facts of the "ministerial" life is what the Psalmist, according to the Prayer Book Version, calls "the sickness that destroyeth in the noonday" (91:6). This "sickness" hits all of us at different times, and in different ways. Sometimes it hits only a few years after our ordination or commissioning. More frequently it hits when we are in our forties or fifties. Sometimes it hits when the end of our ministry is in sight and we start counting the years or months till we draw our pension. The honeymoon period is over. We are on the long slog, the period where the grace that is called for is the grace so often spoken of in the New Testament and generally translated "endurance" (Romans 5:3–4 etc., etc.)—"stickability", "going through with it". Life and ministry are dull, lacking in lustre, compared with what they used to be. We cease to be surprised, to marvel at the sheer grace of God that called us, to praise and thank him for it, to rejoice in it.

In the Pauline literature, this note of surprise is evidently present. Listen to this: "To me, who am less than the least of all saints, is this grace given that I should preach among the Gentiles the unsearchable riches of Christ" (Ephesians 3:8). And to this: "I thank Christ Jesus our Lord for that he counted me faithful, putting me into the ministry" (1 Timothy 1:12). We could give other examples. There is about those passages a kind of awed surprise, a note of thankful astonishment, at the gift of ministry, the most precious thing in the world.

When this disappears, there goes with it that note of expectancy which is, I believe, part and parcel of our Christian faith. My dear friend, Cardinal Suenens, whose books many of you will know, is always talking about "the surprises of the Spirit". He talks about them because he is constantly experiencing them—at the hand of the God who is constantly "making all things new", including our ministries (Revelation 21:5). Lack of expectancy, a kind of *ennui*, is very definitely one of the perils of the ministry.

Sometimes this lack of expectancy is directly connected with the first of the perils which we have been considering, namely *activism*. We are exhausted by our activity, and we can hardly lift up our head to look into the Face of God and be refreshed. Sometimes it is connected with the peril of sloth. We have lost the habit of refreshing ourselves at the fountain-head of life, namely prayer, and with it meditation and reading. Sometimes it is due to a defective doctrine and experience of God the Holy Spirit.

As I do my rounds in the churches, I listen with interest to hear how the introductory clause of the third section of the Nicene Creed is recited. Usually it comes out like this: "And I believe in the Holy Ghost, the Lord-and-giver-of-life." But this is wrong. It should be: "And I believe in the Holy Ghost, the Lord (*comma*), the Giver of Life." The French is clearer: "Je crois en l'Esprit-Saint, qui est Seigneur et qui donne la vie." Two things are predicated in this affirmation about the Holy Spirit. The first is that he is Lord, sharing with the Father and the Son in the title *Kurios*. The second is that he is the Life-giver. Now this is not just a reference to the original creation when, the Word having acted, the Spirit moved like an awesome wind over the waters. It is a reference to the ever-present activity of the Holy Spirit in the *world*—wherever truth and beauty and goodness are present, there the Spirit of God is at work, often using agents who are unaware of his presence and power. It is a reference to the ever-present activity of the Holy Spirit in the *Church*, dividing severally to each member of the Church as he wills (1 Corinthians 12:11). It is a reference to the ever-present activity of the Holy Spirit in *you*, if you are prepared to be a channel of his grace. That Holy Spirit is ready to come to you like the wind by which he is described in Scripture, blowing away the stale and the foetid, refreshing, exhilarating. He is ready to come to you like fire, burning the dross, warming, inflaming, uniting.

For decades some of us have been longing for a renewed understanding of and emphasis on the person and work of the Holy Spirit. That longing has been fulfilled in recent years, though often in ways which we did not expect. (After all, there is a strong element of the unpredictable in the way wind and fire function—that is one of the reasons why we are so afraid of them!) The charismatic movement has come. It is a fact to be reckoned with in any serious ecclesiology. But before we give it an approving nod or a disapproving dismissal, before we list the pros and cons with a kind of cool detachment, let us not think that we can deal with the Spirit thus. It is for *him* to deal with us. You cannot pigeon-hole the Spirit—he has a way of flying out of the pigeon-hole! You cannot measure the force of the Spirit, as you might seek to measure the force of a gale—he has a way of blowing down your little machine! What matters—and what in the long run is the only thing for which we shall be responsible—is not the cool detachment of our assessment of a movement, but our own open-ness to the activity of the Spirit in our own life and ministry.

Was I gratefully and thankfully surprised, when I woke this morning, that God had given me another day in which to exercise my ministry? "To me, who am less than the least of all saints"? Am I on the look-out today for some surprises of the Spirit? Do I believe, really believe, in the Lord, the Life-giver?—believe that he can vivify even a ministry which died years ago, or warm my heart, or renew my prayer-life which cooled a decade back?

We could not do better than to end these lectures, and especially this lecture on glory, with this prayer:

> Almighty Father,
> whose Son was revealed in majesty
> before he suffered death upon the cross;
> give us faith to perceive his glory,
> that we may be strengthened to suffer with him
> and to be changed into his likeness,
> from glory to glory:

Sure Foundation

who is alive and reigns
with you and the Holy Spirit,
one God, now and for ever.

And if, in Pauline fashion, we wished to end on a doxological note, what better than this?:

Now to him who is able to do immeasurably more than all we can ask or conceive, by the power which is at work among us, to him be *glory*, in the Church and in Christ Jesus, from generation to generation evermore! Amen.

Anything to Declare?

In September 1978, the Bishop of Caledonia, the Rt. Reverend Douglas W. Hambidge, called together his clergy and some of his lay workers for a residential conference in Terrace, British Columbia.

I

What do we have to proclaim?

IN SOME QUARTERS today, "proclaiming" is a scarcely respectable word. Those who dislike the word maintain that we are in no position to proclaim. Theology is in such a state of flux that the best of us can do little more than listen— listen, if possible, to what God may be saying to us in the chaos of the late twentieth century; listen to what the strident voices of our times may be screaming at us; listen to the questionings of our people; listen patiently and with deep sympathy; but who are we to *proclaim?*

There is something to be said for this approach. Some of us clergy are bad listeners. Some have practically ceased, if ever they began, to listen to *God*; their lives are such a welter of activity that they say they have not got time to be still and listen to the voice of God. Others have practically ceased, if ever they began, to listen to their *fellow human-beings*. I know more than one clergyman who talk so unceasingly and at such terrrifying

Terrace, British Columbia, 8, 9, 10 September, 1978.

speed that it is almost impossible to get a word in edgeways. But I have known others who, specialising in the gentle art of sympathetic listening and uttering sometimes scarcely a word, have elicited from those who bring their troubles to them, the remark, spoken in deepest seriousness: "Thank you for helping me so much. I feel greatly relieved and helped." A burden seems to have dropped from them.

Then, of course, those who are hesitant about the word "proclamation" have this to be said for them: anyone who ventures to speak about God can only, in one sense, "stutter". Who are we sinful mortals to speak of theological immensities—of God in his blazing holiness, in the eternity of his being, in the majesty of his greatness? Who are we to pontificate about time and eternity, we who are "dust and ashes", or, to put it less biblically and in more modern terms, merely a speck on a world which is less than a speck in a universe of unimaginable vastness? "God is in heaven, and thou upon earth. Therefore let thy words be few" (Ecclesiastes 5:2).

Again, who of us has not felt the inadequacy of the language, for example, of the creeds? It is shorthand language, with all the disadvantages of such a means of expression. "I believe in . . . the resurrection of the body." Well—yes, and no. You do, and you don't. At least, I do and I don't. Together with St Paul, I do not believe that flesh and blood will inherit the kingdom of God (1 Corinthians 15:50). This body, which has served me so well over a few decades, will live and then be discarded never to be resumed. "A spiritual body" (v 44)—whatever that may mean—will be given to me, and the character, the personality, which has been created here will somehow be carried through into the fuller life of the age to come, there to be refined, expanded, renewed—use what words you will. But you cannot say all that in a creed (which is really a hymn), and so you have to use theological shorthand, liable as this is to very great misunderstanding. You stutter!

Let all this be granted, and granted with all gravity. But does it mean that we can do little more than listen, and that, at least for a time, we must ban the word "proclaim" from our vocabulary? I do not believe it for a moment. If I did, I should have to abandon my calling as a priest in the Church of God. For a priest, at least in the understanding of the word in the Anglican

Communion, is a minister of word as well as of sacrament, and even the sacrament of the Eucharist is itself a "proclamation" of the Lord's death till he come (1 Corinthians 11:26).

Let us do a little burrowing into our New Testaments, and see whether they have anything to say on this matter. From one point of view, the early Christians might perhaps have excused themselves if they had said: "We dare not use so confident a word as 'proclamation'. Look at us. We are only a handful of very ordinary men and women—'untrained laymen' (Acts 4:13). Who in the great sophisticated heathen Graeco-Roman world is likely to listen to *us*? Let us quietly go about our work, loving and serving the Lord, but reserving any kind of confident proclamation till he comes in power and great glory, vindicating his cause and us his quiet and listening disciples." But they said nothing of the sort.

They said rather, in effect, "we have a gospel to proclaim" (Bishop George Bell's hymn which begins with these words catches their spirit admirably), and they were so confident about it that they survived—victoriously survived—the fearful shock of the non-appearance of Christ in glory, in their own lifetimes, to which they had looked forward with such keen anticipation (e.g. 1 Thessalonians 4:17).

To our New Testaments, then, we turn. Let us first watch the early Christians at work, as St Luke shows them to us in the Acts.

If we examine the word *katangellein*, "to proclaim" (the word we have just noted in 1 Corinthians 11:26, used of the sacrament of the Eucharist), we get some very interesting results, e.g.:

> Acts 4:2—Peter and John were proclaiming in Jesus the resurrection from the dead.
> 13:5—Barnabas and Saul proclaimed the word of God (i.e. the Christian message, in (of all places!) the Jewish synagogues (cp. 15:36; 17:13 etc.)).
> 13:38—Through this man (Jesus) forgiveness of sins is proclaimed.
> 16:17—These men . . . proclaim . . . the way of salvation.
> 17:3—This Jesus whom I am proclaiming to you.

> 17:23—What you worship as unknown, this I
> proclaim . . .

Resurrection, the Christian message, forgiveness, the way of salvation, Jesus himself—this is the subject matter of the Christian proclamation. "He it is whom we proclaim" (Colossians 1:28).

This is spelled out, not in narrative (as in the Acts) but in doctrinal form in various New Testament passages. We may glance at two of them:

1. I Corinthians 15:3ff. St Paul claims that he is passing on what he himself had received. If we ask "from whom?", we may surmise that he very likely meant the members of the church of Damascus to which he had gone after his dramatic conversion experience. What he had then received—a very few years after the happening of the events themselves—he passed on in the course of his evangelistic work in Corinth about AD 50. This is stated in almost credal form—

> that Christ died for our sins according to the scriptures,
> that he was buried,
> that he was raised,
> that he was seen.

Perhaps we may see in this the core of the creed of the Damascus church—as it has indeed been the core of the Christian proclamation down the ages, and is today.

2. Romans 1:2-4. The gospel, St Paul asserts, is about God's Son: on the human level he was born of David's stock, but on the level of the spirit—the Holy Spirit—he was declared Son of God by a mighty act in that he rose from the dead . . . Jesus Christ our Lord.

Here again we have an almost credal outline. The gospel is seen to be the Person of Christ himself.

This gospel is firmly rooted in history, firmly "earthed". Jesus is of the stock of David. There is an indissoluble link between the historic facts which took place at a given place and time in our world and the present realities of life as we experience it. The gospel is no gospel unless it is concerned with day-to-day living—with race and sex and ecology and politics. (This theme is elaborated in *The Bible and Social Justice (vide supra*, pp 141ff.)

When I was about to be consecrated bishop in the Church of God, my students gave me my pectoral cross. They had the College motto incised upon it—*Vae mihi si non evangelizavero.* The New English Bible translates that verse from 1 Corinthians 9:16 thus: "It would be misery to me not to preach."

"Have you anything to declare?" It is a question which the customs authorities ask us at the airport. It is a question which every preacher, every Christian, must ask himself. His answer must find its focus in "the grace of our Lord Jesus Christ and the love of God and the fellowship of the Holy Spirit". We proclaim from a trinitarian base.

2

How do we proclaim?

1. "What you are speaks so loud that I cannot hear what you say." The words are those of a cynic. But, though spoken negatively, they convey a positive truth and one, moreover, with which the writers of the New Testament would have whole-heartedly agreed. "Though I speak with the tongues of men and of angels and have not love, I am a noisy gong or a clanging cymbal" (1 Corinthians 13:1). You may be a combination of St John Chrysostom the golden-mouthed and John Henry Newman, but if you have not love, you are nothing.

The point is worth pursuing. I turn your attention to a passage in 2 Corinthians 6:3ff.

It is clear that, when St Paul speaks of "trying to commend *ourselves*" (v 4), he has no personal objective in mind. He is only concerned to do so in so far as he is a minister of the gospel, "sharing in God's work" (v 1), a "servant of God" (v 4), an "ambassador of Christ" (5:20), intent upon representing his sovereign worthily. How is he to do this? The answer is outlined in a series of short but pregnant phrases:

v 4. "By our steadfast endurance." The Authorised Version "patience" will not do as a translation. In this noun, we have the idea of "internal stamina" which is never content to leave a task half-fulfilled because it is too tough, but is determined to go on with it "until it is thoroughly finished". Those who work in the northern areas of Canada know something of the meaning of "distress" and "hardships". Great numbers of our fellow-Christians in communist-dominated countries know the meaning of "flogged, imprisoned, mobbed . . . sleepless, starving". Many Church leaders know something about "overworked", and what the "care of all the churches" entails (2 Corinthians 11:28). Steady endurance is the quality that counts and commends.

v 6. "By the *innocence* of our behaviour." The noun occurs only here with certainty in the New Testament. (In some texts it comes also in 11:3 where the New English Bible, in a footnote, translates it as "purity".) The adverb from the same root comes (with a negative) in Philippians 1:17—"from mixed [impure] motives". The adjective occurs eight times in the Epistles in the sense of "pure" (2 Corinthians 7:11; 11:2; Philippians 4:8; 1 Timothy 5:22; Titus 2:5; James 3:17; 1 Peter 3:2; 1 John 3:3).

A canon friend of mine was asked to take a Quiet Day for the clergy. Some of those invited replied to the invitation: "He cannot speak for nuts. But we'll come to see his face." The beauty of holiness, of God's purity, shone through.

v 6. By "our grasp of truth". This New English Bible translation is a somewhat free rendering. The Authorised Version gives a straightforward translation of the Greek—"by knowledge". St Paul is often chary when he writes of knowledge which is little more than head-knowledge, intellectual furniture—"knowledge puffs up, love builds up" (1 Corinthians 8:1). He prefers to speak of knowledge which operates on a practical, spiritual level (as in, e.g., Ephesians 1:17; 4:13; Colossians 1:9–10 etc.). But here, for all his nervousness of mere head-knowledge, he uses the plain, straightforward word. We must "know our stuff". In our own field, we cannot afford to be tiros, amateurs, if we are to commend our calling and our faith.

v 6. By "our patience and kindliness". The two words are used in Romans 2:4 of *God's* patience, and the first word in

1 Timothy 1:16 of *Christ's* patience. Our patience and kindliness are to be a reflection of these qualities as seen in the Father and the Son.

Parochial life gives ample opportunity for the exercise of these qualities! It may be a source of encouragement to remind ourselves, when we find our congregations slow to grasp the truth which is so evident to ourselves, that Jesus more than once faced similar difficulties. "How dull you are! How slow to believe . . . !" (St Luke 24:25).

v 6. "By gifts of the Holy Spirit." The New English Bible rather boldly inserts the words "gifts of". They are not in the original. It would, I think, be possible to join the words "Holy Spirit" to the preceding ones—"through patience, through kindness in the Holy Spirit." That is to say, we commend ourselves (and so, our Lord and his message) only in so far as we are in him and he is in us, and we are open to his power and enabling.

v 6. "By sincere love"—non-hypocritical love, love in which there is no play-acting. ("*Darling*, it is *heavenly* to see you." Aside: "The little *cat!*".) Unhypocritical love is the love of Christ in us, the set of our will for the eternal welfare of another.

v 7. "By declaring the truth"—so the New English Bible, suggesting the "ministry of the word". That may well be right. J. B. Phillips translates "speaking the plain truth", a phrase which gets close to "speaking the truth in love" (Ephesians 4:15). That certainly is a measure of maturity in the friendship of two people or in the relationships of people on a committee or church council. To be able to speak the plain truth about our own problems or about another's weakness, to do so in openness and love, that is a real commendation.

v 7. "By the power of God." This last one in the long series beginning with "by" is the *sine qua non* of them all. All these facets of Christian character which *commend* are only possible by the operation within us and among us of that very power which raised Christ from the dead (Ephesians 1:19–20).

This powerful passage serves to illustrate what we call "proclamation by character". The result of such proclamation by people "penniless" but "owning the world" is that "poor ourselves, we bring wealth to many" (v 10). And that is what we are here for.

2. *We proclaim by ourselves being implicated in society, in the life around us, and in the world beyond our immediate circle.* It is clear that Jesus, the incarnate Lord, the Word made flesh, cared deeply about men's bodies and about their tortured minds. He never dealt with "souls" as if they could somehow be separated off from other parts of their human personality! He expects his followers to do likewise.

The Christian, faced by a situation where the drainage system is so bad that the children's health is imperilled, does not say "God wills it" and betake himself to prayer. He acts, he fights. He takes the matter up with the local council. If a film is being shown at the local cinema which is likely to poison people's minds, he organises against it until it is taken off. That may be negative, but it is "proclamation".

Just because we are Christians, we have an interest in politics, for politics is a sphere where decisions are made which affect the lives of those for whom Christ died and who are precious in God's sight. A necessary result of such care for people is that Christians will often find themselves implicated in difficult situations and involved in controversy. That cannot be helped. That is part of the cost of discipleship. We must be prepared to be the objects of criticism, for Christ's sake. We are at war.

To regard Christianity as just an interesting story of ages long gone by is to engage in a great delusion. That would be the exact reverse of the faith of the incarnate Lord.

Read the story of Martin Niemöller's resistance to the Nazi movement, and you will see the dynamite of the Christian gospel at work resisting evil when the other voices in society, including those of liberal education as represented by the Universities, had been silenced.

Read *The Trial of Beyers Naudè*, and especially the record of a sermon preached by him in 1963 on the text: "We must obey God rather than men"; read of his decision to accept the directorship of the Christian Institute, a decision which deepened his conflict with the State and cost him both his position as a minister in his own Church and his status as an Elder as well; read of his choice between religious conviction and submission to ecclesiastical authority—"by obeying the latter unconditionally I would save my face but lose my soul"—and

you will see something of the cost of commending the gospel.
Read the story of Christian resistance to communist atheism
in Russia and Eastern Europe, to mention only two areas, and
you will see what "resisting unto blood, striving against sin"
involves.

Read the story of the martyrdom of Archbishop Janani
Luwum as he bore his witness to truth and love in the face of the
tyranny of Idi Amin.

Being implicated in society, in the life around us, and in the
world beyond our immediate circle is costly, but it is an integral
part of Christian proclamation.

3. *We proclaim by preaching.* Here I use the word in its
conventional sense of the declaration of the word of God by one
of his ministers in the pulpit.

Having written fairly extensively on this (for example, in *The
Ministry of the Word*, 1945, revised edition 1964 (Lutterworth
Press) and in *On Preaching*, 1978 (SPCK)), I will not elaborate
on this now. Suffice it to mention two things:

(a) In Article XIX the Church is defined as "a congregation of
faithful men, in the which the pure Word of God is preached,
and the Sacraments be duly administered". Anglicanism is seen
at its best when that balance of word and sacrament is maintained and is seen to be maintained. It is a weak and flabby
church which minimises the place and power of preaching.

(b) At a most solemn moment in the services of ordination
and consecration, the bishop gives a present to the man to be
ordained priest or consecrated bishop. It is a Bible. The giving
of that present is an eloquent act. It is as if to say to the man
concerned: "This is yours—to study, to expound, to interpret,
to relate to the life of the individual, of society, of the world.
Take it. Reverence it. Use it."

3

Who does the proclaiming?

In a bewildered world whose inhabitants are puzzled by a
variety of competing philosophies (as well as perplexed by a

divided Church), who does the proclaiming of the Christian faith? How can the authentic note of the Christian gospel be heard? I suggest, just as a beginning for further thought and discussion, four answers:

1. *The converted individual.* What do I mean by the word "converted"? Not by any means necessarily one who looks back to a given date and says, "In that year, on such and such a day, I was converted" (though on that day a meaningful experience may have happened to him). I mean, rather, one who is now— daily, hourly—facing in God's direction.

The Hebrew word generally translated "repent" is a very simple one. It means to "turn round". The man who hitherto has been running away from God now turns round and finds himself—face to face with his Creator and Redeemer. The Hound of Heaven has been after him—

with unperturbèd pace, majestic instancy

even though previously he had been too deaf to hear his footfall. Now eye meets eye. Fear turns to trust, rebellion to penitence, disobedience to the cry "Thy will be done". Conversion has begun.

The Greek word for repentance is a richer, fuller word than the Hebrew. It means a change of *mind*, with the added all-important nuance of a change of heart and action. The whole personality is thus affected. The individual who repents has embarked on a life-long process; there is no end to it this side of eternity (nor presumably on the other side!).

The repenting, "converted" individual, then, is one who now is facing Godwards, upwards, who "minds heavenly things" (Romans 8:5ff), whose "mind" is being constantly remade and his whole nature thus transformed (Romans 12:2). The "upward calling of God" (Philippians 3:14) goes on as long as the disciple breathes. No sooner is one mountain peak scaled than he is enabled, by the very scaling of the peak, to see further peaks beyond, all waiting to be scaled.

This business of conversion from the unholy to the holy is a strenuous process. No wonder that the writer of the Epistle to the Hebrews writes, "pursue holiness" (12:14). And yet, there is something essentially restful about the process, for holiness is the result of being in love with Jesus, of "abiding in the vine" (St John 15:4ff). Holiness is likeness to Jesus, and that is, in a sense, a natural growth for one made in the image of God. The unnatural is the un-holy.

2. *The married couple.* A highly effective form of proclamation is the witness of a husband and wife who share together and pray together. Sometimes this will be spoken proclamation, but often it will not. St Peter writes of the power of a wife's behaviour in winning her husband to the Christian faith, without a word being spoken by her (1 St Peter 3:1). So a married couple's wordless witness is itself proclamation.

Such praying and sharing together is mutually enriching. It does not entail the dominance of one partner and the suppression of the personality of the other. It should lead to freedom of growth for both, not least for the wife who should be encouraged to develop a life of her own and the particular gifts which God has given her. This is a matter which calls for watchfulness on the husband's part, particularly if he is a naturally dominating personality, or if he believes, as he rightly may, that his calling is a divine one which makes imperious demands on his time, energy and concentration.

As they pray and share together, each partner will find his or her own gifts enriched. Their witness will be more than doubly effective, for in the divine arithmetic, one plus one makes more than two! Such joint witness is a form of proclamation whose effectiveness can scarcely be over-estimated.

3. *The local Christian community*, the people of God in their particular setting. We could call this the charismatic community, for, ideally at least, it is the company of people who are open to receive the grace-gifts with which God wants to endow them.

A study of Romans 12:6ff must impress us with the variety of gifts mentioned there. We find, as we should expect to do, such gifts as *prophecy* ("inspired utterance", NEB), *teaching* and *"stirring speech"* (the power to stimulate thought and action). But in the midst of these exciting gifts comes *service* or, as the New English Bible translates it *"administration"*. How right that this often denigrated word finds itself here in such exalted company!

Cardinal Suenens, in his book *A New Pentecost?*, makes the point that the day should come when there is no charismatic movement in the sense in which we now use that phrase, for the Church, in the mind of God, *is* his charismatic movement. Let the Church *be* the Church, in your community, and the proclaiming will be done.

It will be done in a variety of ways. For example, (a) by the sheer *quality of life*, the very exuberance, of the church's members. When they are seen to be the possessors of abundant life (St John 10:10), that will be proclamation in itself.

(b) by the quality of their *worship*. There is an attractive picture of the effect of lively worship on the outsider, given in 1 Corinthians 14:24–25. He enters a place of Christian worship. He hears "something that searches his conscience and brings conviction". He finds that "the secrets of his heart are laid bare". The result is that "he falls down and worships God, crying 'God is certainly among you!' " We may well ask whether the nature of our services is such that there is a similar effect on a visitor. Is there a liveliness, a warmth, a joy, and a sense of awe which is palpable?

(c) by the *social witness* which they bear. The desire to be effectively implicated in the life of the local community, to bear its ills on their hearts and to work towards their alleviation and annihilation—in fact to be Christian humanists precisely because their Master assumed human nature for them and for their salvation—this is proclamation indeed.

Christians in the purposes of God constitute that company wherein racial, social and sexual differences are transcended, his Israel, the Church, destined to be the salt to keep society from going bad, the light to drive out its darkness.

4. *The preacher.* I use the word in the conventional sense of one who has been authorised to exercise this gift in the Church—clergyman, reader, deaconess, and so on. But when I speak of the preacher in this sense, I do not see in my mind's eye a lonely figure in the pulpit. True, he stands there alone—no one else is visibly there with him. True, he has done most of his preparatory work alone—thinking, writing, jettisoning the

chaff, keeping the grain, praying, offering all he has of mind and experience to God. But when he comes to the act of delivery, he is not alone. For preaching is essentially a co-operative action, a function of the *Church*. Half the sermon is given by the congregation, as they pray with and for the preacher, as they offer to God their minds for the apprehension of some new truth and their wills as they seek to translate intellectual truth into volitional activity. Preaching of this calibre is proclamation.

Pursue Holiness

Romans 8:29
God knew his own before ever they were, and also ordained that they should be shaped to the likeness of his Son.
Hebrews 12:14
Pursue . . . holiness (a holy life), without which no man shall see the Lord.

THIS IS A mighty chapter, this eighth chapter of the Epistle to the Romans, from which I have chosen the first of my two texts. It is a chapter which stretches us almost to breaking point, for St Paul deals with the immensities of the gospel—with incarnation and atonement, with sin and salvation, with life in the Spirit, with the secret of prayer, with suffering and glory, with the transformation of the individual and the redemption of the universe. Some chapter this! In it, St Paul peers into the future. But he also—if we may use "temporal" terms—looks into the past, to the "time in eternity"—how silly our language is!—when God made his great plan for his men. "He knew his own", St Paul asserts, "before ever they were", and planned for them.

What was that plan? That they should be great, and men should sing their praises? That they should be successful, and the world would be at their feet? Not so. That would be a simple operation. "That they should be shaped to the likeness of his Son." That is his plan. That is miracle. That is destiny—your destiny—mine. A miraculous destiny.

National Evangelical Anglican Congress, Nottingham, 17 April, 1977.

What picture was in the writer's mind when he wrote the words? Probably that of the potter, with his clay and his wheel, his working and his breaking, his re-shaping and his re-making, till at last, with a sigh of satisfaction he says: "It is finished. I have fashioned it after my own heart and mind. I have embodied my vision in it. It is a part of me. It is after my likeness. It is after the likeness of my Son."

Dare we say that this is the passion in the heart of God—that we should be shaped to the likeness of his son? In a sense, this is almost too wonderful to put into words, and one hesitates. But so it is.

Let us leave it there a moment, and turn to our second text. It is from a writer who takes a very different stance on many matters from that taken by St Paul. But here he is totally at one with him. With an urgency which even St Paul could not beat, the writer says: "*Pursue* holiness". The Authorized Version "follow" does not get the vigour of the verb. The New English Bible "aim at" gets nearer but scarcely captures the sweatiness of the Greek. Here is something elusive. We could so easily miss "the many-splendoured thing"—holiness, the shape of the likeness of the Son of God. And if we *do* miss it, then we go on—engrossed no doubt in the Lord's business—but blind to his beauty; unable to catch the *visio Dei*, unable to *see* the Lord, and therefore unable to reflect his glory.

As I have read about this Congress, as I have prayed for you though absent from you till this evening, I have tried to imagine what it would be like if the two thousand members of this Congress left Nottingham tomorrow all "pursuing holiness" as if that were the one thing above all others which mattered, all in process, unhindered process, of "being shaped to the likeness of God's Son". One thing it would *not* mean is quite clear: it would *not* mean a withdrawal from involvement in the world. It might mean temporary withdrawal while we reviewed our lives to see what it is that so far has been hindering the pursuit of holiness, what has been marring the work of the heavenly Potter in shaping us to the likeness of his Son. It would certainly mean the regular withdrawal for daily communion with the Potter, without which he has scant opportunity to do his work of re-fashioning. But withdrawal from the world into a kind of pietistic individualism—no! For the "Eldest Brother" of whom

St Paul speaks in our passage was, of all men, the most deeply implicated in the sorrows and sicknesses of his brethren—touching the leper, risking the defilement of the strange company which he kept, applying his saliva-moistened clay to the eyes of the blind, bringing sanity and peace to the man named Legion who hitherto had been a mob rather than a man. No wonder that, as people watched him, they thought of the passage in Isaiah which spoke of One who bore men's griefs and carried their sorrows. He stood in with them, with an awe-inspiring intimacy of contact, from baptism to crucifixion. If *his* learning of obedience was gained through his sufferings (Hebrews 5:8), it is likely that our pursuit of holiness will meet with greatest success *in the midst of the conflict*. There, where the battle is hottest, men are looking to see what Jesus is like. *There*, then, his followers must be found, themselves shaped to the likeness of God's Son.

St John shows a profound insight in this matter. In the great chapters of farewell discourses (14–17) he depicts our Lord as about to get to grips with the Prince of this world in the final conflict of Calvary. Our Lord's great passionate desire is that the world be shown that he loves the Father and does exactly as he commands. How is this to happen? It is to be done by his advancing to the fray. "So up, let us go forward to meet him", the Prince of this world (14:31). At the hottest point of the battle, on the cross in fact, his true nature will be seen. And so it is to be in the case of his younger brothers.

If, then, the pursuit of holiness does *not* mean a quietist, individualistic saving of our souls by withdrawal from the world, what *does* it mean? It means an openness to the action of the Spirit who does the shaping of us to the likeness of God's Son. He is the divine Agent—the most uncomfortable Comforter. I use this phrase about the third Person of the blessed Trinity because of the metaphors by which he is described in Scripture. No one who has exposed himself to the rigours of a gale blowing in from the Atlantic could call that a comfortable experience. No one who has seen the purging effect of fire would ever lightly tamper with it. It may well be that those who expose themselves to the action of the Spirit in re-shaping them will perforce find themselves painfully blown about and searingly purified. But that is the basic cost of their "pursuit".

Old, deeply cherished viewpoints may be blown to smithereens. Old prejudices may have to be burnt out; but until the full blast of the wind and fire has been felt, the re-shaping will be held up.

Is not one of the chief lessons which we can learn from a study of the history of the Church just this—that it is the men and women who have been athirst for God, the living God, who have made the deepest impact on the world? Is it not that those who have nourished a passionate love for Jesus Christ have effected most in the lives of their fellows? Is it not that those who have pursued holiness, who were actually being shaped to the likeness of God's Son, have most effectively invaded the forces of evil and beaten the enemy back? Is it not that those who know most, in their own experience, of the wholeness of God are the ones who bring wholeness and sanity, *shalom*, salvation, to the world? You would not be hard put to it to find instance after instance to illustrate this theme—from St Paul and St John down to William Temple and Mother Teresa.

Many of us have, especially in recent years, been wrestling with the problems created by a society which has to so large an extent left God out of its reckoning—a society which corresponds all too closely to that described by St Paul in the words "Godless and hope-less". Some of us have shared a little in the agony which our Lord experienced when he looked out over Jerusalem and wept over it. That is the true and deepest patriotism. What is the Church to do in the face of this spiritual national emergency? Some would feel that the organisation of some great campaign, perhaps on an ecumenical basis, planned centrally at great cost of men and money, is the best way forward. For myself, I believe that, though the day of big meetings is not over, the stimulation of local effort and enterprise, of which there is a very great deal springing up in many parts of the country, would seem to be a more likely way; and the use of the media—press, radio and television—for intelligent teaching about the basics of Christian believing, being, and doing, might well be developed to that end in ways which hitherto have not been explored at any great depth. We must continue to wrestle with this matter; indeed, to agonise over it. We are not making the impact that we should. People—many of whom could not put their desire into words—are wanting, like the Greeks in the

236 *Sure Foundation*

Gospel, to "see Jesus", and they are not seeing him. How can we help them? This is our primary problem, and if we run away from it, we betray the Lord Christ.

Deep in our hearts we know *this*—that the most likely way that people will see Jesus will be in ordinary men and women like ourselves shaped to his likeness. That is about the closest they will get to him—when there is an accent to our speech, a look in our eye, a warmth to our grasp, which will make them say: "You have been with Jesus of Galilee." This, let me repeat, is not a retreat into a pseudo-evangelical pietism; it is sheer down-to-earth reality, as down-to-earth as the Incarnation itself.

Since Thursday, you have been talking, steadily and solidly. Now you stop a while. That is good. It gives the Lord a chance to get a word in! In a few moments, in deep solemnity and silence, we shall receive the tokens of his passion, the broken bread and the outpoured wine. Perhaps he will say to us: "Pursue holiness—it is the one thing that matters above all others. Let me, by the power of my Spirit, fashion you, shape you, after my likeness." And if we dare find words to reply, we might put it like this: "Yes, Lord, I'm ready. Come as the wind. Come as the fire. Let me feel the full force of your blowing and your burning. For their sakes I consecrate myself. Amen."

Tomorrow's Clergy

St Mark 3:13
Jesus called the men he wanted; and they went and joined him.

NEARLY FOUR MONTHS ago, in the Enthrone-
ment Sermon I preached in Canterbury Cathedral, I used these
words:

> We must have a steady supply of parish priests who will
> give themselves wholly to this one thing—the thoughtful
> ministry of the Word, the awesome ministry of the sacra-
> ments, the visiting of the homes of the people, the ceaseless
> ministry of intercession, the equipping of the laity for their
> witness.
>
> Let us then say to our young men today: "There is no
> finer life than that of a parish priest. Covet this calling.
> Train for it. Pour your best into it. Glory in it. Count
> yourself thrice-blessed if you hear God calling you to it."

There are signs that, after long years of decline in the numbers of men coming forward to the ordained ministry, there is
now a steep increase. Whether the upward graph will continue
remains to be seen. I believe it will, and that slowly but surely
we shall begin to see a strengthening of our position and a better
prospect of training the laity for the work of Christian witness
*Festival Service of the Corporation of the Sons of the Clergy, St Paul's
Cathedral, 13 May, 1975.*

237

which was committed to them in their baptism and confirmation.

There are those who say that, in view of economic stringency, we should refuse to accept for training a large number of those who are offering themselves. They say that we shall not be able either to pay for their training or to give them a decent wage once they are ordained. I believe this to be a wrong, indeed a faithless, approach to the matter. If God is answering our prayers and the men are coming forward, who are we to block their way?

But let us not be starry-eyed about this matter. The cost of training grows yearly greater. The battle to keep the clergy's salaries adequate to meet the never-ending rise in the cost of living is exceedingly difficult. Let us make no mistake about this. Here, it seems to me, is a question of obedience on the part of us who are responsible for finding the means for their training and maintenance. Sometimes those who squeal loudest because their parish is amalgamated to the one next door are those who give least to the maintenance of a vigorous ministry at home and overseas. The growing number of men coming forward and the growing cost of training and maintenance—not to mention the cost of grants for widows and dependants—is a call for very careful husbandry of resources, perhaps for a measure of frugality not known before, and for sacrifice on the part of those who have much more money than the clergy have or (speaking for the majority of them) care very much about having.

St Mark tells us that, in the early days of our Lord's ministry, "he called the men he wanted, and they went and joined him." So the apostolic band was formed. He trained these young men. They then went, equipped, authorised, and empowered, and carried on the work which they had watched him do. It was a tough task—they had to wrestle, as he did to the death, with the world's sin and ignorance and disease. It was no job for weaklings. It called out everything they had got, and more, and they found that the "more" was supplied by the inspiration and wonderful activity of the Spirit of Jesus himself.

So it has been down the long centuries of the Church's history. Jesus has been *calling* men. The call has come in a variety of ways—sometimes so personally as to be almost audible to the physical ear; sometimes through the agency of a friend who says: "Do you think *you* might be the man God wants in the ministry?"; sometimes through a dawning realisation of just how wonderful the Christian message is; sometimes through the appalling need of a world where hate and darkness and the sordid reign. Jesus calls. That is still a fact. Do I not know it—because, for nineteen years I trained these men, and for another nineteen and more I have been ordaining them?

Jesus calls. Then it is over to the Church to test that call, and to provide the means by which the call can be answered. To *test*—that is the work of the Advisory Council for the Church's Ministry; many of you will have served on its Boards. To *provide*—that is the task of people like ourselves who have the enormous responsibility of increasing and administering the money which has come down to us over the long years of the history of the Corporation of the Sons of the Clergy.

I speak to you tonight as one who is deeply interested in the work of the Corporation. I speak as one who is appreciative of the link with the Merchant Taylors' Company, of which I am proud to be a Freeman. I speak as one who knows pretty intimately the needs of the clergy at home and can guess how those needs are likely to increase in the immediate future. And I speak as one who, being privileged to travel extensively and see the work of the Church overseas, knows for a fact that the needs abroad are far more clamant, far more desperate, in a sense far more deserving, than they are even in these islands.

So I would say to those who have this work at heart: we shall need you in the future even more than we have done in the past. You will need to be very wise in your stewardship of the money entrusted to you. You will need to be adaptable in the way you distribute that money and alert to world needs and new conditions. The demands, not only on your resources, but on your alertness and on your responsiveness to changing needs, will be very great. But remember that in doing your work you are playing a part in making possible that ongoing work of Christ's Church which he began when "he called the men he wanted and they went and joined him". Surely no age has had greater need of their ministry than has ours—for we are sinners and need God's forgiveness; we are ignorant of the things of God (for all our technical sophistication) and need his wisdom; we are sick, sick to death, and need his healing.

We go to our work in good heart, for we rely on the Spirit of Jesus, the Spirit who animates and revives and enables the Church to be in fact God's redeeming and healing agency in the world. And we pray that he who calls the men he wants will make us more worthy in our work of enabling them to fulfil their calling.

Training for the Ministry

St John 21:15
After breakfast, Jesus said to Simon Peter, "Simon son of John, do you love me more than all else?" "Yes, Lord," he answered, "you know that I love you." "Then feed my lambs," he said.

ONE OF THE most moving moments in the life of an Archbishop—and he has many as he does his rounds in the work of the Church—is that moment, in the service for the Consecration of Bishops, when he listens to the reading of the appointed lections. The first is taken from that passage in the Acts of the Apostles where St Paul bids farewell to the elders of the Church at Ephesus. He will see them no more. The leadership will be in their hands. "Take heed," he says to them, "to yourselves and to all the flock over the which the Holy Ghost hath made you overseers to feed the Church of God, which he hath purchased with his own blood."

The Gospel usually read is taken from that post-Resurrection story which describes how Jesus, having forgiven his faithless disciples, having re-commissioned them, having breathed his life-giving Spirit into them, having shown them the futility of a fish-catching expedition without *him* on board, and having nourished them in his presence, takes Simon Peter aside. One question only does he ask him. It has nothing to do with his shaky past; nothing to do with his orthodoxy. It has simply to

Centenary Service for Wycliffe Hall, Oxford, Cathedral Church of Christ, Oxford, 24 May, 1977.

do with his love. "Simon, son of John, do you love me?" It is a question repeated as often as Peter's denial had been asserted. The old name is used, Simon, not Peter. He is not yet fully the Rock-man. "Simon, son of John, do you love me?" And then the three-fold charge: "Feed my lambs. Tend my sheep. Feed my sheep."

To listen to these readings in the context of a Consecration, and to look back over one's own ministry in that context, is, I repeat, a moving experience.

For there, in those lections, are to be found the essential elements of all true ministry, whether episcopal or priestly— the element of *divine appointment*—no man takes this office upon himself; the element of *pastoral care*—there is a flock, purchased at great cost, which must be taken care of, fed and tended; the element of *total dedication*—"do you love me more than all else?" Given these, even the faltering Simon can be trusted to be first in the apostolic band. Without these, only disaster awaits the flock.

For one hundred years, Wycliffe Hall has stood for these principles, sometimes perhaps falteringly, more often strongly. It has sought to train men in whom the sense of divine appointment is clear—"whom shall I send and who will go for us? Then said I, 'Here am I: send me.' " It has sought to show them what being a shepherd means, not in the sense of shepherds in the lush safety of an English pasture, but rather in the dangerous setting of an Eastern shepherd's life, where wolves abound and food is hard to come by. It has sought to show them what total dedication involves, till they become men who can say: "This one thing I do," men with a passionate love for their Lord and a deep caring for his people.

How immensely the Church of England, and indeed the whole Church of God, has been enriched by this infusion of life-blood into its system which has come through the men who have been trained in the Hall. How we thank God today for its Principals and the members of its staff who, down the years of the century have put first things first—godliness and dedication, prayer and sacrament, scholarship and pastoral care, missionary outreach and evangelistic zeal! How we pray for a continued flow of men like this into our Church—and not only a continued flow but an increasing one.

Let me share with you certain convictions which, if you agree with them, you can turn into prayers to the Lord of the harvest. I do so as one who personally owes much to Wycliffe Hall and to men like Ralph Taylor and Douglas Harrison and Joe Fison who were on the staff in the mid-'thirties. I speak also as one who, for some nineteen years, played a part in the training of men for the Ministry; and for over twenty-one years has been ordaining the products of our theological colleges.

First, let me welcome the fact that, in the realm of training for the Ministry, we are experimenting. No one could accuse the Church of England of being in a rut in this regard at the present moment. We are re-grouping our resources—I prefer to put it this way, rather than to say we are closing down our theological colleges. We are conscious of the fact that the universities, the teacher training colleges, the polytechnics and so on have facilities to offer which we should be very foolish to neglect, resources of personnel and learning which we should eagerly share. Hence the experiments in regional centres. We are engaging in preparing men and women for various kinds of ministry, of which the auxiliary ministry is at the moment the most interesting. This bids fair to use expertise which otherwise might be lost, and to afford a bridge between clergy and laity which hitherto has been all too feeble. The Advisory Council for the Church's Ministry has in recent years shown itself willing to take up and examine ideas which have proved fruitful, and to engage in experiments which will in the long run be for the good of the Church. For that we should be thankful.

There are, however, lions by the way, and we should do well to be aware of their lurking. It would be unwise to neglect the fact that there is something about residential training which cannot be gained apart from it, even by weekends spent periodically together in courses predominantly non-residential. The opportunity to live close to men who, as the Scots have it, are "far ben wi' God"; to sharpen one's brains with men whose theologising is deep and keen, and to do so not only in the lecture-room, but in the leisurely contact of unplanned meeting; to knock off one's ecclesiastical corners by living with men of differing outlooks and convictions—these are but some of the gifts which only residential living can fully bestow.

Nor let it be thought that the auxiliary ministry is a panacea for our ills. An enrichment of our life and a relief to the local situation it will surely be. But we should deceive ourselves if the fact of the inflow of auxiliary ministers led us to any diminution in our determination to recruit and train a steadily increasing flow of men for the full stipendiary ministry. Here it may be I am treading on controversial ground. I would however tread it without apology. The number of ordinations in recent years has been perilously low. The full effect of that has yet to be felt. But it comes at a time when appalling ignorance of the Christian faith exists in these islands and, I believe, at a time when a welcome is increasingly given to an intelligent presentation of that faith. What is needed is not fewer men, or only part-time men, but more men, full-time men (and it may well be, soon, women as well), trained with immense care and even rigour, who will give themselves totally to this one thing—the ministry, in their Master's name, of prayer, of study, of preaching, of sacrament, of visiting, of counselling. Nothing, I believe nothing, can take the place of such people in our communities, and it is folly to think it can.

For many years now we have been praying the Lord of the harvest to send such labourers. There are indications that he is seeing fit to answer that prayer and that the prospects are good. Would it not be an act of unforgivable faithlessness if we were now to say that we must limit the number of men in training, because of financial or other difficulties? Should we not rather regard the present position as a challenge to our faith and our readiness to venture? Could this not be our finest hour? Of course, the financial burden at the centre will be greater. Of course we shall have to find other means of raising the money— for example by allowing and encouraging the parish from which an ordinand comes to make itself responsible for his training. Of course we shall have to encourage the ordinands themselves to engage in sacrifice, as a token of their sense of privilege in being called, by amazing grace, to such a ministry. Of course! Of course! But, whatever happens, we must not say "No" to a man who, called, tested and trained, has what it takes to be a shepherd of the flock of Christ.

"Simon, son of John, do you love me more than all else?" "Yes, Lord, you know I do." Then, Simon, we welcome you— we count you happy that you believe yourself called and chosen.

We will test you, and train you, and care for you, and *give* you—give you so that you may tend the lambs and feed the sheep, bring again the outcasts and seek the lost. You could have no other calling comparable to this. You are a gift of the ascended Christ to his Church. May the Lord of the Church make us worthy of his gift, and use our theological centres and colleges to the best advantage. And what we pray in general we pray, with deep thanksgiving, in particular for this Hall as it begins the second century of its life and work.

The Nature of the Episcopate

The eleventh Lambeth Conference was held in Canterbury in the summer of 1978. For the first time it was residential and outside London. A briefer Conference was held for bishops' wives at Christ Church College, Canterbury.
The first Conference took place in 1867, and there have been meetings held at roughly ten-year intervals since. Seventy-six bishops attended the 1867 Conference, four hundred and seven that of 1978.
The 1978 Conference opened and closed with services in Canterbury Cathedral. This sermon was preached at the opening service on 23 July.

Psalm 85:8
I will hearken what the Lord God will say.

FORTY-EIGHT YEARS ago, William Temple, preaching at the opening of the seventh Lambeth Conference, said these words:

> While we deliberate, God reigns; when we decide wisely, he reigns; when we decide foolishly, he reigns; when we serve him in humble loyalty, he reigns; when we serve him self-assertively, he reigns; when we rebel and seek to withhold our service, he reigns—the Alpha and the Omega, which is, and which was, and which is to come, the Almighty.

Lambeth Conference, Opening Service, Canterbury Cathedral, 23 July, 1978.

246

That is the one sure point at which to begin the eleventh Lambeth Conference. "Lift up your hearts" to the God who reigns, and loves, and cares—for his world, for his Church, for us.

How urgent it is that we should hear what God has to say to us about that world, about that Church, and about us! For, by reason of his very nature, he is the God who *speaks*.

"He spake by the prophets"—so we say in the Creed. He spoke in the Word made flesh—we have preached many sermons on that. He spoke in the formulation of the Creeds. But does he speak to us today? That is a very different matter. Some of us have virtually given up believing that he does. God forgive us. We would not admit it; it would shock our congregations if we did. But we have stopped listening, and our spiritual life has died on us, though we keep up appearances and go through the motions.

But many in this congregation know that God does speak, and that he makes his mind known to his followers—yes, even to us bishops, men who occupy of all positions the most perilous, because the cameras are always on us and we are compelled constantly to utter.

Really to believe that our God is a God who goes on disclosing himself in ever fuller fashion is to be men of hope and expectancy. Really to believe this is to put less trust in human talk and more trust in listening. "My soul is still and waits on God," said the Psalmist. That is why we are meeting residentially for the first time since the Lambeth Conferences started. It is difficult to do much "hearkening to what the Lord God will say" if you have to spend some hours daily going to and from Lambeth. It is easier to hearken if we can daily unite in unhurried worship and slip into the Chapel between sessions. For God has a way of making himself known not in the strong wind, nor in the earthquake, nor in the fire, but in "the voice of a gentle stillness". God never shouts. We often do. That is why we become deaf.

This means that our predominant attitude, during this Conference, must be one of questioning and of obedience; of setting aside our preconceptions and seeking to "understand what the will of the Lord is". We shall do this in corporate worship, in silent withdrawal, in the devotional lectures, and in the give and take of discussion. Much time is set aside for debate—in sections, in groups, in Plenaries. But some of the most profitable work will be done when two or three gather informally and find that the Lord is in their midst.

We noisy, comfortable Westerners have much to learn from our Eastern brothers, materially poorer and often spiritually richer. We who belong to dioceses whose bishops go back to Paulinus and Augustine need to listen to the younger Churches and catch from them the "first, fine, careless rapture" of their deep love of Jesus.

What *is* the office and work of a bishop in the Church of God today? We Anglicans talk much about episcopacy—and rightly so. The fourth section of the Lambeth Quadrilateral, enunciated in the Conference of 1888, dealt with the Historic Episcopate, and is important. Here, in episcopacy, we insist, is an important part of the contribution which we Anglicans have to make to the Catholic Church. But what is the nature of the episcopacy about which we talk so much? What are the genuine characteristic marks of a bishop? In some quarters he must seem to an observer to be a kind of super executive, an organiser-in-chief, given to much talking and little thinking. But *that* of itself is no great gift to bring to the Catholic Church! Such men there are in plenty without our adding to them. On the other hand, is the bishop, like the Holy Spirit whose agent he is, primarily a *paraclete*, in the sense of a stimulator, an enabler, an *animateur*? One who is open to the wind of the Spirit, warmed by the fire of the Spirit, on the look-out for the surprises of the Spirit—a leader in *that* sense? One who is a teacher because he continues to be a learner, a speaker because he is a hearkener? One who is a guardian of the faith, because the faith to him is "the many-splendoured thing" which never ceases to amaze him because of the immensity of its grace as revealed in the Person of Christ incarnate, crucified and risen? A *martyr* perhaps?

As we examine again the nature of episcopacy—and this is one of our main tasks in the Conference—we shall earth our thinking with an earthiness which becomes the followers of an incarnate Lord. We exercise our ministry in a world which "groans and travails together in pain". Gross inequality of opportunity, dense over-population of God's world, threats of atomic war—these are some of the marks of the world in which we work. Our discussions do not take place in a vacuum. They are set in a vortex of problems, but "the Lord who dwelleth on high is mightier". God reigns; and we shall seek to see our problems in the light of his kingship and so get our perspectives right. This is *God's* world.

And this is *God's* Church. That being so, we can go to our work with a quiet confidence. It is not for us to steady the Ark—Uzzah is not the most attractive figure in the Bible, and we might do well to remember his end! "The gates of hell shall not prevail" against the Church of Christ. We can damage that Church by our cocksureness—it is just possible that we have got our minds made up wrongly about some of the issues and that we shall have to revise our views while we are here. We can wound the Church by the narrowness of our vision or the shallowness of our thinking. Above all, we can grieve the Spirit by our lack of love—we shall be tested on that score in the coming weeks. Some of our differences will be resolved as we think and pray together. Some will remain unresolved. That matters little. Differences are not sinful. They can be creative. The one thing that matters above all else is that *nothing* shall break our love for one another. The eyes of the Church all over the world are on us. We shall discuss, debate, agree, differ. We shall, please God, never threaten, or litigate, but always love. We shall go to our task with a song in our hearts, precisely because it is *Christ's* Church that we love—and pray for—and work in; and God's world that we serve.

I will hearken what the Lord God will say.

Speak, Lord, for thy servant is listening.

Tension and Wounds

The General Convention of the Episcopal Church in the United States of America meets every three years and is composed of the House of Bishops and of the House of Deputies. The latter consists of four clerical and four lay Deputies from each diocese and American churches in Europe elected by diocesan conventions. The 1976 Convention was held in Minneapolis. This address was given on September 17, the day after the vote was taken which approved the ordination of women to the priesthood. Prayer Book revision was also taken a stage further at that Convention when the Proposed Book of Common Prayer was authorised for public worship as an alternative to the Book of Common Prayer (1928), for a period of three years.

MAY I SAY how profoundly thankful I am for the spirit in which your debate was conducted yesterday—a spirit of love and courtesy and prayer. The problems which you have been considering have perplexed us for a long time and I have no doubt that tensions will persist and wounds will endure.

I wish therefore to say a word about those two things: tensions and wounds. I said to someone this morning, "How is everybody?" He said, "Just a bit run out." I can understand that so well after the similar debates we have had in England on these matters.

Address to the General Convention of the Episcopal church in the United States of America, Minneapolis, 17 September, 1976.

First, then, a word about *tension*—that can result in bitterness, in division and in threatening; or tension that can result, in the mercy of God, in power and beauty. Look at a violin—the music only comes when the strings are taut. It is *through* the tension that the music comes. I have a feeling, perhaps I should say a deep belief, that out of this long debate, which reached its climax yesterday, music will come; good will come. If you don't see how that can be, I say to you, "nor do I". There was a big division here. But I believe God sees how that can be. If we go forward in love, as I know you will do, then I think something of a new revelation may well await us. But our two unchanging points must be: love of the brethren, and unity of the Church. Hold to these two things tenaciously, and, out of the tension of our debates and our differences, the music will come.

That is the first word I have had on my mind as I have thought of coming to address you. The other word was the word *"wound"*. I realised that I should be speaking to some wounded people this morning. The question is: What will you do with your wound? You could, of course, let it fester. But that you will not do. You could let it become your strength—that I believe you will do.

Look at the prophesy of Hosea. There was a man with a wound, if ever there was one. The wound came out of the tragedy of his own home life and the birth of illegitimate children through his unfaithful wife, Gomer. But as one great commentator has said, the strength of Hosea was precisely in his wound, because he saw, through the break-up of his marriage and his home, right into the heart of God. He saw that, as practically no other of the ancient prophets did. So what must have seemed to him in his human blindness an unrelieved tragedy, one great minus, became in the mercy of God a plus; not a negative, but a positive. A plus is always in the shape of a cross. I want to say to you, my brothers and sisters, my sympathies are with you, but I believe you will see in the coming years, through the love of the brethren and through your passion for the unity of the Church, that what seemed to you an unadulterated minus is made into a plus by the mercy of God and your own preparedness to suffer.

I have been thinking of the extraordinary miracle wrought by our Lord in making a fellowship out of his Twelve. Look at

them—Matthew, the tax gatherer, who earned his living from
the invading power, and was loathed for what he did. But in
that same Twelve was Simon the Zealot, whose political creed
taught him that it would have been a good act to plant a dagger
in the back of one like Matthew. But these two men, politically
poles apart, were drawn together by their love of our Lord
Jesus. Then there was Simon Peter, sincere but rash and im-
petuous; and young John, quiet, thoughtful, mystical. These
men, temperamentally poles apart, were drawn together by
their common love for their Lord. And among the womenfolk
who followed Jesus, there was a Mary Magdalene, who if
tradition is right was a woman of the streets; and Joanna, wife of
Chuza, who came from court circles. These women, socially
poles apart, were drawn together by their love of the Lord
Jesus. Out of that mixed crowd he created a fellowship. This
was miracle.

Then I think of the great Jerusalem quadrilateral. We talk of
the Lambeth quadrilateral, but there was a quadrilateral many
years before that—in Jerusalem! "They continued steadfastly
in the apostolic teaching, in the fellowship, in the breaking of
the bread, and in the prayers." That second item in the Jerusalem quadrilateral, "the fellowship", was simply a continuation and a burgeoning of that fellowship created by our Lord in
the days of his flesh. It was open enough to take in, though at
first with great hesitancy, that stormy petrel, Saul of Tarsus,
and to make him one with them. This too was miracle. But this
is what happens when people, poles apart, have a deep and
burning love for their Lord. This it is which creates out of the
minus of division, a cross-like plus. Loyalty to him, love for one
another, unity in the Church.

Will you suffer a word of warning from one who represents a
Church which has not been as bold as you have in this matter of
the ordination of women, but has shown a typical British conservatism? If any of you reach the point where you cannot put
your arms around the person who you think voted wrongly
yesterday, and say, "My dear brother or sister, I differ from
you, I differed from you yesterday, but I love you dearly in
Christ," then at that point a deep penitence is called for. If you
cannot say, "together we will go out to make new Christians, to
bring in new disciples," then our father below, as C. S. Lewis

used to call the devil, is winning a victory—and that, you will agree with me, must not and shall not happen.

So I pass to something which has interested me deeply, and that is your Venture in Mission. How delighted I was to see that you are setting your hand to this matter in this session of your convention! Jesus, it is recorded, when he saw the crowds, was moved with compassion. His heart went out to them. Our Church is surrounded, in America and throughout the great world, by untold millions who have never as yet even heard the name of Christ, let alone had the opportunity of an intelligent confrontation with him. It is to these that you are seeking to reach out, and I thank God for it.

You are great givers, and I have faith to believe that you will reach your target in the course of a very few years. Are you as good receivers as you are givers? I ask for this reason: we of the Anglican Communion are part of a great world family of some seventy million men and women—a family stretching from the Arctic to the Equator, and from East to West. I believe profoundly that Africa and Asia and Latin America have an immense amount to give to us needy people in the West. My question is: are we humble enough to receive from them, and are we making adequate preparation and financial provision to make that reception possible? I ask that question against the background of a tiny experiment which we carried out in my own diocese of Canterbury a year ago. We asked a priest from the Church of South India, with wide experience also in Africa and in Europe, if he would leave his family and come and live with us in the diocese for a year. This he did. It was a little bit of cross-fertilisation from him to us. We organised no big meetings for him. We asked him to meet little groups in depth. He taught us lessons which very few English people could do. He has taught us how to pray a bit better, how to listen, how to be quiet, how to leave the superficial and go a bit deeper and explore into God. My question is: are we doing enough to get this cross-fertilisation going—to organise it and to finance it— so that we, at the receiving end, get something of the second and third generation joy of an African, and the deep spiritual perception of an Indian? This, it seems to me, is one of the outcomes of believing in the Anglican Communion as a giving and receiving family concern.

Now I turn to another matter to which we must give increasing attention in different parts of the Anglican Communion. That is what I would call the marriage of episcopal leadership with synodical government. I don't think we have got this totally right in the old country yet. We are working at it. We are wrestling with it, and I doubt not that you are doing so in your Church also. I can only tell you that we find increasingly the value of joint, shared debates when bishops, clergy and laity work at the great issues, including the theological issues, together, thus narrowing the gap between the Houses, thus increasing our learning one from another. Our convocations, that is to say our Houses of Clergy, still meet separately from time to time. They are older than our parliamentary government, and we would not think of terminating them. But generally, we meet together, and so misunderstandings between the Houses are avoided—we grow a little less suspicious of one another. We find that we need not be too anxious about our rights in either House; "the worst thing to do with your dignity is to stand on it", as the old saying goes.

My dear friends, let us rejoice in our partnership in a great family—the Anglican Communion. In it, history, going back far beyond Augustine and Paulinus, joins hands with opportunity—to serve God in a world hungry for want of the knowledge of him as he has revealed himself to us in Christ our Lord. Let us go from our convention determined to put first things first—love of the brethren, unity of the Church, worship of the Lord, evangelisation of the world—and to that quadrilateral, let us hold fast in the power of the Holy Spirit.

VIII
PRESIDENTIAL ADDRESSES

Northern Ireland

THE VISIT WHICH I recently paid to Northern Ireland left some lasting impressions on me. It was the second visit which I have paid in recent years to that troubled country. The second visit only served to underline the impressions made during the first. One impression was the deep desire of the ordinary man and woman for peace. It is only a militant minority which is engaged in killing, but it draws its strength from the fears and anxieties in the wider community.

Another impression was of the triumph of compassion in the midst of the forces of destruction. I think not only of the Corrymeela community and others like it, but of the skilled and patient work of doctors and nurses who seek to repair the ghastly physical damage done by bombs and other weapons. I saw this at first hand. I also think of those who refuse to nurse hatred even when their dear ones have been killed—again I saw this at first hand.

All these things—and others like them—are like beams of light in a dark situation, and they should be a stimulus to us all to continue to uphold in our prayers those who are engaged, in whatever way, in the pursuit of peace.

I wish today to make special reference to the British Council of Churches/Irish Council of Churches Joint Consultation which took place in Newcastle, Co. Down, late last April, at which the Archbishop of York and our Secretary-General represented the Church of England. Many of you will have seen the Report of the Joint Consultation, and I would express the hope that those of you who have not yet done so would study it

Presidential Address to the General Synod, 1 July, 1975.

soon and with care, particularly in view of the fact that the Constitutional Convention has opened since our last group of sessions and has got down to work in an atmosphere by no means devoid of hope.

May I make three points for your thought and, where may be, for your action:

1. I hope we may agree that our Government has both a legal and moral responsibility to keep the peace in Northern Ireland while the Province's own people are engaged in seeking an agreed solution in the Convention. Recently the Reverend William Arlow, a Church of Ireland clergyman who has just become General Secretary of the Irish Council of Churches, stated that the Government were contemplating a withdrawal from Northern Ireland if the Constitutional Convention breaks down. I believe we should welcome the Government's subsequent denial that they were contemplating withdrawal, and assure them of our support as they carry out their responsibilities. We can understand the sense of impatience felt by many of our people at the apparent lack of progress, deepening to despair whenever outrages such as that at Birmingham have occurred. We can also appreciate the strain on our soldiers in their difficult task—and here I should like to pay tribute to them for the restrained but effective way in which they carry out that task. Nevertheless suddenly to withdraw our forces would be to invite worse bloodshed than what is now the case. We cannot turn aside simply because the path becomes more arduous.

2. The Joint Consultation, since it was arranged under the auspices of the Irish and British Councils of Churches, had amongst its delegates no members of the Roman Catholic Church and their member Churches. This needs to be taken much further—it may well be, as the Report suggests, by the provision of a centre of reconciliation, a place of contemplation, study and worship in Ireland, and organised by Roman Catholics and Protestants working together. But certainly the BCC and ICC should engage in dialogue with the Roman Catholic Church in Britain and Ireland more closely and at a deeper level than they have done hitherto.

3. This leads me to my third and last point. There are other issues than the Irish Problem facing our society today. He would be a very insensitive man, and this would be a very insensitive Synod, not to be deeply concerned at the serious economic situation in which our country finds itself at the moment and at the state of society generally.

We can be glad that many groups today share effective power. But those who acquire power in the nation also acquire responsibility not simply to protect sectional interests but to care for the whole life of society. This exercise of responsibility calls for a temper of mind and a singleness of heart which spurns arrogance, self-seeking, envy and greed. We are still as a nation groping our way forward to workable arrangements for taking consultation and reaching decisions among those who now share power. These efforts will be frustrated unless the British people are prepared for a cleansing of self, a quickening of conscience and a renewal of faith which alone can exalt our nation.

Our immediate duty as church people, clearly, is to pray earnestly for our country. Doubtless we have been engaged in this essential Christian work. But the need is now urgent. Let us pray for guidance in this time of need, and especially that all who have a lively faith in God may be able more clearly to give an account of the hope that is in them.

Three Journeys

IT SEEMS TO be part of the function of a twentieth-century Archbishop of Canterbury to undertake pretty extensive travels, not only in the Diocese of which he is Bishop nor in the Province of which he is Metropolitan, but in the whole Anglican Communion and far beyond it. I believe it is right that this should be seen to be an important element of his work. I thought it might be of interest to members of General Synod if I told you a little about some of the travels abroad which I have undertaken within the last year and if I passed some comments on them. I mention three journeys.

1. *The Sudan.* It is a remarkable fact that at the turn of this century there were virtually no Christians in this vast country (the largest nation in Africa). Now there is a large and flourishing Church. Its four Bishops are all African. It was my joyful task to inaugurate the Province of the Sudan and to be present at the installation of one of those four Bishops, Elinana Ngalamu, as its first Archbishop.

The circumstances attending the inauguration were somewhat dramatic. A killer plague had broken out in the southern part of the country and there had been many casualties. Juba was cut off—none came in and none went out. President Nimieri, at the end of a reception which he kindly gave us in Khartoum, expressed the view that the plague was sufficiently contained to allow of our venturing in to Juba. He offered his private plane, and we flew the thousand miles south only some
Presidential Address to the General Synod, 6 July, 1977.

twenty-four hours later than had been arranged. We were the first in. The Province was inaugurated among scenes of great jubilation.

I wish that those who doubt the power of the gospel or the vitality of our missionary work could have been present with us in Juba that day. That was last October.

2. In February we set out for a four-and-a-half weeks' tour of *Australasia*. Here again we were in at the start of a new Province of the Anglican Communion—this time Papua New Guinea. Not many decades ago there were head-hunters here. Now, as a result of missionary work in which the Australian Church has played a large part, there is a lively and healthy Church, whose new Archbishop, Geoffrey David Hand, has devoted the major part of his life and practically all his ministry to its service.

From Papua New Guinea we went on to Melanesia, and from Melanesia to Australia whose Primate, Frank Woods, was just about to retire—an ecumenical leader and a man greatly beloved and respected. We visited the great cities—Brisbane, Melbourne, Adelaide, Perth, Darwin, Sydney, Canberra, Newcastle. The visit to Darwin was particularly memorable—I had not visited it on either of my previous journeys to Australia. The scars of the fearful cyclone which hit it on Christmas Eve 1974 were still evident. With typical courage and with the help of the whole Australian Church, a new Cathedral was built strong enough to withstand even another similar disaster. I preached at its Consecration. Memorable, too, was a visit to an Aborigines' settlement at Oenpelli where Christians are seeking to help these people whose history goes back so many thousands of years and whose integration into the life of the Australian continent has been made more difficult than it need be by ill-treatment meted out to them by white men in the past.

So to New Zealand, both of those lush and lovely islands, where our travel and work were greatly facilitated by Government co-operation in transport by plane and car and by the welcoming kindness of the Church.

So home, via Fiji, where we left part of ourselves with those lovely, warm-hearted people.

Wherever we went, there were huge congregations, signs of a lively church life, and a welcome which amazed us by its sincerity and depth. England still means much to these peoples separated geographically from us by thousands of miles. Canterbury, too, means much to them. By this, of course, I do not mean any one incumbent of the office of Archbishop of Canterbury, but Canterbury as the rock whence spiritually they were hewn, the centre, as they regard it, of that great Anglican Communion which, with its seventy million adherents, straddles the world.

In days when our ties could so easily be loosened, I believe the links which bind the Mother Church with the younger Churches should be strengthened. In the hope of doing something in this direction, I undertake these travels. I believe the visit to Australasia made a useful preparation for the Lambeth Conference to be held in a year's time.

3. The eight-day visit to *Rome, Istanbul and Geneva* was a visit very different from the other two which I have described, different in character and in purpose.

Archbishop Fisher's visit, the first visit of an Archbishop of Canterbury to the Pope since the Reformation, was an unofficial one. Archbishop Ramsey's visit was of a more formal nature, as was mine in April. The audience with His Holiness was very cordial, and I believe that relationships between the Church of Rome and the Anglican Communion were taken a step further. Members of General Synod will have seen the relevant documents, and especially the Common Declaration (see Appendix 1, pp 314–317) signed by the Pope and myself after a service in the Sistine Chapel—they are published, together with information about the visits to Istanbul and Geneva, in a booklet called *Pilgrim for Unity* (published jointly by the Catholic Truth Society and SPCK).

I believe it to be important that the work of ARCIC should continue in the coming years. There is much theological work yet to be done. The publication of the three Agreed Statements—on Eucharist, Ministry and Authority—is enough to encourage us to go on further.

The Anglican Centre in Rome is continuing to do valuable work under the guidance of Dr Harry Smythe.

There is a danger of a widening gap in the work of inter-Church relationships, a gap which, if allowed to widen, might well lead to disorder in the Church. I refer to a gap between the thinking of the theologians and the action—or rather, lack of action—on the part of the hierarchy in implementing their thinking. There is a danger of a further gap, viz. between the actions of the people in the pew and the response of the hierarchy. It was to this danger, and the consequent disorder in Church life, that I referred in my sermon in Rome (see pp 117–122) on the eve of the signing of the Common Declaration.

The visit to Istanbul made an Englishman thankful for our own freedom from State pressures. The Patriarch, with whom I had long and friendly talks, works and worships under conditions of very considerable difficulty, as do his fellow bishops, priests and faithful laity. We should keep them in our prayers (for the joint communiqué signed by the Ecumenical Patriarch and myself, see Appendix 2, pp 318–319).

The visit to Geneva and the headquarters of the World Council of Churches was again cordial and happy. It is clear that the World Council looks for the closest co-operation from Britain in its world-wide work, and I hope that we shall do what we can to ensure that there is always a full British representation on its central staff. The fact that the Primate of Canada is Chairman of its Central and Executive Committees, and a very active one at that, means that there is a powerful Anglican presence in Geneva, and that is warmly welcomed.

My time in Geneva included a visit to the Orthodox Centre at Chambésy—a lively and forward-looking factor in Orthodoxy—and a visit to Bossey where Professor Mbiti keeps a valuable work going under threatening clouds of financial difficulty.

I hope I have not bored you with these travel stories. But I felt that, inasmuch as I go in a very real sense as your ambassador, I had a duty to tell you at least a little of what I seek to do in your name and in the Name of our common Lord.

One Church

IF THE LAMBETH Conference last year demonstrated one thing more than another, it was that the Anglican Communion, in spite of all the differences existing between its Provinces, is a brotherhood whose members share each other's joys and griefs, triumphs and defeats. The whole Communion, and for that matter many outside it, have watched with sorrow and sympathy the things which have recently befallen the Bishop in Iran and Mrs Dehqani Tafti and the small Christian community in that country. We unite in the hope that the Iranian Government will do all in its power to protect minorities and to prevent the recurrence of the kind of incidents which have recently occurred there.

If I mention three other leaders in our Communion whose names are often in our minds and in our prayers, it is only to illustrate the fact of our brotherhood which manifests itself particularly when danger lurks or problems multiply. *Bishop Desmond Tutu*, of South Africa, was an outstanding figure at the Lambeth Conference and is loved by many outside this country and his own. He is a man whose discipleship moves him to give brave and costly leadership.

Archbishop Silvanus Wani of Uganda must be bearing heavy burdens at this time. The removal of Idi Amin has not ended the stresses, nor indeed all the bloodshed, in that lovely country. The process of rehabilitation and of unity is a slow and painful one, and the members of the great Church in that country deserve our prayer and support.

Presidential Address to the General Synod, 6 November, 1979.

That also applies to the neighbouring country of the Sudan, whose Province I initiated in 1976. The four African Bishops there, under the leadership of *Elinana Ngalamu*, face difficult problems, not least in the South where the care of great numbers of refugees from Uganda lays heavy burdens on them.

I now turn to say something about Anglican relations with other Churches.

Members of Synod will want to know what progress has been made on the question of the attitude of the Roman Catholic Church to the ordination of women, particularly as I promised at the last group of sessions, in reply to a question from Canon Rhymes, that I would pursue the matter with Cardinal Hume. This I have done, and we have had long talks on this and other matters. The Cardinal took the matter up with His Holiness the Pope personally, and he has referred it to his advisers. We now await further word from him.

There has been much comment upon the three Agreed Statements produced by the Anglican-Roman Catholic International Commission, in this and other Synods, at the Lambeth Conference and at the Anglican Consultative Council. Most of this comment has been generally favourable, but there have been some criticisms. ARCIC is now working on criticisms of the Authority document. It has already published its *Elucidations* on the Eucharist and Ministry Statements which go a long way to answering "Evangelical" Anglican criticism. ARCIC was also asked by this Synod to say something on the theology of the Church. It is now preparing a theological Introduction to the three Statements on this subject. As promised in the original Authority Statement, the Commission is also preparing a continuation of the conclusion of *Authority in the Church* on the specific question of a universal primacy. ARCIC hopes to complete all this in a Final Report by January 1981 at the latest. It will then be up to the Churches of the Anglican Communion and the Roman Catholic Church to take up a definitive attitude to the completed work of the Commission. If there is agreement in faith on these issues, then we look to the next stage on the path towards visible unity.

The Anglican Consultative Council has raised the question of the possibility of a unified Anglican response to the work of ARCIC—the Primates' Meeting will be taking a first look at this

question this month. The ACC has also empowered its Secretary-General to approach the Vatican about ARCIC's successor, and has made the suggestion (already made in this Synod)
that a new International Commission (with some new personnel) should have the responsibility for fostering pastoral relations between the two Churches and for looking at the kind of
unity we are seeking—to spell out an Anglican-Roman Catholic
unity in diversity.

With reference to the Orthodox Church, the Bishop of St
Albans spent some time at the Ecumenical Patriarchate in
Istanbul earlier this year as the guest of the Patriarch Demetrios
and subsequently visited ten autocephalous Churches of Orthodoxy in the Middle East and Eastern Europe. In each case he
had the opportunity of conversation with the Patriarch and his
theological advisers. His object was to report personally on the
Lambeth Conference and on the present situation on the
ordination of women in the Anglican Communion, and to
discuss the future of Anglican-Orthodox conversations. On his
return the Bishop has reported privately to the Archbishops
and the House of Bishops.

The most obvious and encouraging result of these and other
exchanges with Orthodoxy has been the decision to continue in
1980 the international dialogue which was interrupted in 1979.
It is however clear that the Orthodox believe any future discussion of the ordination of women should take place within the
debate about the Ministry. It is agreed that these theological
discussions will have a greater sense of pastoral and practical
realities, but the Orthodox resisted the idea of separating out
the ordination of women for isolated consideration. Any general debate about the ministry of women should, they believe, not
be the subject of tripartite talks but fall, for example, within the
purview of the World Council of Churches.

The death of Archbishop Athenagoras in September robbed
the Church of England of an old and firm friend. We pay tribute
to one who was greatly esteemed in these islands, in America
where he had previously served, and far beyond. We welcome
the enthronement last Sunday of the new Archbishop of
Thyateira and Great Britain, as head of the Greek Church in
these islands. Archbishop Methodios, who was Metropolitan of
the Greek Church in Ethiopia, is one of the leading interpreters

of Anglicanism in Orthodoxy and has taken a major part in the doctrinal discussions. Over recent years he has been a close colleague of the Bishop of St Albans in these matters.

Agreement has been reached for dialogue to take place between the Anglican Communion and the World Alliance of Reformed Churches. A European Regional Anglican-Lutheran dialogue will shortly begin; during my recent visit to Sweden and Finland progress was made in this direction.

Here at home, it is well known that the Churches' Council for Covenanting faces serious difficulties. There is the problem that the Free Churches have women ministers while the Church of England has decided neither to remove the barriers to the ordination of women nor to permit women lawfully ordained abroad to exercise their priesthood in this country. There are at least three other major issues: the mutual recognition of existing ministers; the acceptance of the historic episcopate by the participating Free Churches; and the working out of the appropriate pattern of inter-Church relationships after the Covenant. The CCC is pressing ahead in drafting a Covenant. We hope and pray that it will be successful. It hopes that a report may be presented to the General Synod next July, and then, if the Synod so directs, referred to the dioceses.

In November 1977 this Synod commended the Nationwide Initiative in Evangelism to the dioceses. In January this year the Initiative was committed to God in a service in Lambeth Palace Chapel by leaders of all the main streams of Christianity in this country. These same leaders are asking every local church to use the first Sunday of a new decade, January 6th 1980, as an opportunity to pray especially for the task of evangelism. I hope that the forms of service which have been drawn up by NIE will, after due preparation of the congregations concerned, be very widely used.

In conclusion, and speaking as one who has sat in this Synod and in the body which preceded it for nearly thirty years, may I be allowed to ask you to reflect with me briefly on the situation in which we as a Synod now find ourselves?

I have taken part in all the discussions which led to the formation of the General Synod. I have rejoiced to see an increasing measure of co-operation between the Synod, the Church Commissioners, the Pensions Board and so on. I hope this process will develop further. And I wish here to pay my tribute to the dedication, skill and diligence with which our Secretary-General plays his part in the guidance of our affairs. Synodical government has come into being here in England, and it is going through the painful period of adolescence. We must bear in mind that synodical tidiness and managerial efficiency is only part of what is called for in the life of a healthy Church. Life is larger than logic, and room must be left for development outside the committee room—a large place for inspiration and for the initiative of individuals or groups who do not fit easily into any structure of management but who have ideas which they long to inject into the body of the Church and which the Church sorely needs. Further, very careful thought needs to be given to the place of episcopal leadership in a synodically governed Church—for the Anglican Communion, including that part of it which we here represent, is still, and will, I hope, ever remain, an *episcopal* Church whose members look to the *episcopate* for guidance and stimulation of mind and spirit. Here is at once a matter for hard thinking on the part of the Church and a constant challenge to the episcopate itself.

What do we mean by the word *synod*? "A way of convergence or of consensus" would be a translation not far from the meaning of the two Greek words which make up the word "synod". I must confess, however, that as I have listened to, and taken part in, *some* of our debates, I have doubted whether we have kept close to the spirit of that translation. I take it that the purpose of a debate in a holy synod is for the members so to open up their minds to the Spirit of truth that at the end they can say: "We have the mind of Christ." I take it that this implies the very real possibility that members will be led to change their minds in the course of the debate, as new aspects of truth are presented to them. This means that debating and voting in Synod—contrary to that in other areas of public life—can never be on party lines. But I ask myself—to quote a phrase which I heard the Bishop of Winchester use recently—have we "yet extricated ourselves from the shadow of the Mother of Parliaments"?

May I, treading on delicate ground, utter a warning? I am old enough to remember the bitterness of party strife which obtained when I was ordained in the early nineteen-thirties and which survived, in part, when I first became a member of the

Church Assembly more than a dozen years later. Am I being over-anxious when I say that I have detected certain signs—a cloud no larger, I trust, than the size of a man's hand—of a revival of such a spirit? Were it to develop, it would spell the death of any synodical government worthy of the name, for the protagonists of the parties concerned would come to the debates of the Synod with their minds already made up, their serried ranks determined to vote along pre-determined party lines, and nonsense made of any revelation of the mind of the Spirit through the medium of the debates.

I do not know who will preach the sermon at the opening service of the new Synod. But he could do worse than take for his text the words of St Paul: "Quench not the Spirit." Please God, the members will not do that. But they *could* do so by a revival of party spirit, or by the creation of structures which, good in themselves, became a strait-jacket.

The last paragraph of Edward Carpenter's *Cantuar* has within it a warning to our Church not to become an "inward-looking community preoccupied with its own life". Were we to do so, we should be looked upon by other parts of the Anglican Communion with pity. "Here", they would say, "is the old mother-Church bound by a system like the nation's parliamentary one, a Church let and hindered from striking out boldly on new paths, neither free nor daring in a new and demanding age." We should not be the laughing-stock of our sister-Provinces—they are far too loving for that. But we should be in danger of incurring their pity.

This shall not be. "We believe in the Holy Spirit, the Lord, the Life-giver", and, believing, we hope and rejoice.

The Health of the Anglican Communion

Revelation 21:5
He who sat on the throne said, "Behold!
I am making all things new!"

IF I SPEAK this afternoon primarily to those who are members of the Anglican Consultative Council, representatives of other Churches and Consultants, I am sure that others present will understand. I take it that you are here because you are interested in the work that the Council is meeting to do, and that most of you, if not all, are prepared to help the Council by praying, especially during this week and next, for the guidance of the Holy Spirit in our deliberations. I hope that what I am about to say may lead to a deeper understanding in our work and a more intelligent under-girding of it in prayer.

Since I became a bishop more than twenty-three years ago, I have had the great privilege of travelling extensively in many parts of our Communion and beyond it. What I have to say today is in part the outcome of those travels—the result of pondering on what I have seen and of thinking over conversations I have had all over the world with those engaged on the Master's business.

I want to share with you three matters which should be to the forefront of our thinking, praying and planning, as our twentieth century draws towards its close, and as we look to the work and witness of our Communion in a fast-changing world.

Presidential Address to the Anglican Consultative Council, St Paul's Cathedral, London, Ontario, 8 May, 1979.

1. First let me say something about *conservatism and "openness"* (I use the latter word for want of a better one, and will explain my use of it in a moment). Conservatism is a word frequently used with derogatory over-tones. I do not so use it now. There is a very strong conservatism in the Bible. The Deuteronomist's constant call to "remember", and Jeremiah's injunction to look to the old ways (Jeremiah 6:16) are but two instances of the biblical appreciation of the fact that because a thing is new it is not necessarily right or better than the old. History and tradition cannot be set aside; they are neglected at our peril. There is a "sacred deposit" which it is our solemn trust to guard (2 Timothy 1:13–14).

But alongside this "conservative" emphasis, comforting in its reassurance, lies the more disturbing insistence on a God who does new things, who indeed "makes all things new" (Isaiah 48:6ff; Revelation 21:5). Scientists teach us to think in terms of a continuing, "explosive" creation. Scripture teaches us to think of the Spirit, the Lord, the Life-giver, in eruptive metaphors of wind and fire, doing the unexpected, breaking up old ways, breaking out in new ones.

"Why", I recently asked a priest in West Africa, "did you read the Epistle today in the Authorised Version?" (It was a passage in which St Paul exhorted his readers to "possess his vessel in sanctification and honour . . . not in the lust of concupiscence . . .", and it was clear that the priest did not know what St Paul was talking about, and it was even more unlikely that his people did.) The answer to my question came like a flash—"Tradition," he said. I ventured to point out that some of the harshest things which, according to the Gospels, Jesus ever said were uttered to break up the power of traditions which were crushing the upsurge of new life.

The issue between "conservatism" and "open-ness" is pinpointed for us in the matter of liturgical revision. I do not believe that the future of Anglicanism hangs on whether we address God as "You" or "Thou"! I realise that liturgical revision is a task at once difficult and delicate, calling for good theology and pastoral sensitivity. But it serves to give us a good illustration of the importance of realising that we are at once the heirs of long centuries of experience in worship, enshrined in our ancient forms of worship, and at the same time are servants of the disturbing, burning, blowing Spirit who goes on creating new things and would have his servants show themselves open to do the same. Thank God for tradition—it gives us guidelines. Beware tradition—it can throttle the life out of you!

2. I turn now to another matter which surely must increasingly engage the attention of the Church in coming days. I refer to *the missionary task of the Anglican Communion.*

We have—rightly, I believe—given much time and attention to the creation of new Provinces within our Communion. Within very recent years, I have myself taken part in the creation of the Provinces of the Sudan and Papua New Guinea, and was present, a few weeks ago, with our brethren in Nigeria just after the creation of their new Province. This is all to the good, though we should, perhaps, be careful not to proliferate too many little Provinces before there is serious need for them and before there are leaders to guide them. But—put not your trust in Provinces, for, after all, they are only bits of administrative mechanism. You can have a Rolls-Royce in your garage, but it will stay just there, in your garage, if you haven't got petrol (spirit) with which to run it and an adequate driver at the wheel. We can have Provinces, Lambeth Conferences, meetings of Primates, assemblies of the ACC, all good in their way—but *to what end?* The test question is: "Is the Anglican Church getting on with its missionary task? Is this organisation, are these meetings, means to the fulfilment of the divine command to 'make all nations disciples' of the Lord Jesus, to 'baptise . . . and to teach'?" If they are not, then we had better look to ourselves lest we be engaged on structures and disobedient to the Lord's prime injunction.

The matter takes on particular urgency in view of two factors which mark the life of our world in the closing decades of the twentieth century. I refer *first* to the notable advance, on many fronts, of the Muslim faith. The significance of that in the political field I need not even touch on—our newspapers in recent months have alerted us to it. But I ask: Are we in the Anglican Communion—to look no further afield—equipped to meet this challenge? Do we in the West know how to enter into intelligent and meaningful dialogue with our Muslim neighbours, or do we look resentfully at the mosques which are rising in increasing numbers in our cities and—wish they weren't there? And in Provinces and Dioceses in areas like West Africa, are our bishops, clergy and laity so taught and so equipped that they can face the waves of Muslim advance calm and unafraid? In the field of Christian literature, is there an ample supply both of major works dealing with the Christian-Muslim debate and of paperback and pamphlet material for airport and railway bookstalls, literature which puts the Christian case positively and powerfully? I fear that the answer to this last question is "No". If that is so, is not this a task to which we should address ourselves with renewed energy?

Secondly, I note the proliferation of sects of all kinds, splinter groups, some pernicious, some mad, some a strange mixture of good and bad, but adding to the confusion which faces especially our young people with problems of choice which they are ill-equipped to meet. I ask: why this proliferation? And why are so many led into these organisations? I cannot but feel that all too often the fault lies with *us*—because, while, it may be, we have "baptised" in great numbers (yes, and confirmed), we have not "*taught*"; and because we have not shown that radiance of holiness which is self-authenticating and which commends the Faith. A person well fed does not augment his meals with food from the dustbin. A person well taught in the Catholic faith and the Scriptures, well nourished with the riches of centuries of tradition and worship and writing, is equipped to withstand the blasts of some new-fangled sect or of some ancient heresy dressed up in modern guise. The need for teaching, teaching and more teaching—I see it wherever I go, from Arctic to Equator, not excluding the privileged countries of our Western world.

3. The third matter to which I believe we must increasingly give our attention is the matter of *leadership in our dioceses and Provinces*. First, we must be clear as to what kind of leadership we are looking for; and then we must see to it that our machinery of government is such that the emergence of men and women of that calibre can take place unhindered.

For example, when a bishop has to be chosen (appointed, or elected, or whatever), what marks are we looking for in him?

Must he be of a certain tribe, or are tribal differences, however ancient and honourable they may be, transcended in Christ? Must he be of the right social class? Are we looking for a popular figure who will "go down well" with people? Or for a good organiser who will keep the machine ticking over pleasantly? (What is more comfortably soporific than the purr of a nicely running engine?) Or are we looking for, and content with nothing less than, a man of God, of prayer, of vision, of prophetic insight, of openness to the Spirit, his mind clear, his spirit aflame, a man who thinks—and weeps—and laughs?

Inasmuch, thank God, as leadership of the Church is increasingly in the hands of the laity (a re-discovery of an old truth vouchsafed to our generation), are our structures such as to allow, yes to *encourage*, the emergence of intelligent and positive leadership, irrespective of whether that is found in a man or a woman, a black or a white, a manual labourer or a white-collar worker?

There are obstructions to such emergence among bishops, clergy and laity; and while such obstructions continue there will be a strangulation of new life—and we cannot afford that if we do not want to "grieve the Holy Spirit of God".

I have mentioned only three of the issues which should, I believe, be in our minds as we address ourselves to the agenda of the Anglican Consultative Council this week and next—conservatism and "open-ness"; our missionary task; and leadership. There are many others, perhaps of equal importance, which will suggest themselves to you. When the Lambeth Conference ended in Canterbury last year, the bishops left with a conviction far stronger than it was ten years previously that, in the good purpose of God for his Church, the Anglican Communion had a significant part to play. We parted with a sense of mission, even of destiny. I ask your prayers that, in the coming days, we may discern more clearly what is God's intent for our Communion within the great Catholic Church of Christ, and within the world for which our dear Lord was content to lay down his life.

IX
STARS ON SUNDAY

To set you thinking

I

Who am I?

I'VE CALLED THIS little series: "To set you thinking". I hope each talk *will* set you thinking, and perhaps talking, and then, because talking by itself doesn't get us very far, set you *acting*! I've put our subjects in *question* form. Tonight's is: "Who am I?" Well, the obvious answer is: "I'm Donald Coggan", or in your case "Bill Smith", or "Mary Jones", or whoever.

But I want to look a bit deeper than this. I may be a very ordinary chap, but from one point of view I'm a miracle. I'm much more than the bunch of chemicals that my body is made up of; much more than the bundle of desires which keep on crying out for satisfaction—thirst, hunger, sex and so on; much more than the animals, though I've got a lot in common with them. Well then, who is this *me*? Let me tell you.

The first thing is this: I'm made in such a way that I can answer to God, respond to him in obedience and love. Oh I know that many of us have lived so long without doing anything about this, this capacity for God, that it has almost died on us. It's like a plant that is almost choked by the thorns growing up round it. But it's not *quite* like that yet with most of us. It may be that the reason why you're looking at this programme tonight is so that you may think about this, and stop the dying process before it's too late.

Stars on Sunday, February–March, 1978.

The second thing about me is that I'm made to be like Jesus. One of the early Christians said that God's plan for us is that we should be "shaped to the likeness of God's Son". I like that word "shaped". It makes me think of a potter at work, shaping a plate or a cup after his own plan; or a carpenter working away at his block of wood until the kind of thing emerges from it which he had planned on his drawing-board.

God had his plan for you before you were born.

God still has his plan for you—to be made like his Son, Jesus Christ.

We all of us make a bit of a mess trying to make ourselves. Perhaps it's time we gave him a chance.

2

What is God like?

"What is God like?" That's a very old question. Men have been at it from time immemorial. And they've come up with some pretty queer answers!

Let's be honest and admit that we are not likely to come up with a neat and tidy answer because, on any reckoning, God is far greater than we are, far beyond anything we can say about him; otherwise he wouldn't *be* God.

But that's not all we can say. We can go much further than that. Let's see what light the Bible has to throw on this.

One of the first things it says is that he is a *just* God, a *holy* God. It matters to him how we treat each other—how I behave to my wife or my employer or employee or to the black man down the road. God is concerned about justice and sets his face against sin.

Then, he is a God of *love*. That's the other side of the same coin of his justice and holiness. One of the Old Testament prophets saw this very clearly when his own marriage went wrong. His wife ran off with another fellow. What was he to do? Give her up and never think of her again? He couldn't begin to do that. He couldn't get her out of his mind. He still loved her—loved her dearly. Then it dawned on him—*God* was like that, only more so! He loves us even when we do the dirty on him and hardly give a thought to him.

Well, that's not far from the teaching of *Jesus*. He said that God was like a father whose boy ran away and couldn't care less for the dad he'd left at home. But the father didn't give up loving the boy. The moment "he came to himself", came to his senses, and then began to come back to the father, there he was, waiting for him with open arms.

Or again, Jesus told the story of a farmer who had a hundred sheep. Ninety-nine of them were safe and sound in the sheepfold. One got lost. The farmer was glad about the ninety-nine. But he was infinitely sad about the one which got lost. And off he went—to find it.

God so loved the world—and that includes you and me—that he sent his only son, that whoever puts his trust in him should not perish but have eternal life.

Thank God for *that*!

3

Who is Jesus?

"Who is Jesus?" There's no doubt that he's somebody in whom people are intensely interested. He is the central figure in *Jesus Christ Superstar* and *Godspell*. You may or may not think that those musicals got him right, but they wouldn't have been made if people hadn't been deeply interested in Jesus. What can we say about him?

We would all agree, wouldn't we, that he was a great *teacher*. Some of the people of his own day said that nobody had ever spoken as he did. They were right. Read those parables—it wouldn't be a bad idea to get hold of a Bible and turn up one of the Gospels and read a bit—and you'll find that Jesus had an extraordinary way of talking very simply about profound matters. *He* "set you thinking" all right! Yes, he was a great teacher.

And he has been, down the centuries, a great *example*. One of the first Christians said that he left us an example that we should follow in his steps. When he was reviled, he didn't revile again.

When he suffered, he didn't threaten—and so on. That example has inspired millions of people to heroic service and sacrifice.

But Jesus is much more than a great teacher and a great example. St John, in his Gospel, described him as the *Word* of God. What did he mean?

A word, when you come to think of it, is a bit of a miracle. Let's take an example. If I say the word "scarlet", an idea in my mind is conveyed to you by means of that word. You all see red! If I say "I love you", something very deep down in my heart is conveyed to the person I'm talking to.

God had something in his mind and on his heart which he desperately wanted to say to his children. How was he to get it across? He would do it by a word. He spoke through his messengers, the prophets and others—and something *did* get across. But supposing that that word, that thought in God's mind and that love on his heart, could take the form of a human person, someone who, in flesh and blood, could live and suffer and laugh and die like one of us, wouldn't that be the most effective word ever spoken? That's exactly what happened.

If you want to know what God is like, you look at Jesus. He is what God has to say to men.

He is what God has to say to me.

He is what God has to say to you.

The thing that matters more than anything else on earth is to listen to him—and to answer.

4

What about the Church?

"What about the Church?" Well, what about it? Let's begin back in the days when Jesus was on earth. He gathered round him a group of a dozen men—a mixed bunch they were. Not all ready-made saints, by any means. They had their quarrels and wrong ambitions, like the rest of us. One in fact betrayed Jesus at the end, and then went and committed suicide. But they were the earliest Christian Church. As a matter of fact, I'm very glad they weren't perfect. I'm glad they were ordinary people like

the rest of us. If there had been a perfect Church, it wouldn't have been any use to me, for I'm not perfect, I'm a sinner. If I'm going to be a saint, I must get busy in a Church which is made up of sinners who are saints on the assembly-line.

The original twelve (or, rather, eleven) were joined, after the death and resurrection of Jesus, by others, and the movement spread very rapidly. All over the place, little groups sprang up. They met in one another's homes, round a table with a bottle of wine and a loaf of bread which they shared in recollection of the Lord Jesus who had had a meal like that, just before he died, with his twelve men. They listened to readings from their Bible and to people who told them about Jesus and about what following him would mean in everyday living. Some of these groups were strong; some were weak. But that is how it all began.

Today it's got more complicated. Of course it has—a lot happens in nineteen centuries! The Church has had its quarrels and it's got its divisions. It has plenty to be ashamed of. *And* it's got lots to be thankful for—witness wonderfully borne to its Lord and Master; millions of people all over the world redeemed, restored and forgiven; teaching and healing work gloriously carried out, often at great cost. The Church isn't dead, because its Lord is very much alive.

It's still the place where the followers of Jesus meet to remember him as they share the bread and wine; to listen to him as they hear his word read and explained; to find strength as they pray and confer together as to how best to witness to him in their everyday living.

If you want to be a Christian, it's not a ha'p'orth of good standing on the side-lines and criticising the Church or calling its members a bunch of hypocrites. A solitary Christian is a contradiction in terms. The Church is a family, the family of God, and in that family is the strength every one of us needs. The grace of our Lord Jesus Christ and the love of God are to be found in the *fellowship* which God's Spirit creates.

5

Does God guide people?

When Jesus was teaching about God, he more often than not spoke of him as Father. By that he meant someone who cared very deeply for his children, went out to them in love, and looked for a response of love and obedience from them. Now if that is true—and I believe it *is*—then we should expect that such a God would not only be willing to guide his children when they needed such guidance, but would positively *want* to show them his way and lead them in it. And I believe that, too, is true.

But the question is: How do we *get* that guidance? How does it come through? Let's see if two or three hints will help.

First, if I am to get guidance from God, I must be willing to know his will and ready to do it if and when he shows it to me. That might quite possibly mean a revolution in my life, my way of acting and speaking, my attitude to God, to others, and myself. But if I'm *not* ready for this, I'm not very likely to be at the receiving end when God wants to speak to me. If we are deaf, we musn't think that God is dumb. The fault *could* be ours. If you switch on your radio or television set and nothing happens, it is just possible that the whole BBC or ITV hasn't shut down but that your set has gone wrong!

That takes us on to prayer. Prayer isn't so much asking God for a list of things we want, but quietly asking him: "What do *you* want? What do you want me to be? Or to do? Or to undertake? Or to understand?" Don't be in a frightful hurry. A few minutes spent on your knees or sitting quietly when the children have gone to bed and the day's work is over, asking God those questions—*that* is the kind of prayer that is likely to get an answer. It disperses the fog and lets the sunshine of God's guidance in.

We need, too, the help of Christians who know God better than we do ourselves. I'm not very wise myself, but there's a lot of wisdom in other members of God's family, the Church, and it's mine for the asking.

Guidance—a big subject. But how's that for a start?

6

Why did Jesus die?

A few weeks ago a young man sat down with me in my home and told me his story. He had made an awful mess of his life, and he was in despair. He said to me: "Will God really forgive me all the awful things I've done?" I was able to tell him that God does forgive, and that he longs to re-make lives that we have messed up—longs to and is able to, through the power of Jesus Christ.

Next Friday is Good Friday. It's the day when we think of the death of Jesus on the cross of Calvary. Have you ever wondered why the day that saw that most awful event, when the heavens were darkened and men and women stood aghast at what people could do to so holy and good a person as Jesus— have you ever wondered why we call that day *Good* Friday? Surely it was the most dreadful day that ever happened! The truth is that "Good Friday" means *"God's* Friday" (just as *"Good*-bye" means *"God* be with you"). But why call this day God's Friday? Because we believe that, in some wonderful way, *God* was at work in that tremendous event which took place at the cross of Christ. *"God* was in Christ, reconciling the world to himself."

What do we mean by this? We mean that God did not leave us to our fate, wash his hands of us, when we went wrong. Jesus, the holy and the pure, didn't refuse to have anything to do with us because we are sinners. On the contrary, he stood in with us to the last, bearing our griefs and carrying our sorrows, and by his stripes we are healed.

The truth is that every one of us is in need of him and of the forgiveness and strength which he offers. We may not have made such an open and obvious mess of our lives as the young man I've told you about made of his. But that we've all gone wrong there's not a shadow of doubt, nor that we need the forgiveness of God and a new start.

Do you remember the old hymn that runs:

> There is a green hill far away
> Outside a city wall

Where the dear Lord was crucified
Who died to save us all.

We may not know, we cannot tell
What pains he had to bear,
But we believe it was for us
He hung and suffered there.

Worth thinking about, isn't it, this Holy Week?

7

Is Jesus alive today?

I'm sorry that we've come to the last of this series "to set you thinking". I've enjoyed talking to you. Thank you for letting me into your homes.

It's Good Friday evening. Perhaps you'll think it a bit strange that our question tonight should be: "Is Jesus alive today?", because on Good Friday we think especially of His *death*. Let me explain.

In one of John Masefield's plays, he pictures Pilate's wife, Procula, talking to the centurion, Longinus, who had been present at the death of Jesus. "Do you think he's dead?" says Procula. "No, I don't, lady," said Longinus. "Where is he, then?", asks Procula. And Longinus answers: "Let loose in all the world, lady, where none can stop his truth."

That's what we'll be thinking about next Sunday, Easter Day. But let's begin tonight. The death and resurrection of Jesus go together—inseparably together, thank God. The people who crucified Jesus thought they had done him in and finished him for ever. Even the disciples of Jesus, the people who loved him best, couldn't understand what had happened, and feared that it was all over with him—and with themselves! Then, a few days later, they met him. There is mystery about the exact form in which they met him—but then, life is full of mystery and we needn't be over-worried about that. But that he was alive, and spiritually present with them, in a way more real and living than before his death, of this they had no doubt. "Let loose in all the world"; yes, those early Christians would have liked the way Masefield put it. Wherever they went, he was there, a companion, a guide, a strengthener.

That has been the conviction and the experience of the members of the Christian Church all down the centuries, and is so today. Jesus lives—the conqueror of death, the Lord of life.

> Jesus lives! Our hearts know well
> Nought from us his love shall sever;
> Life, nor death, nor powers of hell
> Tear us from his keeping ever.
> Alleluya.

> Jesus lives! for us he died;
> Then, alone to Jesus living,
> Pure in heart may we abide,
> Glory to our Saviour giving.
> Alleluya.

X
GREAT CHRISTIANS

Lancelot Andrewes

THIS COMMEMORATION ADDRESS is by way of being a salutation. What I mean by that word will become clear as the address develops, an address which will be divided into five parts.

I. *I salute Lancelot Andrewes as a fellow Old Merchant Taylor.* It was in 1926—as near fifty years ago as makes no difference—that I came to this Cathedral, together with my fellow Merchant Taylors, to attend a service in commemoration of the three hundredth anniversary of the death of Lancelot Andrewes. It was fitting that the boys of his school should do him homage in the place where he lies buried, not far from Lower Thames Street where he lived in the parish of St Laurence, Pulteney, and the old house known as the Manor of the Rose where Merchant Taylors' School began its life in 1561 and where the future bishop at the ripe age of six began the second stage of his formal education in the same year.

Richard Mulcaster, first of a long line of headmasters, reigned over the hundred poor scholars for whom the Merchant Taylors' Company conceived it their duty to provide education. Andrewes was for ever grateful to him—Mulcaster's picture hung over the bishop's study door, and to his son Andrewes left a legacy in his will. The reason for his gratitude is not far to seek—Mulcaster discerned in the little boy of six the makings of an unusually fine scholar; he kindled the flame of Andrewes' love of languages, teaching him Hebrew, Greek and Latin as

Commemoration Service, Southwark Cathedral, 24 September, 1975.

289

well as music and dramatic art, "good behaviour and au-
dacitye", not a bad septet on any reckoning.

A much later and a very much less distinguished Old Merchant Taylor welcomes this opportunity of paying a tribute of
gratitude to the Merchant Taylors' Company which for well
over four centuries has continued to care for the education of
tens of thousands of boys who have passed through its school.
The story has been well told by F. W. M. Draper (*Four Centuries of Merchant Taylors' School 1561–1961*, OUP, 1962).

2. *I salute Lancelot Andrewes as a linguist.* He seems to have
been gifted by nature with a love for and a skill at languages. We
have seen how, during his ten years at Merchant Taylors'
School, before going up to Pembroke Hall, Cambridge at the
age of sixteen—he was to become Fellow and then Master of
that College—he began the study of Latin, Greek and Hebrew.
We are not surprised that he was taught the first two; the third
is more unusual, and we may guess that we can detect here an
enthusiasm of Richard Mulcaster. Mulcaster built well: *this* Old
Merchant Taylor entered the Hebrew Class in 1926 and has
been thankful for that privilege ever since. He tries to believe
that Spencer Leeson of blessed memory (Head Master 1927–
1935 and subsequently Head Master of Winchester and Bishop
of Peterborough) was right in closing down that ancient institution of the Hebrew class on the grounds that it encouraged
over-specialisation for its members too early in their careers.
On the other hand it may be argued that its closure has meant
the cessation of a steady stream of young Hebraists, many of
whom have gone on to make distinguished contributions in the
sphere of Old Testament scholarship. Such a loss is a very grave
one. Further, it may be argued—and of this I have no doubt—
that a firm grounding in linguistics is a very sound mental
training; it makes for accuracy, for an abhorrence of slovenli-
ness, for a reverence for words and for clear expression, and
these are no mean factors in education and in preparation for
life and thought.

Andrewes' knowledge of the Biblical tongues laid a sure
foundation for his preaching and he made full use of it. The
preacher today, of course, has life made easy for him. He has his
New English Bible, his Jerusalem Bible, his Revised Standard

Version, his Moffatt, his Knox—it is all there, pre-digested. Other men have wrestled, and we have entered into their wrestlings. So be it, and we are grateful. But I think my dog is the stronger and the healthier for the fact that sometimes I give him a bone and let him lick it, and turn it over, and crunch and chew it. It is better for him than canned food all the time. Need I say more? Hoskyns used to say that it is possible to bury your head in a lexicon and arise in the presence of God. Andrewes would have agreed with him. So would I.

3. *I salute Lancelot Andrewes as a man of the Bible.* So long as people are interested in the English Bible, the King James version of 1611 will have an honoured place in their reckoning. (This is the so-called Authorised Version, inaccurately so called, for it was never officially authorised.) And so long as the King James version is honoured, the name of Lancelot Andrewes will be revered for the outstanding part that he played in its production.

We who live more than three and a half centuries later can easily see how many are the errors of that version. Of course this is so. It could not be otherwise. Semitic scholarship has made an enormous advance since Andrewes laboured at Hebrew. In the best of our modern versions the new discoveries are incorporated—to our lasting advantage.

But two things at least should be said about the 1611 version. The first is this. Begun as it was in 1604 with the full approval and encouragement of King James I, it is remarkable as being the result of the work of a committee, itself divided into six sub-committees, two sitting at Westminster, two at Oxford, and two at Cambridge. "Can any good thing come out of"—a committee, or indeed out of six committees? Yes, it can; and it did. The reasons are not far to seek—the members of these six sub-committees were noted not only for their culture and learning (themselves qualifications absolutely basic to such skilled work) but also for their humility and piety. They said, in the *Preface of the Translators*: "We never thought from the beginning that we should need to make a new translation, nor yet to make of a bad one a good one . . . but to make a good one better, or out of many good ones, one principal good one, not justly to be excepted against: that hath been our endeavour, that our mark." In saying that, they were paying their tribute to William Tyndale above every other English translator, for it has been reckoned that ninety per cent of Tyndale's translation stands unaltered in the verion of 1611. But that is another story.

The second thing to be said about this most influential version of 1611 is this. It was produced at a period in which, as G. M. Trevelyan put it, the English language reached "its brief perfection". This was the age of Shakespeare and Marlowe, of Spenser, Hooker and Bacon. And this was the age which produced, in the well-known words of Macaulay, "a book which, if everything else in our language should perish, would alone suffice to show the whole extent of its beauty and power".

Lancelot Andrewes was chairman of one of the Westminster groups (he was Dean of Westminster in the year 1604 when the project was proposed at the Hampton Court Conference). His group was entrusted with the Old Testament books from Genesis to the end of the Second Book of Kings. Here was ample scope for Andrewes' Hebrew scholarship. He and his colleagues worked in the Jerusalem Chamber in Westminster Abbey, the very room where so much work was to be done later in the production of the Revised Version, and, later still, in the production of the New English Bible. There can be little doubt that his influence extended far beyond these Old Testament books, and that our debt to him in the whole operation is a very big one.

4. *I salute Lancelot Andrewes as an Anglican.* Like Charles Simeon in a later century at King's College, Andrewes in the late sixteenth century at Pembroke Hall laid his foundations well. He joined a small group of senior men who held weekly meetings for prayer and Bible study. Each member had some special task to accomplish—one digging into the meaning of the text, another working at the exegesis, another at the doctrinal import of the passage. This meant that the undergraduate who shortly after graduation was made a Fellow of his College went to his later work well equipped to do the work of a priest and bishop. As a young man of thirty-four, he was assigned the stall of St Pancras in St Paul's Cathedral. This was the stall of the confessor or penitentiary, and Andrewes took his task seriously. At stated times in Lent he would walk about in one of the

aisles of the Cathedral in order to give spiritual counsel and advice to those in need. No suspicion of "Popery" was allowed to deflect him from a task which was close to his heart and which he conceived to be of the essence of his ministry.

In saluting Andrewes as an Anglican, I refer, of course, not only to the great offices which he held, and held with distinction, within the Church of England. In addition to those offices to which I have already referred he was Bishop of Chichester (1605–1609), Bishop of Ely (1609–1618) and Bishop of Winchester (1618 to his death in 1626). That in itself is a fine record, though conceivably by itself it *could* have meant little. That it meant much and that we can salute him as one of the great Anglicans of our long history is due to a variety of reasons.

I shall refer later to the overwhelmingly important fact that he was a man of prayer. This it was which under-girded his whole life and ministry; but I pass that by specifically at the moment.

There is no doubt that Andrewes lived at a time when Anglican faith and worship were experiencing a time of rich flowering. How could it be otherwise, when men like John Donne at St Paul's, Nicholas Ferrar and George Herbert were all making their own particular contributions? Andrewes undoubtedly made his. To his preaching he gave constant and meticulous care, and his congregations knew it and appreciated it. The pulpit was always a power when Andrewes occupied it. Scholarship, shrewdness, sternness, tenderness—all were there when Andrewes preached. "His sermons", said T. S. Eliot, "rank with the finest English prose of their time, of any time" (*For Lancelot Andrewes; Essays on Style and Order*, p 14). "The most conspicuous qualities of the style are three: ordonnance, or arrangement and structure, precision in the use of words, and relevant intensity" (pp 18–19). Intellect and sensitivity were in harmony; and hence arise the particular qualities of his style (p 20).

"Most Reverend Father in God", say the presenting bishops to the Archbishop when a priest is to be consecrated, "we present unto you this godly and well-learned man . . ." Of the godliness of Andrewes we have already spoken. As for scholarship, he was always at his books and at his writing; and this, in spite of almost incessant busyness at the Court where his attendance was constantly demanded and his advice called on. He was an example of that ideal of Anglican ministry which is so clearly and constantly pictured in our Ordinal—a man at his prayers and at his books, "drawing all his studies this one way . . ."

The bishop, too, must be a centre of unity. This Andrewes strove to be. We may be surprised at certain things within Andrewes' life and work—for example at his apparent silence when the fires of Smithfield were re-lit, for the last time, in 1612 and Bartholomew Legate was burnt on a charge, undoubtedly true, of heresy; or at Andrewes' adulation of King James, an adulation no doubt closely linked with his view of the divine right of kings, which in turn was connected with his study of the Old Testament; or, again, at the invective and irony which marked the controversy between the Bishop and Cardinal Bellarmine on doctrinal matters. In all these things he was a man of his age, and some of the issues in which he was forced to take part must have been a sore trial to his scholarly and eirenic spirit. But through it all he sought, as a bishop of the Church, to illustrate, in so far as he could, the principle which he laid down when he said: "There is not a greater bar, a more fatal or forceful opposition to his [the Holy Spirit's] entry than discord or disunited minds."

In his "appeal to antiquity" Andrewes bore witness to his solid position as an Anglican. His was no new Church began during the convulsions of Henry VIII's reign. The English Church is to be traced back to primitive Christianity; it is a true and authentic part of the Holy Catholic Church. It shares in the heritage of the Eastern and Western Churches, their Scriptures, their three creeds, their four General Councils and so on. From that position Andrewes would not, and did not, move.

5. *I salute Lancelot Andrewes as a man of prayer.* Andrewes' *Preces Privatae* bear, of course, the marks of the period in which they were written. A modern might, for example, express surprise at the exaggerated language in which Andrewes speaks of sin and seeks forgiveness. But, it may justly be asked, is this so much a criticism of Andrewes as of ourselves who, lacking Andrewes' concept of the dazzling holiness of God, correspon-

dingly lack a vision of man's, and of our own, unworthiness and sinfulness?

What Robert L. Ottley in his *Life of Lancelot Andrewes* (1894) called "an austere sanctity, which is concealed for the most part under a veil of masculine reserve", is revealed to us in these prayers. Here we have "largeness of sympathy, self-restraint, soberness, fervour, the spirit of 'continuous but not unhopeful penitence'" (p 180). Here are method and orderliness. Here are prayers soaked in the thought and language of Scripture. Here are prayers arising out of the conditions, in Church and State and society, in which he who composed them lived his daily life. Here is wide outreach to all sorts and conditions of men, mentioned in great and moving detail—and all set in the context of the eternal, of worship, of adoration, of eucharistic triumph, of the Church militant and triumphant. Here is the distillation of what Andrewes did during "a great part of five hours every day" which, according to Bishop Buckeridge who preached his funeral sermon, Andrewes spent upon his knees. Here is the secret of how he kept his purity of life in the midst of Court and controversy.

It would border on the trite to draw out in detail from this "salutation" those characteristics of Lancelot Andrewes whose continuance we must seek to ensure in the ministry of the Church in our own day. Scholarship; intense devotion to and study of the Scriptures; loyalty to that part of Christ's Holy Catholic Church to which we as Anglicans belong; prayer as the very life-blood of our work and ministry—these are some of the things which a study of Andrewes' life brings home to us with blinding clarity. Deprive the Church of a ministry like that, and it will not be long before its candlestick is moved from its place. Renew the Church with a ministry like that, and it will go forth conquering and to conquer.

And, lest this seem too remote from most of you who are listening to my words tonight, you will remember, won't you, that there is only one source from which the ministry of our Church can be recruited, and that is—the laity?

Thomas More

Jude 3
Join the struggle in defence of the faith, the faith which God entrusted to his people once and for all.

Romans 14:13
Let us cease judging one another, but rather make this simple judgement: that no obstacle or stumbling-block be placed in a brother's way.

THERE IS LITTLE need to re-tell the story of the life and work of Thomas More in such a place as this, nor to such a congregation as this. Most of us, probably, have seen that fine play *A Man for All Seasons*. And most of us have seen the splendid More Exhibition now on view at the National Portrait Gallery. We may consider ourselves fortunate if we are the possessors of the Exhibition catalogue which bears all the marks of careful scholarship and skilled presentation.

Anyone who lives at Lambeth Palace, as I do, must think with pleasure of the fact that More, at the age of thirteen, was a page-boy to the Archbishop of Canterbury, John Morton, after whom part of that building is named. With some prescience and insight, Morton wrote of the boy: "He is a merry lad who will become a marvellous man." Both adjectives, "merry" and "marvellous", could well be used to describe Thomas when he came to maturity. Anyone who has Canterbury in his diocese,

500th Anniversary of the birth of Thomas More, Chelsea Old Church, London, 5 February, 1978.

as I have, must be allowed at least to mention the fact that, if Chelsea Old Church has the body of More, Canterbury has his head—safely buried in the Roper vault in St Dunstan's Church in our city.

Tomorrow is the five hundredth anniversary of this great man's birth, and we do well to meet together to remember him in the presence of God. In his person, and in this place, we have a special meeting point between Anglicans and Roman Catholics.

As you entered the church this evening, you probably paused to look at the statue—"Sir Thomas More, scholar, statesman, saint"—erected in 1969 in his honour. If you did not, you will doubtless do so on your way home. It would be an interesting exercise, if you felt so inclined, to follow the river as far as the Victoria Embankment Gardens and there to look at another statue, itself a memorial to another great man, a contemporary of More's, William Tyndale. For long he has been a hero of mine, and when I pass his statue I feel moved to stop and do his memory reverence.

Let me very briefly sketch the characters (without re-telling the biographies) of the two men as I see them.

Thomas More's mind was made in the mould of a scholar. He rejoiced in the company of men of letters. When he was a young man of twenty-one, he met Erasmus, and they became life-long friends. John Colet—there is a name still revered in the City of London!—William Grocyn, William Lily, William Latimer, Thomas Linacre—what a galaxy of close friends! They brought to him all the riches of the Renaissance, of the beauty that was Greece and the glory that was Rome. They stimulated the thinking and writing of one another, and their influence can be seen in the Latin orations which More used to make at official receptions. His learning was seasoned with wit, and the undoubted prolixity of his writings, and especially of his controversial works, was relieved by a delightful sense of humour.

He moved with ease in Court circles, and was greatly appreciated there. But, if we are to judge by the fine picture of More in the company of his father, his household and his descendants (by Rowland Lockey, after Holbein), he was happiest of all in his family circle where all the younger members, girls equally with boys, shared in the culture, the wit and the affection of a man of affairs and of deep religious conviction. His religion had under-girded him all his days—in his youth he thought seriously of entering the contemplative life—and at the end sustained him during fifteen months in the Tower and to the last when he laid his head upon the block. It says much for the calibre of the man, for his intellect and for his culture, that Erasmus, on hearing of More's death, said: "I feel as if I had died with More, so closely were our two souls united."

At home with the Bible, with the Fathers, and with the classics, More's was a well-stored mind. But it is in his prayers that one can often see deepest and most clearly into the soul of a man. We listen, not only with pleasure to the linguistic beauty of this prayer composed during his time in the Tower, but with reverence to the note of a deep religion in the heart of the writer:

> Good Lord, give me the grace so to spend my life, that when the day of my death shall come, though I feel pain in my body, I may feel comfort in my soul; and with faithful hope of thy mercy, in due love towards thee and charity towards the world, I may, through thy grace, part hence into thy glory.

William Tyndale's was one of those "deathless minds which leave . . . a path of light"; there is no one whose effect on the growth of the English Bible is comparable to his. Because of the influence which his translation had on the Authorised Version—something between seventy and ninety per cent of that version is pure Tyndale—he can well claim to have enriched our language more than Shakespeare or Bunyan. What drove him on in his work was his passion to make the principles of the Bible available for all to learn. "If God spare my life," he remarked to an ignorant divine in Gloucestershire, "ere many years I will cause a boy that driveth the plough shall know more of the Scriptures than thou dost." He, like More, was influenced by men like Erasmus and Colet. His heart would have warmed to the words that Erasmus wrote in the *Exhortation* with which he prefaced his New Testament of 1516: "I totally dissent from those who are unwilling that the sacred Scriptures, translated in the vulgar tongue, should be read by private individuals. I would wish even all women to read the Gospel, and the Epistles of St Paul. I wish they were translated into all languages of the people. I wish that the husbandman might sing parts of them at his plough, and the weaver at his shuttle, and that the traveller might beguile with their narration the weariness of his way."

So strongly did this passion burn in Tyndale that he was content to spend the last twelve years of his life (1524–36) as an exile on the Continent, for he found "not only that there was no room in my lord of London's palace to translate the New Testament, but also that there was no place to do it in all England". The copies of his first edition, begun in 1525 and completed in 1526, filtering into England hidden in bales of cotton, were burnt at Paul's Cross at the instigation of William Warham, Archbishop of Canterbury, Cuthbert Tunstall, Bishop of London, Thomas Wolsey and Thomas More. He himself was burnt, after being strangled, in 1536 at Vilvorde, but not before he had prayed: "Lord, open the King of England's eyes"—a prayer answered only a year later by the royal recognition of the Coverdale Bible.

More and Tyndale engaged in mighty polemic. More wrote a *Dialogue concerning Heresies.* Tyndale replied with *An Answer unto Sir Thomas More's Dialogue.* More's rebuttal appeared in the form of his eight books of *Confutation of Tyndale's Answer* which occupy something like a thousand pages in the great Yale edition of More's *Works.* To our modern way of looking at controversy, the language used by the two men seems unpleasant in the extreme. More was engaged in a fierce championship of the old religion, and in that championship was happy to pursue his opponent relentlessly with a barrage of polemical artillery. Tyndale did not spare his opponent, and the heat of the battle was fierce. It is astonishing that a man who carried such heavy burdens as More did could engage in so lengthy a refutation of reformist doctrine; but he shared the forebodings of Erasmus and others of a coming widespread religious revolution, and felt it his duty to allow Bishop Tunstall to conscript him to undertake the suppression of heresy by a battle of books.

Here, then, are two sketches, very brief, of two men—both of them scholars enriched by the new learning; both of them deeply concerned to share with others their insights into God's truth; both of them saints, "far ben wi' God" (as the Scots would have it); both of them martyrs for truth as they saw it, laying down their lives within a year of one another for Christ and conscience' sake: but opposed, the one to the other, to the point of prolonged bitterness.

These two men pose a problem, a series of problems, which are not easy of solution. Today we do not engage in prolonged and bitter polemic—or at least not often. We do not kill one another—or at least very rarely—because of theological or intellectual differences. But divisions persist, separations continue, bitterness sometimes develops, and God's heart of love is grieved and the progress of his cause is hindered.

Of course, it would be possible to say: "Let us love one another and leave it at that." But that might be to encourage a mere sentimentality and the sacrifice of truth on the altar of a sloppy *bonhomie*. This would be to do despite to the first of our texts, which ran: "Join the struggle in defence of the faith, the faith which God entrusted to his people once and for all." And that would not do, for truth *matters*. There is what the writer of the Pastoral Epistles calls a sacred "deposit" of truth which it is for us to guard as a sacred thing and to pass on unimpaired to succeeding generations. "O Timothy, keep that which is committed to you"—all too easily it can be eroded. The Catholic faith, the faith of the Church down the ages, enshrined in holy Scripture and outlined in the Creeds and Councils of the Church, is a precious thing. "Keep that which is committed to you."

But what happens to this "sacred deposit" as age succeeds to age? There are accretions which sometimes dim the pristine beauty of the original revelation, and which do not accord with its main tenets. There are new insights and developments of truth, springing legitimately from earlier revelations, which bear every mark of being the result of the activity of the Spirit of Truth. How do we distinguish these from the accretions which fetter and distort? There is the record of the persecution of good men by good men because of differences of belief and of insight. There is the legacy of hatreds which are not forgotten nor, as yet, forgiven, and which make an excuse for a continuation of differences today. It is against a somewhat sordid background that we must heed the injunction: "Join the stuggle in defence of the faith entrusted to God's people once and for all."

Alongside this injunction from the Epistle of Jude we set another, from St Paul: "Let us cease judging one another, but rather make this simple judgement: that no obstacle or stumbling-block be placed in a brother's way." St Paul would be the first to affirm that truth matters. His controversy with St Peter and with his own Jewish people, and his martyrdom for the truth's sake, prove that. But alongside it he puts the command not to judge any man—presumably in a spirit of pride or superiority or bitterness—but, rather, to see to it that no stumbling-block is put in his way. For, however much I may differ from my brother, however difficult it may be for me to see that his apprehension of truth can even approximate to mine, he, like me, is "made in the image of God", and is destined, in St Paul's incomparable phrase, to "be shaped to the likeness of God's Son". We have a common destiny in the Mind of God.

We have looked at two great men, servants of God, at deep variance with one another, but both martyred in a cruel age for the truth as they saw it. What do they say to us? They say, surely, that truth, and not least the truth of the Christian revelation, matters, and matters deeply and intensely. They say, also, that love for one another matters, and matters as deeply and intensely.

If they, Thomas More and William Tyndale, could speak to us tonight, I think they might, in the light of the intervening centuries, tell us how to hold our texts together. They might say two things:

1. See that you love one another fervently. Not sentimentally; God forbid, for that would be a travesty of Christian love. But with the love of brothers in Christ, redeemed, restored, forgiven through him; one in baptism, one (soon, please God) in Eucharist, one in service. See that no obstacles be placed in a brother's way.

2. Be very sensitive to the movement of the Holy Spirit. He is the Spirit of Truth. He may come to us as a still small voice whose word we could all too easily miss. He may come to us like a rushing gale, blowing away our old conceptions, battering

down our old regulations, giving us new insights, and all the time saying to us in his gentle way: "Remember, dear child, you are only a babe. God is very big. You are very small. Walk humbly with your God and don't, please don't, put a stumbling-block in a brother's way."

Charles Simeon

TENS OF THOUSANDS of visitors from all over the world come to this chapel every year. Not many of them notice a vault marked simply "C.S 1836". Indeed, if the initials were explained to them as being those of a man called Charles Simeon, they would not be any the wiser. If, however, they were told that in November 1836 "C.S." had been accorded a funeral the like of which had probably never taken place in Cambridge previously, nor has done since, the visitor might prick up his ears. For that is precisely what happened. It was market day, but the shops were closed. It was term-time, but the lectures were suspended. The nave of this chapel was filled with eight hundred members of the parish of Holy Trinity, a few hundred yards from here—admission was by ticket only! Another eight hundred or so, members of the University, gathered in the College hall. The choir, famous even in those days, did its part; the organist played Handel's *Dead March*. It was, to say the least, a remarkable occasion.

Who was this "C.S."? He was a clergyman who for fifty-four years laboured at Holy Trinity Church, while for the same fifty-four years he was a Fellow of this College. That, on the face of it, sounds pretty mundane, if not dull. Nothing could be further from the truth!

Fifty-seven years before the event which I have described, he had come up as an undergraduate from Eton to this College. Something of a dandy, a great lover of a good horse, a young man of volatile temper and some personal pride, Simeon could

Easter Sunday, King's College, Cambridge, 15 April, 1979.

well have slipped into a life of ease or even of debauchery. The University to which he came was at a low ebb, as was religion within it. But Simeon, though he had to fight battles within himself all his life, became in fact one of the mightiest men in his generation, exercising "a sway in the Church far greater than that of any Primate", if the tribute of Lord Macaulay is to be believed.

He became one of the great *pastors* of his day, though for many years he had to encounter fierce opposition from some of the influential lay people of Holy Trinity Church.

He became one of the great *teachers* of the day, not indeed in the lecture-rooms of the University, but in his own rooms here in this College, where undergraduates would gather to join in his "conversation parties" and to hear him expound the Scriptures in his own inimitable way. Those were the days before theological colleges came into being—all too easily men could slip into Holy Orders with little idea of what that step should mean. Not so those—and they were many—who glimpsed something of the glory, and the demands, of the ministry through the agency of Simeon.

He became one of the great *strategists* of his day, whose influence spread far afield—to India, to Australia—through the men, both clerical and lay, who had dared to be labelled "Simeonites" when they came under his spell in their student days.

So one could go on, describing a man who, on any reckoning, was a "character", but who, for all his eccentricities and failures, was also undoubtedly a saint. A number of books have grown up around him, the best and most recent of which is Hugh Hopkins's biography—not a hagiography but a down-to-earth estimate of a very great man. But I resist the temptation to describe him further—I must rest content with the outline sketch which I have given. Rather, I would put the question: What was it that *made* Charles Simeon what he was?

There is only one point where an answer can be found. Its date and its place can be given. The date was Easter morning, two centuries ago; the place, his rooms here in King's. The story can be quickly told. Three days after his arrival in College, the porter brought him a note. It told him that, as a scholar of the College, he would be expected to attend a service of Holy

Communion in three weeks' time in the Chapel. Nothing could have been further from his mind. But there was the summons—and he was devastated! "Satan was as fit to attend as I", he was to say later on in his life. Apparently he attended the service—indeed, he had to—but with a conscience desperately ill at ease. He read seriously, for the first time in his life, but he was in spiritual despair, not knowing a soul to whom he could turn for counsel and advice. During Holy Week 1779, light began to dawn. Let me give you his own words: "I sought to lay my sins upon the sacred head of Jesus; and on the Wednesday began to have a hope of mercy; on the Thursday that hope increased; on the Friday and Saturday it became more strong; on the Sunday morning, Easter Day, April 4th, I awoke early with these words upon my heart and lips, 'Jesus Christ is risen today! Hallelujah! Hallelujah!' From that hour peace flowed in rich abundance into my soul, and at the Lord's Table in our chapel I had the sweetest access to God through my blessed Saviour."

The language, somewhat strange to us, is the religious language of the late eighteenth century. But the fact which it describes can only be seen as the experience of a revolution which altered the whole trend of Simeon's life. "Conversion" is not a bad word for it—it was a "turning round" to face the Christ from whom hitherto he had been running away. It was a deliverance from the service of self to the service of his Lord. It was a life-commitment—without reservation.

It is that event which we celebrate in this great service today—an event which was literally *crucial*, the crux which gave meaning to his life and power to his ministry, the meeting with the Christ of the cross and of the resurrection. But that was only the beginning. If we are to answer the question: "What was it that *made* Simeon the man that he was?", we must bear in our mind's eye the narrow path on the lead roof of this College on which he would pace up and down, for him "the secret place of the Most High", where he would daily hold communion with his Lord. He had a habit of rising early—at 4 a.m.—lighting his own fire, and spending four hours in Bible study, meditation and prayer, in his room and on the roof, before embarking on the tasks of the day. In such ways and in such places men of God are made.

One other factor must be mentioned as being integral to the

making of Charles Simeon. It was his intense belief in the value—yes, I would go further and say the holiness—of the Christian ministry. Though he would have loved the application of the word "evangelical" to himself, he was not a party man. But he was a great Church of England man, and he loved its ministry with a deep love. A friend of his said that, if you wanted to find Mr Simeon, he would either be by the sick-bed of a parishioner or out riding his horse—and the riding of the horse might well be in order to see that the people of the surrounding villages were getting relief during a bread-famine. He gloried in the privilege of visiting his people. He gloried in the opportunity of preaching—and of teaching others how to preach. He gloried in the sacrament of the Holy Communion, the service honoured with "Christ's peculiar presence", as he said. He magnified Christ, and he magnified his office. He would be happy today to see that more men are coming forward to the sacred ministry, and I have no doubt he would put to them this test for their ministry, the test he applied to all his sermons—will it "humble the sinner, exalt the Saviour, and promote holiness"? Not a bad test by any reckoning!

How terrible that a preacher on an occasion such as this should have no text! What would "C.S." have said? No; I have kept it to the end, so that you will remember it if you forget all else. "Come after me", said Jesus, "and I will make you fishers of men" (St Matthew 4:19). Charles Simeon "came" and "was made"—made into a fisher of men who in turn influenced others in great numbers across the globe.

Still they "come", thank God. For some, their conversion is dramatic, like Simeon's; for some, it is more gradual but none the less real, a turning round, a deliverance from self, a commitment without reservation and for life. Still they are being "made"—into fishers of men; learning the discipline of prayer and communion with their Lord. Still they are being sent— some into the parishes, some into the professions, some into the far parts of the earth, ordained and lay, there to bear their witness, in life and in death, to the risen Lord—and no going back on it! *Christ is risen!* Thanks be to God!

Max Warren

2 Corinthians 12:9
My grace is sufficient for thee;
for my strength is made perfect in weakness.
Acts 6:5
A man full of faith and of the Holy Spirit.

IF MAX WARREN had had a share in the planning of this service, the last thing which he would have desired of the address would have been that it should be a eulogy of Max Warren. Nor shall it be. Rather he would have wished that it should be a thanksgiving to the Lord, the Life-giver, who, in his case, brought the new life into being through the love of deeply committed Christian parents, and then kept on giving abundance of life, spiritual and mental, which overflowed to the blessing of others.

What I shall try to say will be—if you will forgive so apparently cold a word—"analytical"; an attempt to get to the root of what it was that God found in Max, created and developed in him, which he could take up and make a means of grace to others. For the same Holy Spirit, the Spirit of Jesus, who inspired this particular son of his, is the Life-giver at work in the hearts of all who obey him. Here is a ground of hope for us all.

I re-read a large part of *Crowded Canvas* (Hodder and Stoughton, 1974), Max's autobiography, on a recent visit to Russia and Armenia. I had enjoyed it at a first reading. I

Memorial Service, Westminster Abbey, 11 October, 1977.

appreciated it more at the second. It is a lovely book. Let me tell
you some of the marks of the man's character as a disciple of
Jesus and a leader of his people which struck me most powerfully.

I noted, first of all, the *humility* of the man. I doubt whether
he realised fully how able he was. But he knew that the gifts
which he possessed were just that, *gifts, charismata,* dispensed
by a lavish God and to be used to his glory. True humility is not
to be found in denying that you possess the particular gifts that
are yours. It is to be found in acknowledging those gifts to the
full, glorying in them, developing them, and handing them
back to the God who gave them to you to do what he will with
them.

I noted, secondly, the *alertness of his mind.* There was nothing
stagnant here. On the contrary, there was a mind well trained
and disciplined, which was constantly stimulated by discourse,
by reading, by friendships of all kinds throughout the world,
by new ideas, vistas, visions. The word "excited" recurs
frequently in his story. Fun had a way of bubbling up pretty
frequently when he was about, and thankfulness even in the
tough passages of life—and he had these in plenty—was only
just round the corner.

The basis of his reading was the Bible. Here was the great
stimulus to his thinking and reading, a never-drying spring to
thought and action. There was no obscurantism in his Bible
reading— truth was welcome from whatever source it might
come. Max did much to open intellectual windows for multitudes who, without his example and inspiration, might have
been content with narrower visions and to draw from shallower
wells. From his basic biblical work he ranged out, through the
Fathers, over the mountains of man's history in all its shame
and all its glory, over the growth of the Christian Church, over
the wealth of literature which succeeding generations and a
variety of nations have left as a legacy to mankind. His training in
history at Cambridge stood him in good stead. His world-wide
journeys, especially during his twenty-one years as General
Secretary of the Church Missionary Society, served to feed his
avid mind. But even more exciting than the reading of books, or
indeed the writing of them, was the stimulus of friendships with
an innumerable company of people to whom he listened—he

was a sensitive and attentive listener—people with whom he
talked on journeys, discussed in committees, debated in groups
such as those provided by the College of Preachers or the
Evangelical Fellowship of Theological Literature, or whom he
entertained in a series of homes where his hospitality and that of
his wife seemed never to end.

In re-reading *Crowded Canvas*, I noted, thirdly, Max's deep
sense of responsibility. Ian Bradley in a recent book seeks to
analyse the effects of the evangelical movement during the first
half of the nineteenth century. It is significant that he entitles
his book *The Call to Seriousness*. It was this call to seriousness
which the Victorians found so compelling, which influenced
their missionary zeal and gave point to their campaigns against
vice at home and slavery abroad. Combined with his sense of
fun, balanced by it, Max had a deep sense of the seriousness
which is entailed in being a slave of Jesus Christ. And small
wonder. For if the distinctive mark of the human is his answerability, his capacity to respond to his Creator and Redeemer
God, if it is this above all else which marks him off from the
other members of the animal creation, then there must be in any
man of stature an under-girding seriousness in his attitude to
life in its entirety. He is answerable to God—in worship, in his
attitude to his fellow-humans, in what he makes of his own life
in its vertical and its horizontal dimensions, in the way he treats
God's world.

This "seriousness"—to use Bradley's word—led Max to de-
termine, as the most natural thing in the world, to give his life to
missionary service abroad—a determination frustrated (or,
rather, as events were later to prove, gloriously fulfilled) by a
long period of sickness during his twenties. It led him to a deep
concern for the welfare of the whole man, whether he was
ministering to the Hausa people in Nigeria, to the youth of the
diocese of Winchester, to the undergraduates of Cambridge, to
the world-wide clientele of the Church Missionary Society, or
to the thousands who thronged this Abbey during the decade he
spent here before his retirement. This "seriousness" led him to
a deep concern with the political aspects of life at home and
abroad, for here are the corridors of power where men's fates
are decided and their conditions of living are determined.

Lastly, I noted the *prophetic nature of his ministry*. "Come up

hither and I will show thee things which must be hereafter."
This was the message which came to the writer of the book of
the Revelation. "Come up hither"—that is the essence of being
a prophet. From that height alone is the air clear enough to
discern what is going on below. Max's ability to see the pattern
of history and to perceive what might well be the major issues
which would face the Church in years still distant derived from
"coming up hither". He could look at those issues in their
immensity and complexity with a calm confidence because he
believed passionately in the total adequacy of the gospel. That
gospel was—for him—centred firmly in the Person of Christ.
He had been grasped by him and he wanted others to have the
opportunity of consciously coming within the orbit of that
embrace. There is something deeply significant in the fact that
the last book he wrote—the last of a long series—was, in a
sense, an *apologia pro vita sua*, and had as its title: *I Believe in the
Great Commission* (Hodder and Stoughton, 1976). Because he
had been laid hold of by One whose name is Love, he became
not only one of the great missionary statesmen of the century—
a prophet in that sense—but also a great lover. Prophets are not
always specialists in love—they sometimes find it easier to
denounce institutions or even to threaten them than tenderly to
care for individuals. Max somehow combined the vision of the
seer, the prophet, with the care of the pastor and the lover of
souls.

If we ask the secret of this rare combination of gifts, we find
it, I doubt not, in his prayer life. He did not find prayer
easy—which is a comfort to us lesser mortals. He did not adapt
easily to the pattern of other men's praying. But pray he did,
and that constantly, and I suspect that his intercession list, and
his use of that list, could we but see it, would shame most of us.

There was his power. And in his home, as in his God, was his
peace. His was a shared life, and our love and sympathy and
gratitude go out tonight to Mary who shared his life so richly
and so deeply—to her and to Rosemary and to Pat.

"My strength", said our first text, "is made perfect in weakness." Max's life was one long illustration of that. "A man full
of faith and of the Holy Spirit," said our second text. "*Whose
faith follow*", in the power and the joy of that same Spirit.

XI

EXPECTANS
EXPECTAVI

Expectans expectavi

These verses, set to music by Charles Wood, have had a special meaning for me, for they were sung, among other occasions, in Bradford Cathedral (1956), York Minster (1961) and Canterbury Cathedral (1975) at my enthronement.

They were written by Charles Hamilton Sorley, son of W. R. Sorley, Professor of Philosophy at Cambridge. Born in 1895, Sorley was educated at Marlborough and won a scholarship to University College, Oxford. He was commissioned into the Suffolk Regiment in 1914 and, as a Captain, was killed in the Battle of Loos on 13 October, 1915.

This sanctuary of my soul
Unwitting I keep white and whole
Unlatched and lit, if thou should'st care
To enter or to tarry there.

With parted lips and outstretched hands
And listening ears thy servant stands.
Call thou early, call thou late,
To thy great service dedicate.

Appendix 1
Common Declaration of Archbishop Coggan and Pope Paul VI

1. After four hundred years of estrangement, it is now the third time in seventeen years than an Archbishop of Canterbury and the Pope embrace in Christian friendship in the city of Rome. Since the visit of Archbishop Ramsey eleven years have passed, and much has happened in that time to fulfil the hopes then expressed and to cause us to thank God.

2. As the Roman Catholic Church and the constituent Churches of the Anglican Communion have sought to grow in mutual understanding and Christian love, they have come to recognise, to value and to give thanks for a common faith in God our Father, in our Lord Jesus Christ, and in the Holy Spirit; our common baptism into Christ; our sharing of the Holy Scriptures, of the Apostles' and Nicene Creeds, the Chalcedonian definition, and the teaching of the Fathers; our common Christian inheritance for many centuries with its living traditions of liturgy, theology, spirituality and mission.

3. At the same time in fulfilment of the pledge of eleven years ago to "a serious dialogue which, founded on the Gospels and on the ancient common traditions, may lead to that unity in truth for which Christ prayed" (Common Declaration 1966). Anglican and Roman Catholic theologians have faced calmly and objectively the historical and doctrinal differences which have divided us. Without compromising their respective allegiances, they have addressed these problems together, and in the process they have discovered theological convergences often as unexpected as they were happy.

314

4. The Anglican/Roman Catholic International Commission has produced three documents: on the Eucharist, on Ministry and Ordination and on Church and Authority. We now recommend that the work it has begun be pursued, through the procedures appropriate to our respective Communions, so that both of them may be led along the path towards unity.

The moment will shortly come when the respective Authorities must evaluate the conclusions.

5. The response of both Communions to the work and fruits of theological dialogue will be measured by the practical response of the faithful to the task of restoring unity, which as the Second Vatican Council says "involves the whole Church, faithful and clergy alike" and "extends to everyone according to the talents of each". (*Unitatis Redintegratio.* N.5.) We rejoice that this practical response has manifested itself in so many forms of pastoral cooperation in many parts of the world; in meetings of bishops, clergy and faithful.

6. In mixed marriages between Anglicans and Roman Catholics, where the tragedy of our separation at the sacrament of union is seen most starkly, cooperation in pastoral care (*Matrimonia Mixta*, para 14) in many places has borne fruit in increased understanding. Serious dialogue has cleared away many misconceptions and shown that we still share much that is deep-rooted in the Christian tradition and ideal of marriage, though important differences persist, particularly regarding remarriage after divorce. We are following attentively the work thus far accomplished in this dialogue by the Joint Commission on the Theology of Marriage and its Application to Mixed Marriages. It has stressed the need for fidelity and witness to the ideal of marriage, set forth in the New Testament and constantly taught in Christian tradition. We have a common duty to defend this tradition and ideal and the moral values which derive from it.

7. All such cooperation, which must continue to grow and spread, is the true setting for continued dialogue and for the general extension and appreciation of its fruits, and so for progress towards that goal which is Christ's will—the restoration of complete communion in faith and sacramental life.

8. Our call to this is one with the sublime Christian vocation itself which is a call to communion; as St John says "that which we have seen and heard we proclaim also to you, so that you may have fellowship with us; and our fellowship is with the Father and his Son Jesus Christ" (1 St John 1:3). If we are to maintain progress in doctrinal convergence and move forward resolutely to the communion of mind and heart for which Christ prayed we must ponder still further his intentions in founding the Church and face courageously their requirements.

9. It is this communion with God in Christ through faith and through baptism and self-giving to him that stands at the centre of our witness to the world, even while between us communion remains imperfect. Our divisions hinder this witness, hinder the work of Christ (*Evangelii Nuntiandi* 77) but they do not close all roads we may travel together. In a spirit of prayer and of submission to God's will we must collaborate more earnestly in a "greater common witness to Christ before the world in the very work of evangelisation" (*Evangelii Nuntiandi*, ibid.). It is our desire that the means of this collaboration be sought: the increasing spiritual hunger in all parts of God's world invites us to such a common pilgrimage.

This collaboration pursued to the limit allowed by truth and loyalty, will create the climate in which dialogue and doctrinal convergence can bear fruit. While this fruit is ripening, serious obstacles remain both of the past and of recent origin. Many in both communions are asking themselves whether they have a common faith sufficient to be translated into communion of life, worship and mission. Only the communions themselves through their pastoral authorities can give that answer. When the moment comes to do so, may the answer shine through in spirit and in truth, not obscured by the enmities, the prejudices and the suspicions of the past.

10. To this we are bound to look forward and to spare no effort to bring it closer: to be baptised into Christ is to be baptised into hope—"and hope does not disappoint us because God's love has been poured into our hearts through the Holy Spirit which has been given us" (Romans 5:5).

11. Christian hope manifests itself in prayer and action—in prudence but also in courage. We pledge ourselves and exhort the faithful of the Roman Catholic Church and of the Anglican

Communion to live and work courageously in this hope of reconciliation and unity in our common Lord.

From the Vatican, 29 April, 1977

Donald Cantuar: Paulus P.P. VI

Appendix 2
Joint Communiqué from Archbishop Coggan and Patriarch Demetrios

Continuing one of the most ancient traditions of the Christian Church, that of having meetings between the Orthodox and the Anglican Churches, and especially between the Ecumenical Patriarchate and the See of Canterbury, in the mystical presence of our risen common Lord Jesus Christ, we, the humble representatives of the two Churches, have met anew and in brotherly love, and in faithfulness to truth we have examined our progress towards the unity of the two Churches and towards Christian unity in general.

Although we, the leaders of the two Churches and the ecclesiastical and theological consultants around us, have left the sacred question of the theological dialogue between the two Churches to the Commission concerned, nevertheless we have declared our firm wish that the dialogue should be continued constructively on the good foundations already laid, and every effort be made for the removal of obstacles to its successful progress.

The most specific difficulty during the meeting was the ordination of women, which the Ecumenical Patriarchate officially declared to be unacceptable to the Orthodox Church.

The answer of the Archbishop of Canterbury was that the Anglican Church was not seeking the agreement of the Orthodox Church on this subject, but was hoping for understanding of it.

The two leaders agreed that the official dialogue between the Anglicans and Orthodox should continue, as being one of the most promising ways of resolving the problems which divide the two Churches as well as the rediscovery of those things which unite them, but they also hoped that the agreements already reached by this Commission would be more widely shared among the faithful of our two Churches, for the promotion of the Ecumenical Movement and Christian Unity.

According to the ancient tradition of the undivided Church the Christian faith is sustained when believers support each other in understanding and love. It is for this reason that we want the fruit of the dialogue to be widely shared by the faithful people of both Churches.

The two leaders, taking advantage of their spiritual and historical meetings, wish to declare that their care and vigilance extend beyond the interests and problems of both Anglican and Orthodox, and are extended to Ecumenical Christianity and furthermore embrace the general good of the whole of humanity.

For this reason the two leaders express their unshakeable conviction that all Christians should cooperate with all religious groups for the preservation of love and peace among men throughout the world, the elimination of racial and religious discrimination and the safeguard of religious freedom, so that it may be seen that this world is indeed God's world.

Fanar, 1 May, 1977

Donald Cantuar: Demetrios of Constantinople